Kant's
ETHICAL PHILOSOPHY

Immanuel Kant

ETHICAL PHILOSOPHY

second edition

the complete texts of

GROUNDING for the METAPHYSICS of MORALS

and

METAPHYSICAL PRINCIPLES OF VIRTUE
(Part II of *The Metaphysics of Morals*)

with

On a Supposed Right to Lie Because of Philanthropic Concerns

translation by JAMES W. ELLINGTON

introduction by WARNER A. WICK

HACKETT PUBLISHING COMPANY
INDIANAPOLIS/CAMBRIDGE

Immanuel Kant: 1724–1804

Grounding for the Metaphysics of Morals
was originally published in 1785

The Metaphysical Principles of Virtue
was originally published in 1797

Cover design by Richard L. Listenberger
Interior design by James N. Rogers, Starr Koester Atkinson

Printed in the United States of America

For further information, please address
  Hackett Publishing Company, Inc.
  Box 44937, Indianapolis, Indiana 46244-0937

ISBN: 0-87220-320-4 paperbound
ISBN: 0-87220-321-2 clothbound

Library of Congress Catalog Card Number: 94-079516

The paper used in this pubication meets the minimum requirements of
American National Standard for Information Sciences—Permanence of
Paper for Printed Library Materials, ANSI Z39,48-1984.

CONTENTS

TRANSLATOR'S FOREWORD

My translation of Kant's *Metaphysical Principles of Virtue* (Part II of the *Metaphysics of Morals*) originally appeared in 1964 in the Library of Liberal Arts series. It is here reprinted and has been preceded by my translation of Kant's more famous *Grounding for the Metaphysics of Morals*, which first appeared in 1981 in the Hackett Publishing Company series of philosophical classics.

The translation of the *Grounding* is based on Paul Menzer's text (Berlin, 1911) as it appears in Volume Four of the Königliche Preussische Akademie der Wissenschaften edition of Kant's works. Karl Vorländer's German text (Leipzig, 1906), as it appears in Volume Three of the Philosophische Bibliothek edition of Kant's works, was also consulted. The translation of the *Metaphysical Principles of Virtue* is based on Paul Natorp's text (Berlin, 1914) as it appears in Volume Six of the Akademie edition. Karl Vorländer's text (Leipzig, 1907), as it appears in Volume Three of the Philosophische Bibliothek edition, was also consulted. For the most part I followed the reading of Kant's second edition (1803) of the *Metaphysische Anfangsgründe der Tugendlehre*, and where the text of the first edition (1797) varied significantly from the second, I have mentioned this in a footnote. Page numbers of the Akademie edition, the standard reference for Kant's works, appear in the present translations as marginal numbers. All material interpolated by me in text or notes has been bracketed.

The *Grundlegung zur Metaphysik der Sitten* has been translated many times. Three of the most memorable translations are by T. K. Abbott, H. J. Paton, and Lewis W. Beck. The literature devoted to the *Grundlegung* and to various aspects thereof is enormous. I shall mention only A. R. C. Duncan's *Practical Reason and Morality. A Study of Immanuel Kant's Foundations for the Metaphysics of Morals* (Edinburgh, 1957); H. J. Paton's *The*

Categorical Imperative. A Study in Kant's Moral Philosophy (London, 1947) and *The Moral Law*. *Kant's Groundwork of the Metaphysics of Morals* (London, 1948); and Robert Paul Wolff's *The Autonomy of Reason. A Commentary on Kant's Groundwork of the Metaphysics of Morals* (New York, 1973) and *Foundations of the Metaphysics of Morals with Critical Essays* (Indianapolis, 1969).

The Metaphysical Principles of Virtue was translated in part by Semple in 1836, but this is actually more a paraphrase than a translation and contains many inaccuracies. Abbott did a reasonably good translation of the general Introduction to *The Metaphysics of Morals* and the Preface and Introduction to *The Metaphysical Principles of Virtue,* and I have often found his translation helpful in my own labors. These are the only English translations till my own and that of Mary J. Gregor (New York, 1964). Joseph Tissot did a complete French translation of *The Metaphysics of Morals,* which appeared in 1837 under the title *Principes Métaphysiques de la Morale;* and Giovanni Vidari did a complete Italian translation in 1925, *La Metafisica dei Costumi.*

Although *The Metaphysics of Morals* is often mentioned in books on Kant's ethical theory, there are very few commentaries on or works exclusively about it, or about either of its parts. I have found only Georg S. A. Mellin's *Marginalien und Register zu Kants metaphysischen Anfangsgründen der Sittenlehre,* and Julius Hermann von Kirchmann's *Erläuterungen zu Kants Grundlegung zur Metaphysik der Sitten und zu Kants Metaphysik der Sitten* in Volume 59, Section One of the Philosophische Bibliothek series. In English there is Mary Gregor's excellent *Laws of Freedom* (Oxford, 1963).

Generations of scholars and students have been so preoccupied with the *Grounding* and with the *Critique of Practical Reason* that the *Metaphysics of Morals* has remained a relatively neglected work. T. K. Abbott in 1879 combined the first two works in a volume entitled *Kant's Theory of Ethics.* A little more than a century later I am combining the first with Part II of the third in a volume entitled *Kant's Ethical Philosophy.* My reasons for doing so are indicated by Kant himself in the *Grounding* (1785) at Akademie 421, where in a footnote he mentions the yet-to-be-written *Metaphysics of Morals* (1797). Immediately following he considers four duties (not to commit suicide, not to break promises, not to let one's talents rust, and not to neglect others in need) as instances of the application of the general categorical imperative to particular ethical duties. *The Metaphysical Principles of Virtue* sets forth the complete and systematic specification of the categorical imperative (formulated in the *Grounding*) to particular ethical duties. To combine the *Grundlegung* with the *Tugendlehre* means to go from the general to the specific.

Scholars and students have far more often taken Abbott's road and gone from the *Grounding* to the *Critique of Practical Reason*, where the categorical imperative is justified and where the treatment is even more abstract than in the *Grounding*. Subsequently and consequently, Kant is often accused of being a formalist with his head in the clouds and of being utterly incapable of dealing with specific down-to-earth cases, i.e., he is accused of propounding a moral theory for rational beings in general and not one for human beings in particular. I am not chastising Abbott for combining the *Grounding* and the *Critique;* but when readers concentrate on these two justly famous works without considering the *Metaphysics of Morals,* they inevitably get a lopsided view of Kant's practical philosophy. Both the *Grounding* and the *Critique* are concerned with what today would be called meta-ethics, and both works are slanted in the direction of high-level abstractions. The *Metaphysics of Morals* is concerned with normative ethics, and here Kant treats of the varied problems of moral judgment and of choice in concrete situations. Moral philosophy is a complex subject, and Kant treats it systematically in these various works as he deals with one topic at a time. The following essay by Warner Wick, entitled "Kant's Moral Philosophy," explains how these three treatises fit together to comprise the full and balanced view of Kant's philosophy of morality.

University of Connecticut   JAMES W. ELLINGTON
Storrs

INTRODUCTION

KANT'S MORAL PHILOSOPHY

Immanuel Kant's greatness as a moral philosopher is rarely disputed and his importance never, even among those who think his teachings grandly misconceived. Yet his substantive moral doctrines, as opposed to his statement and defense of the abstract principles on which those doctrines depend, are not generally known or are "known" in sketchy and distorted forms. This is unfortunate, for the chief interest of practical principles lies in the modes of life and action that they determine. It is also a hindrance to an understanding of the philosophical issues, for the meaning of principles is much clearer when we understand them in the light of their applications and consequences.

An obvious explanation of this odd state of affairs, as far as the English-speaking world is concerned, is that the books in which Kant set forth his specific views about rights and duties, about justice and virtue, have never been generally available in English. His moral "doctrine" (or what many philosophers today would call his "normative ethics" in contrast to his "meta-ethical" treatment of its foundations and method) was expounded in *The Metaphysics of Morals* (*Metaphysik der Sitten*, 1797). It had two main parts, *The Metaphysical Principles of Right* (*Metaphysische Anfangsgründe der Rechtslehre*) and this book, *The Metaphysical Principles of Virtue* (*Metaphysische Anfangsgründe der Tugendlehre*)[1] Semple made a partial translation of the *Tugendlehre* in 1836. Not until the present translation and that of M. J. Gregor (1964) has a complete English translation been available. Hastie

[1] Full justice to the suffix, *-lehre*, would require us to say "the doctrine of right" and "the doctrine of virtue," but if that point is kept in mind, the shorter titles will do.

made a partial translation of the *Rechtslehre* in the latter part of the last century, while John Ladd made a much better partial translation in 1965.

This explanation itself needs explaining, for why should such important works by such an outstanding philosopher have been so long neglected? They have not been widely read in other countries either, so that the problem has not been merely one of language, nor one of the accidents of publishing. Much of the explanation is to be found in the way Kant organized his writings in moral philosophy.

The plain truth is that there is no short and authoritative statement of Kant's ethical theory as a whole, and the two works that are most commonly used for that purpose are not well suited to it. These two — *The Grounding for the Metaphysics of Morals (Grundlegung zur Metaphysik der Sitten)* and the *Critique of Practical Reason*—are both so important in their own ways that one cannot quarrel with the practice of reading them first, the former for Kant's characteristic conception of moral philosophy as falling within the scope of a single principle of "pure reason," and the latter for an investigation of the grounds on which such a principle can be justified as a determinant of action. But these treatises are misleading unless one heeds Kant's warning that each is addressed to a very limited but basic question; for the varied problems of moral judgment and choice in concrete situations are treated as incidental to the special problem about moral principles with which each is primarily concerned. Both are very great works indeed, doubtless worthy of more attention than *The Metaphysics of Morals* proper, which Kant himself described as having "a more simple character," not demanding the "necessarily subtle discussions" of the others. But all the same, to know only these two is to get a lopsided view, distorted in the direction of high-level abstractions; and one is all the more misled if he is not aware that they form only part of the picture.

Moral philosophy is a complex subject, and it is one of Kant's virtues as a philosopher that he thinks and writes systematically, dealing with one problem at a time but not neglecting to explain as he goes along how the different problems are related to each other. In his own words, "philosophy is distinguished from ordinary rational knowledge by its treatment in a separate science of what the latter comprehends only confusedly."[2] To take advantage of his excellence, then, one should read him systematically; and this requires at least an awareness that his separate ethical writings are not so many independent assaults on the same complex of problems—for instance, on "the problems of ethics" in general. Kant calls his shots. So, if I may vary the metaphor, the reader should watch for the many signposts and frontier markers that Kant provides to guide him through the various parts of the realm of moral philosophy. Since Kant's scope is considerable, an exploration of the whole territory would be a long journey. But even on a short trip it is important to have a sound orientation, with a sense of how what one is seeing is related to other areas that may be explored on other occasions.

In the sections that follow I will try to give a bird's-eye view of Kant's moral philosophy, so that the contribution of *The Metaphysical Principles of Virtue* may be understood in its proper setting. Having done that, I will proceed with some introductory remarks about the distinctive features of that work itself.

I

Kant's Preface tells us that the aim of *The Grounding for the Metaphysics of Morals* (which will be referred to as *Grounding*), with which the study of his moral philosophy is best

---

[2] In the Preface to his *Grundlegung zur Metaphysik der Sitten,* translated by James W. Ellington, *Grounding for the Metaphysics of Morals,* (Hackett Publishing Co.: Indianapolis, 1981), Akademie edn. 390. Because of the variety of editions, the page number of the standard Akademie edition will be added. These appear in the margin or at the top of the page in most recent translations, including the present one.

uni
7Gw

begun, is "nothing more than seeking out and establishing the supreme principle of morality, and this constitutes by itself a task which is complete in its purpose and should be kept separate from every other moral inquiry."[3] His method

method

of procedure is what he calls "analytic," beginning with representative cases of everyday moral judgments that we should find familiar and analyzing them in order to discover their underlying principle.

The kind of principle to be looked for is neither a neatly stated axiom nor a copy-book maxim, nor should it be expected to be completely expressible in any one formulation. It is rather a common presumption of all moral judgments, a working criterion that any rational agent supposedly employs as a guide in making his own choices and judgments without necessarily being able to make it explicit—rather like our "knowing how" to speak our mother tongues correctly and to recognize mistakes in grammar and syntax without "knowing," in the sense of being able to formulate, the rules that we follow so confidently. Kant insists that it would be silly to claim to have "discovered" such a principle as something really new. "Who," he says, "would think of introducing a new principle of all morality and making himself as it were the first discoverer of it, as if all the world before him were ignorant of what duty was, or had been in thoroughgoing error?"[4] But still, if there is a consistent standard that is reflected with varying degrees of clarity by our judgments, it would be both practically helpful and theoretically instructive to formulate it with as much precision as possible.

one
principle

Kant's conclusion is that there is one supreme principle for the whole field of morals, including the philosophy of law as well as the ethical demands of personal integrity and social

---

[3] *Ibid.*, Ak. 392.

[4] In the Preface to the *Critique of Practical Reason*, translated by Thomas Kingsmill Abbott, *Kant's Critique of Practical Reason and Other Works on the Theory of Ethics* (Longmans, Green and Co., Ltd.: London, 1927), p. 93, note, Ak. 8.

intercourse. This is the famous "categorical imperative." It can be stated in several forms that are in an important respect equivalent. Each formulation is expressed in quite different terms, bringing out different considerations that are relevant to any moral decision, but to understand what is involved in acting as one of the formulas requires is to see that it means acting according to each of the others as well, so that they all "amount to the same thing" as determinants of action and in that sense express one principle rather than several.

At the risk of confusing the reader by reversing Kant's order of exposition and compressing into a few paragraphs what he takes many pages to say, let me begin at the end, first sketching the outcome of his analysis and then turning back to show how each formulation of the categorical imperative adds a new element to our understanding of its significance. I think this will be the best procedure for a short summary, for we learn about a complex subject more easily if we first get a rough idea of the whole and then look to the relations of the elements that make it up.

conclusion In summary then, Kant's conclusion is that morality demands that we act on the sort of policies which, if adopted by everyone, would generate a community of free and equal members, each of whom would in the process of realizing his own purposes also further the aims of his fellows.[5] As an ideal, such a moral community is not fully realizable, but it both defines the objective of the moral law, and is at the same time applicable to everyday situations in that we ought never act in a way that would be incompatible with it. Its basis is the idea of *autonomy*, or freedom under self-imposed law, according to which each person freely submits to self-discipline under the same rules he would prescribe for others, so

    [5] In Kant's technical language, which will become clearer as we proceed, "morality consists in the relation of all action to that legislation whereby alone a kingdom of ends is possible." *Grounding*, Ak. 434.

that everyone would act as a law unto himself, or "autonomously," and yet also in cooperative harmony with everybody
else.

This ideal might become more concrete for us if we think
of a string quartet as a rough approximation to a moral community. The members mutually agree upon the parts and
scores they will play; the immediate aim of each is to play
his own part as best he can; and the better he plays, the more
his playing harmonizes with the others and the more enjoy-
able it becomes, both to himself and to them. It is significant
that there need be no conductor or "boss" of the operation,
and that the satisfaction of playing well is sufficient incentive
for one's efforts, even though some may also work hard for mu-
sically (or morally) irrelevant motives like money or applause.

Such a "kingdom of ends," as Kant calls this sort of free
association of equals, would be both an "open" society, en-
couraging variety and innovation, and also a rigorously demanding one. Think again of the string quartet. There is no
one best score to serve as the "law" that coordinates the players' activities: any score with a certain formal organization
will serve. But some compositions are more interesting than
others, and some both demand more of the players and are at
the same time more rewarding in the way they extend and
perfect everyone's skill and enjoyment. The rule of law, like
the quartet form, is capable of such indefinite variation and
development. Balancing this openness is an uncompromising
rigor that takes two forms, each corresponding to one of the
two kinds of duties that will be outlined later—the positive
and broadly indeterminate ones, and the strict and determinate duties whose force is chiefly negative. Positively, each
player commits himself to do his best. Playing well, of course,
is a matter of degree, and since no performance is ever "good
enough"—short of perfection, which is impossible—one's obligation in this respect is limitless and indefinite. Negatively,
however, a player is obligated in a strict and definite sense: no
one may do anything which, if done by the others too, would
be incompatible with the common enterprise. To coast

through a hard passage, or to go off on a tack of one's own, would be subversive in principle even if no one happened to hear the resulting sour notes. In the same fashion, a moral community demands the utmost (but indefinite) effort to live up to the spirit of its constitution; and it strictly and definitely prohibits any willful breach in the law, for that would subvert the condition of its existence.

So much for the initial sketch: now let us investigate its elements. Our ideal moral community has *law* as its formal ordering principle; and a law must apply universally, making no exceptions within its jurisdiction. Any acceptable course of action, then, must accord with the idea of legality by being acceptable for all similar persons in like circumstances. If something is right for me, or is demanded of me as my duty, it must be right for or demanded of everyone unless there is a reason why my case is peculiar. Even so, the reason for my being an exception must be based on general grounds, covering anyone answering to a certain description, and not just me. I will let the reader learn from Kant how this requirement of universality can be found in our ordinary judgments and how, once derived, it can be confirmed by examples from each of the main classes of duties. It will be sufficient now to notice that we appeal to it whenever we test an act or proposal by asking, "What if everybody did that?" or by looking for precedents; for if a decision was right once it should be right still, unless the situation has changed in some material respect. At any rate, expressed in general form, it is the first of Kant's versions of the categorical imperative: Act only on a maxim that you can at the same time will to become a universal law.

Several short comments are in order. This is an "imperative": not a statement of fact, but a directive to act in a certain way, which also forbids whatever is inconsistent with that action. In the second place, it is "categorical" or unqualified, as opposed to hypothetical or conditional, both in its logical form and its rational purport. It says flatly, "Act thus," not, "Act thus *if* you want to keep out of trouble, to get ahead in the world, or whatever." In other words, that something is the right thing to do (or that to do otherwise would be wrong) is sufficient reason for doing it. It might happen to be to my advantage too, but whether it is or not makes no difference to my moral obligations. Thirdly, the requirement that one's "maxim" be generalizable as a universal law needs further explanation.

A maxim is a rule. Everything in nature, Kant says, *happens* according to rules (i.e., the "laws of nature"), but only rational agents can *act* according to rules, for that entails self-determined behavior guided by a general concept, like deciding to take two left turns followed by one to the right and then stopping at the next corner. A maxim is simply the rule we follow in any deliberately intentional act. When made explicit, it expresses "what we are doing"; and made fully explicit, it would have to mention our purpose, the means by which we expect to achieve it, and the relevant circumstances. Too sketchy a formulation may be deceptive. A good example would be the gangster who said he was "only making a living"; for anybody has a right to do that, though not by preying upon law-abiding citizens. The reason is that *everybody* cannot prey upon law-abiding citizens, for that is self-contradictory. Or consider the liar who said he only lied "to protect an innocent man." We are apt to think that protecting the innocent is surely a commendable occupation, worthy enough to justify some winking at the proprieties. But let us look deeper into the liar's maxim, specifying the means he proposes to use. Now clearly any maxim about lying will have to include the rule of *lying in order to achieve something that depends upon the lie's being believed*. Otherwise, it would be pointless. But surely, to seek credibility by lying is not a policy that can be *universally* adopted! No rational agent *can* will that maxim as a universal law, for in its universal form it is self-contradictory. A lie can work only if enough people tell the truth to make truthfulness the normal expectation, just as the gangster can succeed only if most people are law-abiding. These miscreants act unfairly in that their maxims require that other people act differently—which is only another way of saying they cannot will that their maxims should at the same time become universal laws.

To return to our ideal of a moral community, we next note that it not only has a "form," that of legality, a species of the general form of rational order; but also a "matter," its free and equal members and the purposes they pursue. Their equal freedom means that none of them may coercively or deceptively subject others to their own private interests. The integrity of each, in his right to seek his own ends as long as he does not violate anyone else's rights, must be respected. Therefore the second formulation of the categorical imperative is: Act so as to treat humanity in oneself and others only as an end in itself, and never merely as a means. To treat a person merely as a means is not to treat him as a human being—that is, a self-determining rational agent—but as a "thing" without purposes of its own, like the proverbial doormat.

Much as this second formulation differs from the first, it is not hard to see that it follows from the first and is indeed equivalent to it. To treat someone as a mere means is to regard his purposes as if they did not count—as if he were just an object that entered one's calculations as an instrument to be used or as an obstacle to be pushed aside. Now any maxim formulating such treatment entails, when it is universalized, that one be willing to be treated that way in return. But that is a contradiction, for it can be no one's purpose that his purpose count as nothing. It follows, then, according to the *first* formulation of the categorical imperative, that a violation of the *second* must be wrong, and therefore that everyone ought to be treated as an end in himself, subject to no one's arbitrary will. The implication also works in the opposite direction. As we saw, a violation of the first formulation always involves making oneself an exception to rules (e.g., of truth-telling or law-abidingness) which must be generally observed, and which one's victims have to assume will be observed, if one's purpose is to succeed. Thus we use others' aims and expectations not as our own but as mere instruments of our schemes; we exploit them, which is exactly what the second formulation prohibits. Therefore, since the *second* forbids any breach of the *first,* it follows from the second that we ought to act only on maxims that we can will as universal laws. The two formulas mutually imply each other, which makes them equivalent in content if not in expression.

mutual implication

We ought, then, to treat each other as ends, as self-determining equals mutually obligated to act only on maxims that everyone could observe without conflict. These elements together constitute the idea of a system in which everyone is not only subject to the rule of law but is also, through the maxims on which he acts, its co-author or legislator; and this common adherence to its constitutive principle makes the system a community. Any external power who presumed to "lay down the law" *for* us without subjecting himself to it in turn would not be treating us as ends in ourselves, nor would he be regarding his maxims as universal laws. He might use threats to make us "cooperate" with his plans, and he might think he was doing it for our benefit. But he would remain a tyrant, condemned by the requirements of the moral law; and he would be totally incapable of putting us under any moral obligation, for we would obey him, if at all, only from fear or canniness. The same considerations condemn the vulgar conception of God as the sort of "lawgiver" who issues arbitrary commands with threats of hell-fire, saying in effect, "Do it or be damned." We may, then, "be obliged" to do something against our will, but we must freely *assume an obligation* that is morally binding. Thus the third element of the supreme moral principle, which Kant calls "the ultimate condition of its harmony with universal practical reason," is the idea of the will of every rational agent as *autonomous,* giving laws to itself. This yields a third formulation of the categorical imperative. Act so that your will can at the same time regard itself as giving in its maxims universal laws.

autonomous will

CI no 3

This point, that the idea of morality involves autonomy, provides the clearest proof that a moral imperative must be categorical. Any rule that meets the formal conditions of le-

duty

gality and justice may be enforced by rewards and punishments (although the converse is not true, for tyranny uses the same incentives). However, anyone who obeys the law for the reward, or to avoid penalties, does so on non-moral grounds, for it is not "doing the right thing" that he values, but rather the pay-off. Someone else may conform to the same law for positively immoral reasons, taking care to be outwardly respectable and even hiring a team of lawyers to help him observe the letter of the law, but only in order to be more secure and undisturbed in his iniquity. He too values conformity (or the appearance of it) for its pay-off, and if either of these people calculated that legality "did not pay," his maxim would recommend disregarding it. Both act as they do on the same kind of principle, which is a hypothetical imperative. More generally, a will that acts on a hypothetical imperative can obey a law only for an extraneous or ulterior motive; it cannot act autonomously, from regard for the law to which it submits, but subordinates the law to another purpose. But this amounts to saying that a principle of moral action, which is necessarily autonomous and dependent on no ulterior motive, must be a categorical, not a hypothetical imperative.

We have by this time gone through the principal elements of the supreme moral principle, which together define the ideal of a moral community with which we began our exposition. As Kant says, if we abstract from the individual differences of its members and their aims, "then it will be possible to think of a whole of all ends in systematic connection (a whole both of rational beings as ends in themselves and also of the particular ends which each may set for himself); that is, one can think of a kingdom of ends that is possible on the aforesaid principles."[6] And so, to put this sublime conception in one bare formula, "morality consists in the relation of all action to that legislation whereby alone a kingdom of ends is possible."

The special problem of the *Grounding* was "seeking out and establishing the supreme principle of morality." That has now been accomplished to the extent of making explicit

[6] *Ibid.*, Ak. 433.

the working criterion reflected in typical moral judgments and giving it alternative formulations that express its different aspects. Kant summarizes his analytical investigation this way, "that the above principle of autonomy is the sole principle of morals can quite well be shown by mere analysis of the concepts of morality; for thereby the principle of morals is found to be necessarily a categorical imperative, which commands nothing more nor less than this very autonomy."[7] To put the matter this way is to emphasize the order of discovery, going from ordinary conceptions to their principle, which is thus "established" as the presupposition of the moral ideals we in fact have, and on the validity of which their validity in turn depends.

But what about the principle of autonomy itself? It requires another kind of examination, for while "the autonomous personality" is much in favor these days, autonomy in the sense required for the foundation of a categorical imperative is thought more often than not to be an obvious impossibility. Consequently, as Kant says, to prove that moral obligation is no "chimerical idea" or "creation of the brain," its principle has to be "established" in a further sense, which will allow us to reason from the principle to what depends on it, rather than in the opposite direction as we have done in the foregoing analysis. In short, if autonomy is a valid conception, then the categorical imperative and all the subordinate principles and doctrines of ethics and jurisprudence are also valid. But how are we to justify the principle of autonomy? The solution of this problem is the task of the *Critique of Practical Reason*, for which the third section of the *Grounding* prepares the way.

II

This need to justify the principle of autonomy is not just a technical question of interest to academic philosophers. As anyone who has thought much about moral problems will

[7] *Ibid.*, Ak. 440.

recognize, there are natural objections to any notion of a categorical imperative. Some of them are practical, arising when we think of reasons why we should do one thing rather than another. Others are theoretical, based on the assumptions we make whenever we set out to explain human behavior scientifically. Let us take up the practical ones first.

As we have seen, our ordinary moral thinking assumes that to act on moral grounds is to act on a categorical imperative, "because it is right," regardless of other considerations. But even as we recognize the force of this requirement, we also tend to ask, "But why should I be moral?" That is, are there not reasons, other than the rightness of it, for doing what is right? If there are, and if they are the "real" reasons for what we do, the apparently categorical, or unconditional, imperative is subject to hypothetical conditions after all. But if there are no such further reasons, why should an intelligent person ever submit to the restraints of morality and justice? These questions are as old as moral reflection, and I think any candid person will realize that they become more urgent as the decisions we face become more difficult.

These questions express what Kant called the "internal conflict of practical reason": we think we ought to do our duty for duty's sake, yet with the other halves of our minds we think this is not a good enough reason, because there "ought" to be something in it for us. It is the old conflict between duty and self-interest. In short, we want to say both that there must be, and that there cannot be, a categorical imperative. How is a categorical imperative possible? This is another way of asking for the justification of the principle of autonomy, and is the problem of the *Critique of Practical Reason*.

A few cases will illustrate our practical interest in explaining away the rigors of morality by giving them a fundamentally non-moral complexion. "The right thing" is often demanding and difficult, and seems more likely to serve the interests of some other person or group, who may not be worthy of our sacrifices, than to do us any good. What if our notions of what is right are simply reflections of outmoded

customs that we have so "internalized" through upbringing
and habit that to act otherwise arouses guilt feelings? "The
heathen in his blindness bows down to wood and stone," as
the old hymn says, and perhaps we too are victims of super-
stition. What if our moral code only expresses the ideology
and interests of a particular class, so that to follow it would
be to make ourselves instruments of purposes we would not
wish to serve? Or again, if my mother hated my father, and
I grew up in a slum, how can I be expected to honor the authority figures of "a world I never made"? And finally, although as children we may have been carried away with admiration for the heroes we read about, what are we to say
when psychology explains their courage as an expression of
the death instinct, an acting out of their narcissism, or something perhaps less damaging to human pride but no less incompatible with the moral point of view?

The "moral" of such considerations—which often occur to
us with special vividness when we first encounter the sophisti-
cation of college—is that it is foolish to knock ourselves out to
do what we have been brought up to regard as our duties, or
to punish ourselves with feelings of guilt for our failures to
do so. Would it not be more intelligent to conclude that
what we call morality and immorality are only the more and
the less accepted ways of responding to social forces or to
inner drives and conflicts? Why not relax and enjoy as best we
can whatever kind of life circumstances may provide? Is there
any reason why I should be moral unless there is something
to be gained by it in the way of comfort, security, or enjoyment?

As if the voice of self-interest did not provide sufficient reasons for wishing to give morality's claims a non-moral interpretation, our ability to explain human behavior scientifically
and our understanding of the conditions under which such
explanations are possible combine to give us persuasive theoretic reasons for doubting the necessity, and even the possibility, of any categorical imperative.

In Kant's terms, this theoretical point can be stated very

simply. [To understand human behavior, or anything else, is to know its causes.] And we come to know causes by discovering laws of nature that relate events to other events which are their conditions. To be sure, we are not in fact able to give scientific explanations for everything that people do, just as we cannot fully explain every change in the weather; but we must assume that whatever people do *has* such an explanation whether we know what it is or not, just as we assume that there must be sufficient reasons why the weather changed unexpectedly yesterday, even though we cannot identify all of them. To assume anything else is to believe in miracles, which is to subvert the whole idea of science and the intelligibility of nature. Finally, to find an event or series of them, and a law that so relates them as to explain why someone did something, is to discover some psychological phenomenon— some drive, desire, or interest—that serves as the cause of the action. And this amounts to showing that the act, if intentional, was determined by a hypothetical imperative: *given* such a motive, the act followed and is thereby explained. The same outcome might have been explained, and have been caused, by a different interest or desire; but *some* such condition is necessary both for its occurrence and for its explanation.

This conclusion is a general one, independent of any particular explanatory theory; for whether one's view of human motivation be Freudian, behaviorist, or of some other persuasion, all take it to be obvious that we act only for a reason that Kant would classify as a hypothetical imperative. [In the practical conflict between moral and non-moral reasons for action, our interest in scientific inquiry and explanation supports the latter.] For it insists that *there must always be non-moral reasons sufficient to explain every action,* so that for theoretic purposes the assumption of a categorical imperative is uncalled for and therefore implausible.

The tenor of both the theoretical and the practical objections is to recommend what are at best the externals of morality, as conformity to society's rules, but at the price of destroying its distinctive character. For if what we have re-garded as the moral law is not a categorical imperative, but only one of several rules for adjusting to the world, sin is no more than bad judgment; punishment can be justified as a corrective, channeling behavior in more desirable directions (as mild electric shocks condition a laboratory rat), but not as redress owed for wrongs done; and a sense of guilt becomes a morbid tendency to cry over spilt milk.

Although the viability of our ordinary moral conceptions, and of the categorical imperative as their principle, may ap-pear pretty dubious, the reader should not abandon himself to despair (or to glee if that is the way his prejudices incline him). He should first be clear about the sort of question we are asking when we want to know how a categorical impera-tive is possible, if it is. Since this is the special problem of the *Critique of Practical Reason,* it will be worth some time and thought.

It is primarily a question about the possibility of doing whatever we do for a special kind of reason, despite the pres-ence of reasons of other kinds. Suppose I happen to be so constituted as to be uncomfortable if those near me are un-happy, and suppose I accordingly endeavor to ease their dis-comfort and mine at the same time. Although this may be "the right thing to do," my efforts are not prompted by a moral reason if they are merely attempts to put myself at ease. For what if I happened to have the opposite kind of constitu-tion, incapable of feeling easy if others are happier than I? Then, for exactly the same sort of reason, I would add to their troubles—definitely not "the right thing to do." In either case I would have acted on a hypothetical imperative, for a reason that was contingent upon the propensities of my "nature." This is not a moral reason for doing anything, although what is done for such reasons may incidentally coincide with what is right. A moral reason would at least have to be independent of the tendencies we inherit or acquire, enabling us to judge inclinations rather than merely to serve them. How then shall we characterize the kind of reason that qualifies as moral, and whose possibility is the possibility of a categorical imperative?

Kant's answer is at first sight surprising. The issue, he says, is "whether pure reason can be practical." In other words, it is whether purely rational considerations are sufficient to determine our actions, not only in the sense of providing a rule that would distinguish right from wrong *if* we wished to act accordingly, but also by supplying a sufficient incentive for doing it. By "purely rational" considerations, Kant means reasons that are independent of the facts of experience, reasons that are a priori as opposed to empirical; and this way of formulating the issue is connected with and will help explain his otherwise puzzling use of the terms "metaphysics" and "metaphysical" in moral philosophy, and not only in what is usually called metaphysics. As he explains in the Preface to the *Grounding* (which has "metaphysics" in its full title), this term refers to the pure, or a priori, part of any systematic body of doctrine. And since Kant holds that both natural science and morals must include a priori principles, he speaks of both a metaphysics of nature and a metaphysics of morals. In these terms, then, the question whether pure reason can be practical has to do with the existence and validity of the categorical imperative as a pure or "metaphysical" practical principle; and Kant has been making the further point that unless such a principle can be valid, moral philosophy cannot exist as a distinct discipline, but will be one of the varieties of applied science or technology. Consequently, moral philosophy depends entirely on its pure part.

The special problem of the *Critique of Practical Reason* can now be stated in three ways: What is the justification of the principle of autonomy? How is a categorical imperative possible? Can pure reason be practical? They are all equivalent in the respect that a satisfactory answer to one of them will be an answer to the others as well; but the last is the most fundamental formulation, calling for a systematic critical examination of the role of intelligence in action (i.e., of practical reason), and in particular for a clarification of the differences between empirical and a priori grounds of choice. Accordingly, the first part of the *Critique* sets out to establish a mutual implication between the possibility of a categorical imperative (and with it the validity of the common moral ideas analyzed in the *Grounding*) and the possibility of action determined by reason alone, or "the autonomy of pure reason." The two stand or fall together.

Although these rather rarefied philosophical questions about the powers of "pure reason" may seem remote from the moral concerns of everyday life, the connection should become evident after another look at the practical and theoretical objections to the categorical imperative with which we began this section. We shall find that they are easily translatable into issues about a priori versus empirically conditioned reasons for action.

When somebody demands reasons for doing what is right, he is clearly asking for reasons other than its rightness—for reasons that will "justify" doing his duty by connecting it with his personal interests. But what defines self-interest? Roughly speaking, there are two kinds of possibilities. One would be that everyone's "true" interest is the cultivation of virtue, the perfection of his moral character. While this may be true, it answers the question, "Why should I be moral?" by begging it; for this only says that the true interests of all of us are defined by the moral ideal. The other possibility would be that each person's "interest" lies in the fulfillment of whatever his many interests happen to be. This Kant calls his happiness. Everybody always seeks happiness in this sense; for here happiness just means the maximum satisfaction of whatever desires one has. It follows that while everyone's interests are the same in name (happiness), they differ in fact; and this difference is almost without limit, because the specific content of happiness varies with the temperaments, circumstances, and histories of each individual. But this is to say that happiness must be an empirical concept, and that any appeal to one's desire for happiness as a reason for doing something, or to any particular interest among the many that constitute his happiness, is an appeal to an empirical principle which is a hypothetical imperative of the form, "To achieve the empirically defined objective X, do Y." And conversely, every hypothetical imperative is an empirically conditioned rule depending on the contingent ingredients of someone's personal conception of happiness.

The argument that a categorical imperative depends on the power of pure reason to determine action can now be stated succinctly. What we call *action* in contrast to unintentional or automatic *movement* is always "rational" in the sense that it is guided by a conception of what we are doing. Such a conception can be formulated as a rule or maxim which must be either categorical or hypothetical, for these exhaust the logical possibilities. If the rule is hypothetical, the act is determined by an empirical condition, and vice versa. Therefore the possibility of acting on a categorical imperative is equivalent to the possibility of an action that is *not* determined by an empirical condition—one that is not done for the sake of what someone has learned to think will help make him happy. This conclusion squares with our common belief that although everybody wants to be happy (by definition), we can and sometimes ought to disregard considerations of happiness. But that entails a belief in the possibility of acting on a maxim that is both rational and independent of empirical conditions.

We should now have a better understanding of what it means to say that our conception of morality depends on "whether pure reason can be practical." And we can also see that "the internal conflict of practical reason" between moral and non-moral reasons for action has to do with whether the maxims on which we act must have empirical conditions or whether they may be purely a priori.

In similar fashion, the theoretical objection to a categorical imperative can be expressed in terms of the same opposition between empirical and pure practical principles. For purposes of science we must assume that everything that happens in nature and in human behavior can be explained by empirical conditions according to the "laws of nature." And in particular, this means that there must always be sufficient empirical (and therefore non-moral) reasons for everything we do. Thus from the standpoint of science, there is no need for such a metaphysical principle as the categorical imperative.

Kant meets this objection head on, endorsing the sufficiency of empirical explanations in science. Indeed, the arguments for the theoretical adequacy of what we should now call the behavioral sciences are all Kant's own and are fundamental to his theory of scientific knowledge. Nevertheless, he insists that these arguments have nothing to do with the categorical imperative as a moral principle. Our knowledge of men and the world is useful in the application of moral principles, but it is irrelevant to questions about their nature and validity, just as moral considerations based on the categorical imperative are beside the point when we wish to explain the course of events. The empirical sciences of behavior are incomplete, but their gaps need to be filled by further empirical knowledge and are not of a kind that can be bridged by non-scientific principles.

Still, it is not enough to say that science and moral philosophy can somehow avoid clashing with each other. We need to understand how they can be compatible. Let us recall first that the question of the *Critique* was said to be whether we can act for a certain kind of reason, i.e., a moral reason, even though there may, and indeed must, be other reasons for doing what we do. The point at issue, then, is whether the inevitable empirical reasons appropriate to scientific explanation must always be regarded as the "real" ones. We can illustrate it by an example drawn from Kant.

Think of a shopkeeper who sells candy to children, whom it would be easy to cheat. He acknowledges an obligation to treat them honestly, as even the weak and unwary deserve. It is also in his interest to do so, for reasons of prudence and good business. Moreover, he has a warm, sympathetic disposition and is especially fond of children. Assuming then that he has both a direct desire and an indirect interest prompting him to give them their money's worth, must we say that he *could not* do it simply because it is right, but must do so, if he does, either from sympathy, from regard for his long-run advantage, or for some comparable reason? The question is whether he *could* act solely out of concern for justice, not whether he probably would, or even how he (or we) could be sure that he did.

I think that we would say it at least makes sense to maintain he could, and that we would still say so even if he had been a crafty misanthrope whose inclinations were all against his doing the right thing instead of being in favor of it. But in saying so, what empirical evidence could we cite in our support?

There is, and there can be, no such evidence. There can be empirical evidence only for behavior that is itself describable in empirical terms, such as for giving or not giving the children full measure for their pennies. Before the fact, there would be empirical evidence for a prediction that our shopkeeper probably would or would not act in certain verifiable ways, based on his sympathetic nature, his prudence, or the opposite qualities; and after the fact, the same traits could be cited to explain what he had been observed to do. But no such evidence affects the question whether he could, would, or did treat the children justly out of regard for justice as opposed to a direct inclination or a calculated advantage. The reason is that empirical evidence for such conclusions *makes no sense,* for one cannot be observed to act justly or morally in the way in which one can be observed to eat heartily or to seek the company of the opposite sex. At best one can be observed to behave in outward conformity to the rules of justice. But that is a point on which a shady character who conforms in order to keep out of trouble and a merely compulsive conformist are equally indistinguishable from an upright man.

Kant's essential claim, based on his careful analysis of the meaning of moral concepts, is that these concepts require us to act *from* a special incentive (respect for the idea of lawfulness) *according to* a purely intellectual standard (the capacity of one's maxim to be a universal law) and *for the sake of* a purely ideal end (a self-regulating community of the free). Since not one of these ideas could be adequately exemplified in experience, they could not have been derived from experience and must consequently be a priori concepts in Kant's sense of the term. Therefore questions about the empirical grounds for predicting or explaining the observable aspects of action are irrelevant to questions about the possibility of its moral aspects.

When we grant the possibility of acting for strictly moral reasons, then, we also necessarily grant the impossibility of showing whether anyone has actually done so, for the available evidence is relevant only to assigning reasons of other kinds. So far as other people are concerned, we can tell when they perform outwardly as justice requires. This is sufficient to determine whether they do what is right in what Kant calls the legal sense; but we cannot tell whether their reasons are honorable, dishonorable, or indifferent in the moral sense of these terms. And as for ourselves, we know the reasons which ought to guide us, and we can try to do as they require; but as we are aware when we are conscious of self-serving motives that incline us in the same direction, we can never be sure which factors have been decisive.

These conclusions about the meaning and possibility of acting for moral reasons are instructive in clarifying the sense in which the categorical imperative is a practical principle. It provides criteria for *deciding* what we ought to do by specifying an end, a rule, and an incentive. But as a principle that is primarily practical, it is of limited use in making judgments about moral character, whether our own or other people's; for while such judgments are sometimes able to assign blame, they can never determine merit. Thus any overt act that is inconsistent with the intellectual standard of lawfulness (such as cheating on a contract) is unjust. It is morally as well as legally wrong because it could not have been done for a morally acceptable reason. (The relief of suffering can-

but how do we assess what should make into a universalisable moral law if not refering to empirical stuff? A priori?

not justify deceit; for although sympathy is a commendable motive, we saw in Section I why no maxim that entails having one's way by lying can be a universal law, and this condemns the well-meaning liar along with the malicious one.) But whereas injustice implies moral wrong, justice and legality, however punctiliously observed, are morally indeterminate. The hypocrite and the pharisee may deceive themselves and their psychoanalysts about their motives, just as they do the rest of us. Thus neither as imperfectly self-conscious agents nor as observers of other people can we be sure when something has been done for the reasons it ought to be done. Moral merit could be known only to God, "the searcher of hearts," although we know well enough what we must do to deserve it.)

Thus, to repeat, the validity of the categorical imperative implies that reasons for action may be independent of empirical influences. (If there is any justification for what we assume whenever we make a practical decision, we *can* act on grounds of reason alone. But if the same overt act can have both empirical and a priori grounds, how are we to understand the relation between these two levels of determination?)

For Kant this is a question of "transcendental freedom," concerning how, as rational agents, we can be free from determination by empirical causes, while as products of nature we are still subject to natural causes. (Kant's solution is to say that for practical purposes we can be sure *that* we are free; but we cannot fully understand *how* transcendental freedom is possible, for we are able to understand only what we can explain according to the canons of empirical science. Beyond that, human limitations are such that we can know only that transcendental freedom is not impossible. The long argument of the *Critique* is devoted to these two points, one positive and one negative: we know we are autonomous, capable of acting according to rules we conceive for ourselves, so that the categorical imperative is vindicated as a guide for action; but since knowledge too is an expression of the transcendental autonomy of intelligence, we cannot lift ourselves by our boot-straps and achieve full knowledge of the ultimate grounds of both knowledge and action.

Since the function of an introduction is to introduce the reader to a study, not to substitute for it, I will not try to distill the argument of the *Critique* in support of these propositions any more than I did the analytic exercise of the *Grounding*. But because it seems both dogmatic and anti-climactic to say that transcendental freedom must be accepted even though it is ultimately unintelligible, let me conclude this section with a few paragraphs to show that nobody can avoid accepting the autonomy of intelligence; for even to deny it, if the denial makes sense, is to endorse it by what we do if not in what we say.

Let us compare what we necessarily assume when we try to make a decision that is morally right with what we assume in efforts to arrive at assertions that are true—which is to be "right" in the sense appropriate to the aims of knowledge. The comparison is instructive because scientific inquiry is also an intelligent activity, governed by intellectual standards that define its aim and method. We shall find that science too has its counterpart of the categorical imperative; that in science our thinking has reasons that are either autonomously rational or empirical, of which however only the former are scientifically relevant; and that scientific knowledge is as indebted to transcendental freedom as is doing one's duty.

Consider what we commit ourselves to when we make a choice. When I decide what to do, I do not wonder, or try to predict, what I shall eventually do, for nobody can decide and wonder about the same eventuality. Deciding makes sense only on the assumption that I really can determine what to do, for reasons I recognize as cogent, and that what I do will not be simply the outcome of the influences impinging upon me. Predicting what I shall do, on the other hand, makes sense only to the degree that I am *not* an agent but a spectator, observing the course of events and estimating the evidence favoring one outcome as more likely than another. Thus we are not thought to be reliable predictors of our own behavior for the obvious reason that, having formulated a predictive hypothesis about what I shall do, I can usually make it true (as I might well be tempted to do)—destroying the scientific objectivity of the prediction whenever I assert myself as an agent.

In parallel fashion, when I inquire about the truth of a proposition, I do not try to predict my eventual opinion about it. The two activities are incompatible, guided by quite different considerations and concerned with different objects. The former makes sense only if I can draw a responsible conclusion according to intellectual canons of evidence proper to the subject of inquiry, and consequently, if what I think need not be simply the outcome of psychological influences on my state of mind. A prediction of my opinion, on the other hand, would have to be based on the psychological determinants of my thinking, not on evidence about its subject matter. Furthermore, even if I could predict some of my opinions by regarding myself as a passive observer of the conditions of their formation, I must still, in the respect in which I am the maker and not the object of my prediction, regard myself as an autonomous inquirer independent of the processes about which I inquire.

To be sure, every thought, whether true or false, and whether relevant or irrelevant, is as predictable and explicable as any other when regarded as a psychological process in the context of other psychological processes. But the difference between truth and error, as states of mind, is not determinable by their empirical causes: it is not as truth and cogency, but only as states of mind, that truth and cogency have psychological causes. For instance, suppose the simple case of someone who habitually believes what he is told. His credulity explains his opinions. Some of them will doubtless happen to be true. But their cause is irrelevant to their truth, for he believes his false opinions for exactly the same reason that he believes the true ones. They are true, when they are, because of their conformity to the canons of knowledge and the nature of their objects—of which he may lack the foggiest notion. More important still, to believe or to say what happens to be true does not establish that one *knows* anything. Though our credulous friend (and many students who take examinations) can give "the right answer" to selected questions, nobody succeeds in *being* right about them until he understands the questions and can tell what is right about their answers, that is, until he can cite the reasons why certain propositions are true, which are often entirely different from the reasons why they are believed.

Here then are some instructive parallels between knowledge and morality. Beliefs are held, and actions done, for all sorts of reasons. But opinions do not qualify as knowledge unless they not only are true but are held for the appropriate reasons, just as acts do not qualify as morally right unless they not only conform to the right rule but are also done for the right reason. In both cases, the empirical causes of action and belief are irrelevant to their scientific and moral significance. We have seen that talk of morality would be pointless if it were only a matter of the influences that cause me to do one thing while impelling you to do another. All talk of knowledge would be no less pointless if there were nothing to it but causal influences that induce me to say or think *this* while causing you to opine *that.* Nor in that case would it even make sense to talk of thinking or having an opinion, which entail reference to an object and to the objective of being right about it.

It should therefore be evident that knowledge is as dependent on the autonomy of intelligence as morality is. In the former case, to be right in the appropriate respects is to judge for truth's sake according to standards which intelligence autonomously determines for itself. These range from the necessary and a priori principles of logic to the more special canons that emerge from the continuous self-criticism of the sciences concerned with particular subject matters. Being morally right is to respect the moral standards which intelligence sets for itself. The categorical imperative defines the universally necessary criteria; and we shall presently see how this one principle can generate a whole body of doctrine applicable to the broad fields of law and morality as well as to their subdivisions.

Finally, knowledge has its own counterpart of the categorical imperative. Why should I care about the truth? To be sure, "knowledge is power" and therefore useful, as conformity to society's rules of propriety is often useful. But not always or without qualification. There is no general reason for respecting the discipline of truth if by a "reason" one means an ulterior motive distinct from the regard for truth itself; and the question, "Why should I be rational, respecting the standards of truth?" is as inane as "Why should I be moral by respecting the moral law?" Why indeed? If one has to ask why he should respect the truth, there is no answer that he would understand, for there is no way to make use of a reason except by the principles he professes to lack. Yet since he *does* ask, he presumably wants an answer that is true and to the point, so that his question must be disingenuous after all.

It follows, if I have made myself clear in speaking for Kant, that to assert any proposition entails what he calls the autonomy of pure reason, for without it, assertion and truth make no sense. Therefore to deny that autonomy is to involve oneself in a contradiction—not, to be sure, in the words one says, but in the implications of the act of saying it.

III

All this, however interesting and "philosophical," has been prologue. For Kant, *doctrine,* the systematic presentation of a kind of knowledge, is to be distinguished from *critique,* the reflective examination of principles, which characteristically concerns itself with the scope and limits of one of the major uses of intelligence, e.g., the *Critique of Pure [Speculative] Reason,* the *Critique of Practical Reason,* and the *Critique of Judgment.* Thus, having analyzed the ordinary conceptions of morality in order to identify their supreme principle, and having provided a critical justification of that principle by examining the place of reason in action,[8] we are ready to sketch the outlines of moral philosophy as a substantive intellectual discipline. This is the business of *The Metaphysics of Morals,* or (to combine the longer titles of its two divisions) *The Metaphysical Principles of the Doctrines of Right and of Virtue.*

We shall be concerned primarily with the "metaphysical" or a priori principles that give any body of doctrine its articulate structure and with which, according to Kant, the exposition of any developed science should begin. *The Metaphysics of Morals* thus has a place in morals corresponding to that held in natural philosophy by *The Metaphysical Foundations of Natural Science,* which is midway between the transcendental reflections of the *Critique of Pure Reason* and the detailed investigations of empirical physics, biology, and psychology. However, apart from these similarities between the parts of natural and moral philosophy, moral doctrine, as we have seen in the preceding section, is peculiarly dependent on its a priori principles and, as we shall see presently, owes relatively little to empirical inquiries.

The metaphysical parts of natural and moral philosophy, which are intermediate between transcendental critique and empirical applications, both make use of empirical *concepts;* but this does not make their *propositions* empirical in the sense of being dependent on empirical evidence and therefore contingently true. If, for example, we take the empirical concepts of matter and motion and apply the transcendental principles of the *Critique of Pure Reason* to them, we can derive some a priori laws of nature—e.g., nothing happens to a ma-

---

[8] The justification provided by a critique is not a strict proof that demonstrates a conclusion by deducing it from premises; for, since it is the first principle or principles of an entire area of knowledge that need to be established, there are no prior premises from which to deduce them. The strategy is rather an indirect one, showing (as we indicated roughly at the end of Section II above) that the principles in question have to be accepted because to deny them leads in one way or another to contradiction or absurdity.

terial object except according to causal laws—which the empirical laws of physics illustrate in an indefinite variety of ways. In moral philosophy likewise we need some empirical concepts in order to relate the fundamental law to "the human condition." Covering rational agents as such, the moral law makes no distinction between God, to whom it would be absurd to ascribe duties, and agents like us, whose relation to the law is always one of obligation. Indeed, the concept of duty makes sense only for agents whose desires and interests may urge action contrary to the law, so that they must choose not only among actions but among different reasons for acting. The concepts of desire and its many species are of course empirical; and such concepts, in conjunction with the supreme moral principle, yield the specific classes of duties which make up moral doctrine proper.

But whereas the empirical laws of nature, subordinate to a few metaphysical principles, account for most of natural science, moral philosophy is peculiar in that its a priori part exhausts what can be called doctrine in the strict sense. To be sure, moral philosophy does have an empirical part, which Kant calls "practical anthropology," but since morals are concerned with what ought to be done, rather than with explaining what actually is done, the contribution of moral anthropology is only supplementary. That is, telling us why we often fail to do as we ought, it helps us foresee the conditions under which we are most likely to succeed. In this it is like the socio-psychological supplement to logic, which explains our tendencies to slip into irrelevance and other fallacies when we should be following the a priori laws of logic. In both disciplines, experience helps us avoid the commonest pitfalls as well as take advantage of opportunities to apply the a priori rules which jointly constitute the substantive doctrine.

Our task, then, is to proceed from the principle of autonomy, as the supreme principle of practical reason in general, to specific rules of duty and eventually down to cases. This is of crucial importance, since the point of moral philosophy, as Marx observed in a different connection, is less to understand the world than to change it by affecting what we do. Problems of action are concrete, always having to do with what is here and now, and opportunities never repeat themselves. Scientific problems, on the other hand, are about individual events and processes only insofar as they are repeatable and illustrate general laws that can be expressed in timeless formulas. Choices cannot be deferred (since to avoid choosing is really to have chosen to let circumstances take their course), and once made, they are irretrievable; but we have all the time in the world to refine and test scientific hypotheses. In short, while the aim of science is understanding through general propositions, moral philosophy is for the sake of what can be realized in action amid changing circumstances.

Crucial as they are for any moralist, these considerations are especially critical in discussions of Kant, for he is often accused of failing to show how his principles can be brought to bear on cases. It is said that the categorical imperative is an empty formula, that it has no power to determine rules specific enough to guide us in concrete situations, and that the precepts Kant seems to recognize are laid down as inflexible prescriptions ill adapted to the fluid situations we face and the diverse values among which we must choose. There is some excuse for these accusations if they come from someone who is acquainted only with the *Grounding* and the *Critique,* for both concentrate on the categorical imperative as a universal principle, for reasons that should now be clear. A knowledge of *The Metaphysics of Morals,* however, and especially of *The Metaphysical Principles of Virtue,* should encourage a more balanced perspective; for although they deal principally with general categories of duties, their orientation is toward the specifics of action, and in the latter treatise we find Kant paying a good deal of attention to what he calls "casuistical questions."

For example, a hasty reader of the *Grounding,* noting Kant's harsh remarks about suicide, might conclude that Kant regards deliberately causing one's own death as wrong under any circumstances. Yet *The Metaphysical Principles of Virtue* presents the problem of Frederick the Great, who always carried poison on his military campaigns so that, should he be captured, he could foil attempts to use him as a hostage to extort dishonorable concessions from Prussia. What about that? The point to remember is that the moral qualities of what one does are not settled by such general descriptions as "voluntarily causing one's own death," but rather by the maxim on which one acts. There is clearly a lot of difference between selfishly "ducking out while I am still ahead of the game" and regretting "that I have but one life to lay down for my country," as Nathan Hale expressed it. The purpose, the circumstances, and therefore the maxim that formulated one's choice, would be quite different in the two cases.

Proceeding now to the applications of the moral law, we find that the field of its legislation has two principal subdivisions. The first is the province of justice and legality, which Kant calls right (*Recht*), while the second is that of the ethical in the narrow sense, or virtue (*Tugend*). They may roughly be distinguished by saying that to render or withhold what one owes, and to observe or violate someone's rights, are matters of justice and injustice, involving external and public performances that can be rewarded or punished; whereas virtue and vice, and merit and depravity are internal and personal things, beyond the reach of even "the long arm of the law." Think first of fraud, embezzlement, and assault: each of them violates someone's rights, and their contraries all reduce to the same thing, to observance of the law, which is not anything to boast about since it is the least that is required of everybody, and is normally enforced by penalties in any case. Now think of malice, self-indulgence, and envy. They may or may not be "acted out" in unjust treatment of others, yet all are vices of the most corrosive sort that corrupt the motivations in a person's character. There is no point in passing laws against them. Moreover, their opposites do not simply reduce to "doing right" in obedience to the law, but are quite different forms of virtue or moral excellence, all deserving of merit "over and above the call of duty," in the sense in which

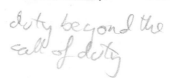
duty beyond the call of duty

duty is owed by everyone; and like their opposite vices, the
virtues are also internal dispositions. We "have a right" not
to be saints or heroes as long as we do not infringe the rights
of others. So much is legality. But from the moral point of
view it is not enough to stand on one's rights and refrain from
breaking the law. Virtue includes helpfulness, respect for the
aspirations as well as the rights of others, and in general a
conscientious respect for the dignity of persons and the spirit
of the law.

The essence of this distinction between what is right and
what is virtuous, or between the realms of legality and morality, whose principal features we have just noted, is formulated
by Kant with considerable economy and elegance in terms
of the concept of legislation, which contains two elements: a rule to be followed, and an incentive to follow it.
Legislation that both makes something a duty and makes its
being a duty the appropriate reason for doing it, is ethical;
and the agreement of action with the law, in *both* letter and
spirit, is its morality. In contrast, legislation that attaches
other incentives, like rewards and punishments, as sanctions
for what it commands as a duty, is juridical; and the agreement of an act with the law, apart from one's reason for doing
it, is its legality. Ethical legislation, then, is necessarily internal, while the juridical variety is external in a double sense:
it establishes an incentive that is "external" to the action that
it enjoins, and only the external and public aspects of action
fall within its jurisdiction. Evil intentions are immoral, but
they are not in themselves illegal. Thus it is a fundamental
tenet of our law that a man is legally accountable only for his
acts: his thoughts are his own business, and he has a right to
them however wrong or mistaken they may be.

The fundamental distinction, then, is between the fields of
legality and morality, defined in terms of the two types of
legislation and the different kinds of obligation that they generate. Duties, as they fall under these distinct species of legislation, do not divide so neatly. This is because "duty is the
matter of obligation," or the thing we are required to do; and

the same duty may be commanded by both kinds of legislation. To fulfill a contract is required by law as enforced by the courts; but there is also a moral obligation to honor one's agreements, which would remain even if the law of contracts were never codified or enforced. Hence the Stoic saying that the good man does of his own accord what others do only under legal constraint, so that if the laws were abolished, the man of virtue would continue to live as before.

In view of this complication, Kant classifies all duties which *can* fall within the scope of external juridical legislation as "legal," reserving the class of "ethical" duties for those which are *only* possible through internal ethical legislation. Promise-keeping, then, is a juridical duty. Nevertheless, he adds, "all duties belong to ethics just because they are duties," so that even those which are primarily and directly legal are "adopted" by ethical legislation, requiring that we do them for moral reasons and not only from fear of the police.

Rechtslehre applies whenever external legislation does. It is subject to the categorical imperative, which can here be adapted to the limitations of legality so as to become the *supreme principle of right:* Act externally so that the free use of your choice may not interfere with the freedom of any man as far as it agrees with universal law. Such a principle is entirely formal, paying no heed to the matter, or ends, of action except insofar as it restricts the manner in which they may be rightly pursued. As Kant observes, innumerable purposes are always occuring to us, and the juridical question is only whether their realization is possible through maxims that are compatible with the standards of legality. If they are—and only if they are—we have a right to proceed.

We have a right, I should have said, according to the principles of natural law. Law which can be recognized as such by reason alone is *natural,* and is the same everywhere because reason is the same everywhere. However, there is also *positive* law, which requires or prohibits action which otherwise would have been legally indifferent. There would be no obligation to obtain a driver's license or to pay an income tax unless some legislative body had so decreed, whereas the obligation to carry out one's agreements does not depend on any particular legislative enactment but holds wherever men have dealings with one another. Natural and positive law are closely related, however, for not every decree or enactment backed by sanctions deserves to be called a law or to be recognized as generating an obligation. Might alone does not make right, so that positive legislation must be consistent with natural law—and therefore with the supreme principle of right and the categorical imperative—in order to be valid.

Positive law, then, the law of external constraint by authority, is subordinate to and depends upon the universal law of reason. And therefore, as should become apparent as we reflect upon it, all legality depends eventually upon the moral law and the internal self-constraint that ethical legislation imposes. This amounts to saying that if there were no ethical duties arising from specifically ethical legislation, there could not be any duties at all: the notion of duty or obligation would make no sense. The idea of duty is essentially ethical, and without an underlying ethical principle the rule of law would be merely a matter of power, not of right.

In order to see this, we might think of a despotic ruler and his decrees. If he is powerful enough, and ruthless enough, his subjects may be "obliged" to do as he commands. This is far from saying that they ought to, or "have an obligation to," but rather, only that they ought to *if* they are to avoid the consequences of his displeasure. Here again we confront the now familiar distinction between hypothetical and categorical imperatives, of which the former can take us no further than counsels of prudent self-interest. Our despot has power, to be sure, but no authority. How does he acquire authority? In short, what must happen in order for us to be able to say that we ought to obey him—that we may not only *be* obliged to, but that we *have* an obligation to?

The long and the short of it is that no one can be compelled to have duties or to recognize an obligation. The concept of duty does involve constraint, for it implies that there is something we ought or ought not to do, regardless of our wishes. But it also includes the idea of freedom. Consequently, says Kant, "the notion of duty can only contain *self-constraint* (by the idea of the law itself)," for there is no way to combine constraint with freedom except through moral autonomy. The concept of duty, as we said above, is *essentially* ethical. Its legal use borrows its significance from ethics. Therefore a ruler has authority, and can impose duties through positive law, only if he legislates justly, according to principles which are at once rational and moral. And of course in doing so he would no longer be a despot. As Thomas Jefferson put it in the Declaration of Independence, all men have certain rights according to natural law, and "it is to secure these rights that governments are instituted among men." Moreover, he added, governments "derive their just powers"—that is, not merely their power but their authority—"from the consent of the governed," who obligate *themselves* to obey the laws. It should be observed of course that "consent" here does not mean just any favorable sentiment or "pro-attitude," but rather the recognition of a rational norm or principle. That is the point of the reference to natural law. Governments may derive overwhelming power from the concurrent interests of majorities; but these are not "just powers" unless they are consistent with the freedom of minorities to pursue their interests too, within the limits of legality as defined by the principle of right.

We have seen that ethical obligations, and the ethical legislation that generates them, are distinguished by the incentive or reason for doing what is required. One's legal obligations may be fully discharged if they are done for fear of reprisals, or because they may fall in line with what one wanted to do anyway, or for any other reason; whereas ethical obligations are not discharged unless they are done out of respect for the law, because it is right to do them. To do them for such a reason is an act of *virtue* (*Tugend*), involving merit over and above the negative "virtue" of being free from blame. The concept of virtue has significance only in ethics, as distinct from jurisprudence, and the content of ethical legislation constitutes the *doctrine of virtue* (*Tugendlehre*) just as that of juridical legislation is the *doctrine of right* (*Rechtslehre*).

Acts of virtue are of two kinds. Virtue of the first sort arises when we carry out our legally determined obligations on ethical grounds. In this we do no different sort of thing (materially considered), but only add an ethical significance to the duties of right by doing them in a different way and for a different reason. As Kant remarks, there is only one virtue of this sort, associated with one comprehensive ethical duty. This is to do one's legal duties from respect for the rational principle that makes them duties, or for duty's sake. But in the second place there are acts of virtue that arise from the recognition of an entirely different order of duties, involving the pursuit of certain peculiarly moral ends that are distinguishable from the general aim of doing right (which is also distinctively ethical because it is an end only as a result of ethical legislation). The moral law determines several such ends which it is a duty to make the objects of our endeavors, and these give rise to the second kind of ethical duty, called *duties of virtue* (*Tugendpflichten*).

Ethical legislation then, which is the ground of both types of virtue, always determines ends that are peculiarly ethical instead of merely requiring that we seek what ends we please within the limits of the law. Now the concept of a moral end is of great importance, both in itself and for an understanding of Kant's moral philosophy. It is important in its own right because it is necessarily connected with the idea of a categorical imperative, without which all obligations would be contingent and instrumental. There is a widespread tendency to think of moral and legal codes as rules that do no more than impose a degree of order and harmony upon the pursuit of happiness, rather as the traffic laws regulate and facilitate driving, so that their value would be instrumental rather than substantive. But in seeing no point in doing something for duty's sake, this view not only abolishes the distinction between legal and ethical obligations, but also undermines the integrity of moral philosophy as a whole by making the dif-

ference between technical and moral imperatives equally unintelligible.

The idea of a moral end is also important for an understanding of Kant because he is often regarded as a mere "formalist" who has nothing to say about moral values over and
above that of being dutiful in general—an apparently empty
ideal—and who further, as if to make a virtue of this weakness,
seems to insist that a rational ethics can have nothing to do
with such ends. But this is a misunderstanding of his fundamental point that to use the purposes we happen to have as
the determinants of all our maxims is to act only on hypothetical imperatives. In the language of the *Critique,* all materially and empirically determined practical principles are
heteronomous; whereas duty in any form is impossible without autonomy. But autonomy is not the same as purposeless-
ness. Kant is careful to explain that we never act without an
end, just as we never act without a maxim. The important
question is not whether we always act for a purpose when we
choose deliberately—which would be a pseudo-question—but
it is about the varieties of ends, and whether they always determine our maxims, as in issues of skill and prudence, or
whether the order of determination can run in the opposite
direction.

Since the concept of a moral end is so important, it would
be well to notice some of its special features. In the first place,
the general idea of acting for an end already presupposes
freedom and is to that degree connected with moral autonomy. Coercion, for example, can succeed only when what we
are to be "forced" to do is a condition of achieving some objective that we are unwilling to renounce. Thus, since everybody naturally wants to stay alive, other things being equal,
we can be forced to do many things "on pain of death." But
should someone decide that other things are more important
to him than saving his skin, as happens frequently enough, he
can no longer be coerced by that sort of threat. We are always
in principle able to adopt our own goals, even though we do
not always succeed in surmounting the obstacles in the way,

or in withstanding the distractions and temptations that urge us in other directions. Now we have seen that legal obligations depend on there being such a thing as an ethical obligation, and since an ethical obligation depends on our freely acknowledging the aim of doing as the law requires, the reason why obligations cannot be forced upon us is that no one can be forced to act for one end rather than another.

While a moral end is one which we must be entirely free to make our own or not, it is also true that it must be, in at least one respect, a "necessary" end; for the alternatives are not of equal status. We *ought* to adopt one and repudiate the other as morally impossible. Duty and obligation have a kind of objective necessity, constraining us in a particular direction. How is this moral necessity compatible with moral freedom? Here it is easy to become confused by words. Moral freedom is opposed to the inevitability of natural necessity: as a rational agent I do not have to respond to the strongest impulse as a weathervane swings with the strongest puff. On the other hand, the morally necessary does not necessarily happen, either always or for the most part. It *ought to,* but it does not *have to;* and the fact that we always can do the "morally impossible" is part of the meaning of obligation. That is why a divine will, by definition lacking all incentives to stray from the law, can have no duties. (This is like our "obligation" to obey the objectively necessary laws of logic: none is more necessary than the law of non-contradiction; yet people contradict themselves all the time, and if they could not, the ideal of rational consistency would be meaningless.) The main idea here should be familiar by this time. The constraint involved in moral necessity can only be self-constraint according to an objective principle; and this is possible only through the autonomy of ethical legislation. Thus once more, all of moral philosophy, comprising both jurisprudence and ethics in the narrower sense, depends on the principle of autonomy which the *Grounding* identified and the *Critique* justified as the supreme principle of morals.

It is this notion of self-constraint according to the moral law, which is possible only through the free acknowledgment of moral action as an end in itself, that leads to the identification of further "ends which are at the same time duties."

In order to see how such ends can be identified, let us recall how the second formulation of the categorical imperative was shown to follow from the first. If one acted as if his maxims were at the same time to be observed by everyone as universal laws, it would follow as a consequence that he would also treat humanity in himself and others as an end in itself. For to treat someone merely as a means would be to act on a maxim that could not without contradiction be regarded as a universal law: it would mean being willing to have one's own purposes pushed aside whenever they were in anybody's way, and to act for a purpose that necessarily implied its frustration is a contradiction. This shows how we can start from a "formal" principle like the first version of the categorical imperative and arrive at the "material" obligation to honor rational agents as ends in themselves. Moral maxims can determine a moral end which it is a duty to protect and promote.

But what does it mean to treat humanity in oneself and others as an end in itself? How does one go about doing it? Let us begin with duties to others. First, then, we have a duty to respect other people's autonomy and integrity as persons, and not manipulate them as if they were purposeless things. So far as overt action is concerned, this is the same as to treat them justly, not interfering with their equal freedom. Since all substantive duties having to do with justice are duties of right, virtue enters the picture only when we ask about the spirit in which justice is done. The ethical obligation to respect the moral law carries with it a duty to respect the dignity of other rational agents who are, like ourselves, the sources as well as the subjects of the law we all acknowledge. This is a strictly determinate or "perfect" duty and is primarily negative, forbidding action in a spirit that would be incompatible with a moral community. It is an ethical duty, but not a duty of virtue involving an end other than that of acting justly.

How else can we treat others as ends in themselves? Obviously, by making their purposes our purposes, so far as theirs are consistent with the law, following the Biblical injunction to regard a neighbor's interests as we do our own.[9] But to further the aims of others is to promote their happiness, their welfare. Hence the welfare of mankind generally is an end that is also a duty. This, as a duty of virtue proper, has several features that are characteristic of the species. In the first place, it is an indeterminate and "imperfect" rather than a strict and "perfect" duty. It sets forth an end that is to be striven for, but it does not specify any particular action for the sake of that end. As Kant sometimes expresses it, the duties of virtue determine certain maxims of action, but not particular actions themselves, as legal duties do. A legal contract specifies the way it is to be carried out, but it is up to us to decide how we can best contribute to the general welfare. We may be well advised, for example, to concentrate our efforts on the well-being of our families, friends, and neighbors—not because their interests are more important in themselves than those of a faraway tribe of bushmen, but because we are better acquainted with the needs and problems of those who are near to us, and because we are in a better position to give them effective help.[10]

[9] This too is a consequence of the categorical imperative in its first form, according to which I may pursue my own interests only through maxims that can at the same time be followed by everyone as universal laws. This requires recognizing that my interests have neither more nor less priority than any other person's interests. Hence I ought to regard the latter as if they were my own.

[10] It is interesting that "the welfare of mankind" recalls "the greatest good of the greatest number," which utilitarians take to be the foundation of all moral judgments. But the difference of Kant's position is instructive. That an endeavor to promote human welfare when we can is a duty, although an indeterminate one, follows from the categorical imperative, a strictly determinate principle of practical reason. The idea

In the second place, such indeterminate duties not only allow us considerable leeway in achieving their objectives, but they are indefinite in the further sense that what they demand is also without assignable limits. We can never say, "There, I have at last done all that I ought to do for other people," for to decide to stop being kind and friendly is absurd, and actual hardship has always been so great that no individual effort can make a noticeable difference in its quantity. And thirdly, duties of virtue go beyond what others have a right to claim from us. The world may rightfully insist on just and impartial dealing, but beneficence like the good Samaritan's achieves merit "beyond the call of duty," in the respect in which duty is what we owe to others in recognition of their just claims.

We also have duties to, or with regard to, ourselves; and they too can best be approached by way of the general command to treat the humanity in ourselves, as well as in others, as an end in itself. Duties to ourselves are always ethical duties, for the idea of a legal duty to oneself is nonsense. The possibility of enforcement by external sanctions is an essential characteristic of legal duties, and it would be odd to the point of insanity to go to law to compel myself to do anything. And while other people may hail me into court to answer for my negligence, they may do so only on the ground that I have neglected to observe someone else's rights. But although duties to ourselves can not be juridical, they may be both strict and broad, perfectly and imperfectly determinate, just like duties to others. And again, only the broad and "imperfect" ones are duties of virtue.

"Perfect" duties to ourselves, like those to others, are negative and restrictive, forbidding us to subordinate the value of our person and qualities to any casual purpose. We may not

---

of a maximum of human satisfactions, however, is inherently indefinite—how is one to tell whether the total consequences of a decision are more likely to add to or detract from the sum of happiness? It is therefore useless as a *principle* for determining choices generally, quite apart from its shortcomings as an empirical principle that can yield only hypothetical imperatives.

degrade our humanity to the level of a thing, as we do when, for example, we debauch our bodies or befuddle our minds in pursuit of the pleasures of food and drink or of drugs and sex, or even when we ruin our health and fray our tempers in chasing fame and the almighty dollar. The point is not that such behavior often injures or inconveniences other people, or that it is unwise and in the long run self-defeating—which it usually is—but that it is a kind of sacrilege, perverting what is distinctively human for the sake of what is merely animal. This is supported by our unsophisticated moral judgments, which react to a self-made derelict not only with pity, but with a degree of disgust that cannot be accounted for by the fact that this man has made himself a useless burden to society and is in arrears in his obligations to his family and acquaintances. None of this implies, however, that there is anything wrong about enjoying the normal pleasures of the senses or the fun of exercising one's skills at top form. Indeed, the contrary is true; but that topic falls under the next heading of expanding and perfecting one's humanity rather than the present one of preventing its abuse. In contrast to these negative duties, then, are the positive obligations that implement the endeavor to develop and perfect our human qualities, which endeavor the Greeks called the pursuit of virtue, or of human excellence, as an end in itself.

According to the majestically cryptic opening sentence of the First Section of the *Grounding*, "There is no possibility of thinking of anything at all in the world, or even out of it, which can be regarded as good without qualification, except a *good will*";[11] and to have a good will is simply to have a character whose aims and choices are in complete accord with the moral law. The supreme value of a good will follows from the fundamental idea of morality as taking precedence over all other interests, for as should now be evident, the point of the categorical imperative is that other values can only be conditional. The goodness of a divine will, which could not do evil because it has no wants that could run counter to the law of

[11] *Grounding*, Ak. 393.

reason, would be holiness: the goodness of a human will, subject as it is to all manner of needs, fatigues, and distractions, is moral virtue. For us, moral perfection can be no more than an ideal to be approximated, so that Kant describes virtue as a condition of continuous progression. The practical alternatives are either degeneration or self-improvement.

Under this general duty to perfect ourselves, care for our moral characters clearly comes first because of the supreme and unconditioned value of a good will; but physical and intellectual development also define indeterminate duties of virtue. The latter are both good in themselves and invaluable allies of a good character. While it is no doubt obvious that disciplined "brains and brawn" are helpful ornaments of a good character, just as they make a bad one more dangerously evil, it may help to clarify their place in the moral spectrum, as well as to illustrate further the difference between justice and virtue, if we review the much disputed topic of "good intentions" versus "results" as measures of moral value.

Kant is often considered the moralist who stakes everything on good intentions; and if this were a simple all-or-nothing question, that would be the correct view. The maxim on which one acts is the crucial determinant of moral quality, and a judgment based on consequences alone allows for no distinction between legality and virtue, or even between acts that are morally significant in the broad sense and those of skill or prudent self-interest. It would doubtless be "a good thing," for example, if I were to endow a scholarship for poor boys—good for them at any rate—but what about the ethical significance of what I did? It *might* have been an act of pure benevolence. But it might also have been done in fulfillment of a promise made when, desperate to obtain an education for myself, I accepted help on condition that twenty years later I would contribute as much as I could afford to a scholarship fund. If that were my reason, the moral picture would be rather different, though not to my discredit. Again, it might have been an act of personal vanity, a display of narcissism proclaiming, "What a good boy am I!" And finally, it might have been a move to build my prestige in a campaign for office or status. The good or bad consequences, both for me and for others, could well be identical in all these cases, but not the moral complexion of my "philanthropy."

Yet it would be too simple to leave the matter there, resting on intentions alone. What if the terms of the scholarship were badly conceived? Benevolence of the purest dye can do much harm when it is not supported by intelligence and sound information. Physical competence too is often necessary if we are to meet our minimal obligations; and something more than competence may be needed to accomplish anything of positive merit. Thus, good intentions are absolutely essential; but they are not always enough. Here some distinctions will be helpful. Intentions are sufficient in judging issues of justice, provided the agent is at least aware of what he is doing. Kant says that if an act is legally obligatory, its consequences are irrelevant to questions of praise or blame. Thus a policeman whose business is to lock up miscreants need not concern himself about how a prisoner's wife and children are going to make out during their breadwinner's absence; nor will he gain any special merit if, in making a capture, he helps to restore a great deal of loot. That is all in the day's work; and his proper stance, which will be recognized by readers of good detective stories, is to say, "I only seen my duty and I done it." Good intentions are not sufficient, however, when we aim to do more than we owe under the rules; for then consequences are imputable as part of the moral evidence. Anyone who aspires to be not only scrupulously honest but helpful or heroic had better not botch the job.

Although concerns for the state of our knowledge, and for physical and intellectual alertness, are required for their usefulness in doing one's duties to others, they are primarily duties to oneself, to which we should redirect our attention. The most important thing about this class of duties is that in them ethical duties reach their culmination: if there were no duties to oneself, Kant says, there could be no ethical duties, and indeed—since all duties depend on ethical duties—no duties of any kind. This is a strong statement, and at first sight a paradoxical one; but it is simply a consequence of the principle of autonomy, for all morality is a matter of self-dedication ("commitment" is the fashionable word) to the ideal defined by the moral law. We accomplish nothing of moral significance until we take this vital step, and we can take it for the sake of no one but ourselves and our self-respect. It may seem plausible to speak of trying to "be good" for the sake of someone else, but the suggestion rests on a confusion. If the point is to please, in the hope of winning approval or affection, it is just another self-seeking device; and though one may consequently "be good" in a manner of speaking, it will amount to no more than going through the legally correct moves for the sake of a non-moral end.

The comprehensive demand of the moral point of view, then, in contrast to that of conformity to the rules, is to realize a state of virtue in one's own character as the basis of all his actions. In an important sense this is not a duty "owed to" anyone, for only legal duties are of that sort; but it is a duty with regard to oneself and its object is oneself. It is only my actions and my character for which the moral law can make me responsible.

For despite the Mrs. Grundys and the other busybodies of the world, we can neither improve nor corrupt other people's characters in any direct or decisive fashion. That is something each person must do for himself; for he alone is responsible for the inward determinants of his choices, and it is these freely adopted aims and maxims that determine the moral qualities of life and action. To be sure, we can affect the morals of others in two sorts of ways, but both of them are roundabout and uncertain.

We can influence people in the direction of outward correctness by a judicious manipulation of rewards and punishments, which may include prospects of pleasure and deprivation having all degrees of severity and subtlety. These are all forms of external constraint. Even when they are most successful they fall far short of inducing morality. But constraint is a necessary first step in moral education. The human race had to be domesticated before it could become fully human, and in bringing up children we try to put them through the stages, from savagery to external conformity and on to autonomy, that the species followed in its rise to civilization and occasional nobility.[12]

Beyond such inducements through bribery and threats (however mild or disguised), we can only provide opportunities for moral choice, models for imitation, informed advice, and Socratic questioning, all in the hope that the beneficiaries of our concern will "get the idea" and become fully autonomous. In short, "You can lead a horse to water but you can't make him drink," and the all-important step in the moral improvement of our children and associates comes when they undergo a radical transformation that can neither be externally controlled nor reliably detected—when they take the initiative in doing the right thing, no longer for the reward or in order to please papa, but because they recognize the rightness of it. From that point onward moral education can be more intellectual, for much of it will consist in bringing out the implications of the fundamental principle, once it has been recognized—rather as we have been doing in this essay.

In summary, it should not be hard to see why the duties of virtue all fall under the two main headings of the welfare of others, and one's own perfection, with the latter taking precedence. Perfection of character (i.e., a good will) is the primary moral end, but other people's perfection is not in our power and cannot be our responsibility except through the negative duty to do nothing that would tempt them from the straight and narrow path. A concern for the general welfare is a duty, but an interest in one's own well-being will take care

---

12 In his essay on *Perpetual Peace*, Kant says that peace among men can never come through moral regeneration alone (as is the current hope of the Moral Rearmament movement). What is needed first is the growth of a world commonwealth under law. While such a legal order cannot cause a moral transformation, it is a foundation on which such a change might occur.

of itself, more in need of restraint within the bounds of the law than of stimulation or of reinforcement by any law of duty.

We have now, without trying to be exhaustive in detail, run through the principal varieties of duties that arise from the two kinds of practical legislation. Duties may be legal or ethical; and the latter may be perfect or imperfect (i.e., determinate or indeterminate) with regard to ourselves and others. We have also seen, when considering the difference between juridical and ethical legislation, that each may generate the same material duty—the fulfillment of an agreement, for example—notwithstanding the real distinction between the grounds of its being a duty. In comparable fashion we should now notice how the same actions may implement several kinds of duties, and consequently how the distinctions with which we have been concerned are primarily analytical, making explicit the different grounds and aspects of moral action but not necessarily requiring a proliferation of separate acts to match each morally relevant aspect of a situation that calls for a decision. As in reading Plato's *Protagoras*, we shall be reminded of the respect in which Socrates could maintain that "virtue is one" even though there is also good reason for distinguishing several virtues.

In the first place, then, the ethical duty to act always from respect for moral principle comprehends all of one's juridical duties too. To act virtuously while observing regulations to the letter calls for no separate performance. We should also notice parenthetically that the family of juridical duties includes not only those defined by statutory and common law in the literal sense, but also those determined by conventional and customary rules and enforced by a variety of sanctions, so long as they are in accord with the principle of right. Aside from our common obligations as citizens, each of us is rightfully expected to fulfill the special obligations of his role in society and to meet the usual standards of good manners and public decorum. The sanctions that enforce the latter are neither criminal proceedings nor a liability to be sued, but

such informal pressures as the prospect of being passed over
for promotion, being fired, left off an invitation list, or ostra-
cized from a particular social circle. The relevant principles
are identical amid the multiplicity of their applications, and
the whole body of social regulations, so far as they are just
and fair, takes on an ethical significance through the duty to
carry out its obligations responsibly and conscientiously.

The next thing to notice is that when we are conscientious
about even so small a thing as thanking someone for a favor,
we may be discharging several kinds of duty at once, such
as observing an ancient and perhaps chiefly ceremonial social
rite, helping to make social intercourse more agreeable and to
that degree doing something about our ethical duty to further
the happiness of others, and perhaps most important, honoring our ethical duty to be—in this modest way as in others—
a person worthy of respect. In general, one of the best ways
to "perfect myself" is to respect the integrity of others and to
take an interest in the things that interest them.

A final illustration may tie up a number of loose ends. A
trade or profession is normally governed by a body of rules
and accepted practices that are designed to foster its standards
of performance; and society usually contrives to make it
worthwhile for an individual worker to organize his activities
accordingly. So much is "compulsion" if you like. But as
standards become better understood and internalized through
practice, and as skill is developed, one begins to be a true
"professional," following the rules autonomously through a
transformation that is the specialist's analogue of the general
shift from legal constraint to ethical autonomy. The work
then tends to become rewarding in itself, no longer just a way
to make a living, and performance usually improves still further, perhaps even to the extent of making contributions to
"the state of the art." Thus an interest in the advancement of
technology and in the intrinsic rewards of skill supervenes
upon the goads of economic necessity. But skill is a form of human excellence. In the practice of a profession, one also per-

fects his powers; and in doing so conscientiously, one does something for his moral character as well as for his technical proficiency. Furthermore, most people can do more for the welfare of society by doing their jobs faithfully and well than by any other method; for we are more effective in roles where we can perform as professionals than where we are only novices. Thus in this sort of situation—admittedly not one in which everyone is fortunate enough to find himself, but such as would be typical of a world organized on rational principles—all our practical categories would overlap. That is, in giving his job the best that is in him, a man could further his private interests, meet his external obligations, display and perfect his skill, promote the general welfare, and enhance his dignity as a moral agent. Although the distinct elements of self-interest, external obligation, and moral virtue can and should be discriminated, they may all be exhibited in the same activities, just as they are all governed by the same comprehensive principle, the autonomy of human intelligence.

EPILOGUE

In the foregoing I have not given a literally sequential exposition of Kant's ethical writings, although I have been as faithful to their substance as I could, and can support each important assertion by citing chapter and verse. It would be unprofitable to the reader to go over the same ground twice in the same way, and one always becomes better acquainted with an object if he can observe it from more than one perspective. In the case of Kant, however, there are further reasons for what may seem to have been a willfully free treatment. One is a teacher's interest in circumventing the difficulties of Kant's intricate technical apparatus by helping students see it as a system of interlocking guides to his astounding analytical power, instead of as a net designed to entangle them. The other reason is more philosophical, and I can best explain it by means of one of Kant's own distinctions.

In the part of the *Critique of Pure Reason* called "The Architectonic of Pure Reason," where Kant outlines the grand design of the critical philosophy, he says that knowledge may be either "historical" or "rational." These names are not very helpful, but he describes the former as being *ex datis*, confined to what has been presented to us through instruction, while the latter is *ex principiis*, based on the proper principles of its subject matter. An example of the difference would be that between the knowledge of chemistry one gets from reading a textbook and the sort possessed by a research chemist. The term "principles" in this context does not refer to statements, but to the grounds of statements; for the principles of chemistry are not what can be written in a book but what is discovered in nature, which statements attempt to formulate. One who has learned a doctrine as it has been presented to him, who understands it and can respond correctly to questions about what he has learned only so long as they are framed in the terms to which he has become accustomed, has historical knowledge in this sense. It is a good enough sort of knowledge for the purpose of passing certain kinds of examinations, but otherwise the student is its prisoner: he cannot translate what he knows into his own words, pursue its further implications, or expound it in a systematic order that differs from the one he has learned. Kant describes him as "a plaster cast of a living man." He is still in a state of tutelage, and enlightenment is the process of achieving freedom from tutelage by making one's knowledge autonomously rational rather than dependently historical.[13]

In accordance with this distinction, Kant writes for an audience that has, or at least is well on its way toward, rational knowledge. He wants his reader to grasp the principles that underlie the various ways in which the truths of a discipline may be presented, and in order to encourage him to do so

[13] See Kant's essay, "What is Enlightenment?" which relates the so-called Age of Enlightenment of the eighteenth century to his own general theme of the autonomy of reason.

Kant assumes that the reader has a rudimentary acquaintance with the basic points and understands them sufficiently to take his own part in developing their consequences without having to have them spelled out in laborious detail. Perhaps he goes too far, as in taking it for granted that anyone can see how the different formulations of the categorical imperative are different but equivalent versions of the same principle (which generations of students and scholars have been unable to do). He is doubtless also in such command of his material, so obvious to him, that he is a poor judge of the places where his reader may need help if he is not to get lost. That is a common failing of the great. And finally it is worth mentioning that the resulting difficulty people have with Kant is more acute when philosophical interests focus on language and its forms, as they have for some time in the English-speaking world; for he took relatively little interest in modes of expression as opposed to what he would call the ideas expressed (though of course the two are necessarily related). His logical theory, for example, is formulated in a way that is now regarded as old-fashioned; for he speaks of concepts, judgments, and inferences rather than words and symbols, sentences and statement-forms, and the kind of argument-form that can be checked mechanically or programmed on a computer.

Kant's work, therefore, ought to be capable of being presented in a variety of orders and of being formulated in several substantially equivalent ways; and if he is not mistaken, alternative expositions should contribute to the reader's understanding rather than the reverse. I have written my own expository essay accordingly, aiming especially to reveal the unity and integrity of doctrine that is to be found in his separate treatises and his often sketchy transitions of argument. I have used ordinary language wherever I could, noting its relation to Kant's technical terms, so as to show that his work is not an esoteric invention but a classic effort to clarify themes and problems that arise whenever men reflect upon the grounds and objectives of rational choice. Most of all, I have emphasized the systematic character of his thought, and especially the dependence of the whole structure of moral philosophy on the categorical imperative as the fundamental principle of the autonomy of reason in action.

WARNER WICK

The University of Chicago

GROUNDING

FOR THE

METAPHYSICS OF MORALS

Grundlegung

zur

Metaphysik

der Sitten

von

Immanuel Kant.

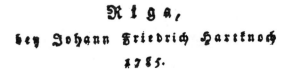

Riga,
bey Johann Friedrich Hartknoch
1785.

Ancient Greek philosophy was divided into three sciences: physics, ethics, and logic. This division is perfectly suitable to the nature of the subject, and the only improvement that can be made in it is perhaps only to supply its principle so that there will be a possibility on the one hand of insuring its completeness and on the other of correctly determining its necessary subdivisions.

All rational knowledge is either material and concerned with some object, or formal and concerned only with the form of understanding and of reason themselves and with the universal rules of thought in general without regard to differences of its objects. Formal philosophy is called logic. Material philosophy, however, has to do with determinate objects and with the laws to which these objects are subject; and such philosophy is divided into two parts, because these laws are either laws of nature or laws of freedom. The science of the former is called physics, while that of the latter is called ethics; they are also called doctrine of nature and doctrine of morals respectively.

Logic cannot have any empirical part, i.e., a part in which the universal and necessary laws of thought would be based on grounds taken from experience; for in that case it would not be logic, i.e., a canon for understanding and reason, which is valid for all thinking and which has to be demonstrated.[1] Natural and moral philosophy, on the contrary, can each have an empirical part. The former has to because it must determine the laws of nature as an object of experience, and the latter because it must determine the will of man insofar as the will is affected by nature. The laws of the former are those according to which everything does happen, while the laws of the latter are those according to which everything ought to happen, although these moral laws also consider the conditions under which what ought to happen frequently does not.

All philosophy insofar as it is founded on experience may be called empirical, while that which sets forth its doctrines as founded entirely on a priori principles may be called pure. The latter, when merely formal, is called logic; but when limited to determinate objects of the understanding, it is called metaphysics.

In this way there arises the idea of a twofold metaphysics: a metaphysics of nature and a metaphysics of morals.[2] Physics will thus

388

1. [Kant's *Logic* was first published in 1800 in a version edited by Gottlob Benjamin Jasche, who was one of Kant's students.]

2. [*The Metaphysical Foundations of Natural Science* was published in 1786. *The Metaphysics of Morals* appeared in 1797.]

have its empirical part, but also a rational one. Ethics will too, though here the empirical part might more specifically be called practical anthropology,[3] while the rational part might properly be called morals.

All industries, crafts, and arts have gained by the division of labor, viz., one man does not do everything, but each confines himself to a certain kind of work that is distinguished from all other kinds by the treatment it requires, so that the work may be done with the highest perfection and with greater ease. Where work is not so distinguished and divided, where everyone is a jack of all trades, there industry remains sunk in the greatest barbarism. Whether or not pure philosophy in all its parts requires its own special man might well be in itself a subject worthy of consideration. Would not the whole of this learned industry be better off if those who are accustomed, as the public taste demands, to purvey a mixture of the empirical with the rational in all sorts of proportions unknown even to themselves and who style themselves independent thinkers, while giving the name of hair-splitters to those who apply themselves to the purely rational part, were to be given warning about pursuing simultaneously two jobs which are quite different in their technique, and each of which perhaps requires a special talent that when combined with the other talent produces nothing but bungling? But I only ask here whether the nature of science does not require that the empirical part always be carefully separated from the rational part. Should not physics proper (i.e., empirical physics) be preceded by a metaphysics of nature, and practical anthropology by a metaphysics of morals? Both of these metaphysics must be carefully purified of everything empirical in order to know how much pure reason can accomplish in each case and from what sources it draws its a priori teaching, whether such teaching be conducted by all moralists (whose name is legion) or only by some who feel a calling thereto.

Since I am here primarily concerned with moral philosophy, the foregoing question will be limited to a consideration of whether or not there is the utmost necessity for working out for once a pure moral philosophy that is wholly cleared of everything which can only be empirical and can only belong to anthropology. That there must be such a philosophy is evident from the common idea of duty and of moral laws. Everyone must admit that if a law is to be morally valid, i.e., is to be valid as a ground of obligation, then it must carry with it absolute necessity. He must admit that the command, "Thou shalt not lie," does not hold only for men, as if other rational beings had no need to abide by it, and so with all the other moral laws properly so called. And he must concede that the ground of obligation here must therefore be sought not in the nature of man nor in the circumstances of the world in which man is placed, but must be sought a priori solely in the concepts of pure reason; he must grant that every other precept which is founded on principles of mere experience—even a precept that may in certain respects be universal—

---

3. [*Anthropology from a Pragmatic Point of View* first appeared in 1798.]

insofar as it rests in the least on empirical grounds—perhaps only in its motive—can indeed be called a practical rule, but never a moral law.

Thus not only are moral laws together with their principles essentially different from every kind of practical cognition in which there is anything empirical, but all moral philosophy rests entirely on its pure part. When applied to man, it does not in the least borrow from acquaintance with him (anthropology) but gives a priori laws to him as a rational being. To be sure, these laws require, furthermore, a power of judgment sharpened by experience, partly in order to distinguish in what cases they are applicable, and partly to gain for them access to the human will as well as influence for putting them into practice. For man is affected by so many inclinations that, even though he is indeed capable of the idea of a pure practical reason, he is not so easily able to make that idea effective *in concreto* in the conduct of his life.

A metaphysics of morals is thus indispensably necessary, not merely because of motives of speculation regarding the source of practical principles which are present a priori in our reason, but because morals themselves are liable to all kinds of corruption as long as the guide and supreme norm for correctly estimating them are missing. For in the case of what is to be morally good, that it conforms to the moral law is not enough; it must also be done for the sake of the moral law. Otherwise that conformity is only very contingent and uncertain, since the non-moral ground may now and then produce actions that conform with the law but quite often produces actions that are contrary to the law. Now the moral law in its purity and genuineness (which is of the utmost concern in the practical realm) can be sought nowhere but in a pure philosophy. Therefore, pure philosophy (metaphysics) must precede; without it there can be no moral philosophy at all. That philosophy which mixes pure principles with empirical ones does not deserve the name of philosophy (for philosophy is distinguished from ordinary rational knowledge by its treatment in a separate science of what the latter comprehends only confusedly). Still less does it deserve the name of moral philosophy, since by this very confusion it spoils even the purity of morals and counteracts its own end.

There must be no thought that what is required here is already contained in the propaedeutic that precedes the celebrated Wolff's moral philosophy, i.e., in what he calls *Universal Practical Philosophy*,[4] and that hence there is no need to break entirely new ground. Just because his work was to be a universal practical philosophy, it has not taken into consideration any special kind of will, such as one determined solely by a priori principles without any empirical motives and which could be called a pure will, but has considered volition in general, together with all the

390

4.[This work of Christian Wolff was published in 1738–39; this and other of his works served for many years as the standard philosophy textbooks in German universities. Wolff's philosophy was founded on that of Leibniz.]

actions and conditions belonging to it under this general signification. And thereby does his propaedeutic differ from a metaphysics of morals in the same way that general logic, which expounds the acts and rules of thinking in general, differs from transcendental philosophy, which treats merely of the particular acts and rules of pure thinking, i.e., of that thinking whereby objects are cognized completely a priori. For the metaphysics of morals has to investigate the idea and principles of a possible pure will and not the actions and conditions of human volition as such, which are for the most part drawn from psychology. Moral laws and duty are discussed in this universal practical philosophy (though quite improperly), but this is no objection to what has been said about such philosophy. For the authors of this science remain true to their idea of it on the following point also: they do not distinguish the motives which, as such, are presented completely a priori by reason alone and are properly moral from the empirical motives which the understanding raises to general concepts merely by the comparison of experiences. Rather, they consider motives irrespective of any difference in their source; and inasmuch as they regard all motives as being homogeneous, they consider nothing but their relative strength or weakness. In this way they frame their concept of obligation, which is certainly not moral, but is all that can be expected from a philosophy which never decides regarding the origin of all possible practical concepts whether they are a priori or merely a posteriori.

391

I intend some day to publish a metaphysics of morals,[5] but as a preliminary to that I now issue this *Grounding* [1785]. Indeed there is properly no other foundation for such a metaphysics than a critical examination of pure practical reason, just as there is properly no other foundation for a metaphysics [of nature] than the critical examination of pure speculative reason, which has already been published.[6] But, in the first place, the former critique is not so absolutely necessary as the latter one, because human reason can, even in the most ordinary mind, be easily brought in moral matters to a high degree of correctness and precision, while on the other hand in its theoretical but pure use it is wholly dialectical. In the second place, if a critical examination of pure practical reason is to be complete, then there must, in my view, be the possibility at the same time of showing the unity of practical and speculative reason in a common principle; for in the final analysis there can be only one and the same reason, which is to be differentiated solely in its application. But there is no possibility here of bringing my work to such completeness, without introducing considerations of an entirely different kind and without thereby confusing the reader. Instead of calling the present work a *Critique of Pure Practical Reason*, I have, therefore, adopted the title

---

5. [This appeared in 1797.]

6. [The first edition of the *Critique of Pure Reason* appeared in 1781, while the second edition appeared in 1787. The *Critique of Practical Reason* was published in 1788.]

Grounding for the Metaphysics of Morals [*Grundlegung zur Metaphysik der Sitten.*][7]

But, in the third place, since a metaphysics of morals, despite the forbidding title, is nevertheless capable of a high degree of popularity and adaptation to the ordinary understanding, I find it useful to separate from the aforementioned metaphysics this preliminary work on its foundation [*Grundlage*] in order later to have no need to introduce unavoidable subtleties into doctrines that are easier to grasp.

392

The present *Grounding* [*Grundlegung*] is, however, intended for nothing more than seeking out and establishing the supreme principle of morality. This constitutes by itself a task which is complete in its purpose and should be kept separate from every other moral inquiry. The application of this supreme principle to the whole ethical system would, to be sure, shed much light on my conclusions regarding this central question, which is important but has not heretofore been at all satisfactorily discussed; and the adequacy manifested by the principle throughout such application would provide strong confirmation for the principle. Nevertheless, I must forego this advantage, which after all would be more gratifying for myself than helpful for others, since ease of use and apparent adequacy of a principle do not provide any certain proof of its soundness, but do awaken, rather, a certain bias which prevents any rigorous examination and estimation of it for itself without any regard to its consequences.

The method adopted in this work is, I believe, one that is most suitable if we proceed analytically from ordinary knowledge to a determination of the supreme principle and then back again synthetically from an examination of this principle and its sources to ordinary knowledge where its application is found. Therefore, the division turns out to be the following:

1. First Section.   Transition from the Ordinary Rational Knowledge of Morality to the Philosophical

2. Second Section.   Transition from Popular Moral Philosophy to a Metaphysics of Morals

3. Third Section.   Final Step from a Metaphysics of Morals to a Critique of Pure Practical Reason.

7. [This might be translated as *Laying the Foundation for the Metaphysics of Morals*. But for the sake of brevity *Grounding for the Metaphysics of Morals* has been chosen.]

TRANSITION FROM THE ORDINARY RATIONAL KNOWLEDGE OF MORALITY TO THE PHILOSOPHICAL

There is no possibility of thinking of anything at all in the world, or even out of it, which can be regarded as good without qualification, except a *good will*. Intelligence, wit, judgment, and whatever talents of the mind one might want to name are doubtless in many respects good and desirable, as are such qualities of temperament as courage, resolution, perseverance. But they can also become extremely bad and harmful if the will, which is to make use of these gifts of nature and which in its special constitution is called character, is not good. The same holds with gifts of fortune; power, riches, honor, even health, and that complete well-being and contentment with one's condition which is called happiness make for pride and often hereby even arrogance, unless there is a good will to correct their influence on the mind and herewith also to rectify the whole principle of action and make it universally conformable to its end. The sight of a being who is not graced by any touch of a pure and good will but who yet enjoys an uninterrupted prosperity can never delight a rational and impartial spectator. Thus a good will seems to constitute the indispensable condition of being even worthy of happiness.

Some qualities are even conducive to this good will itself and can facilitate its work. Nevertheless, they have no intrinsic unconditional 394 worth; but they always presuppose, rather, a good will, which restricts the high esteem in which they are otherwise rightly held, and does not permit them to be regarded as absolutely good. Moderation in emotions and passions, self-control, and calm deliberation are not only good in many respects but even seem to constitute part of the intrinsic worth of a person. But they are far from being rightly called good without qualification (however unconditionally they were commended by the ancients). For without the principles of a good will, they can become extremely bad; the coolness of a villain makes him not only much more dangerous but also immediately more abominable in our eyes than he would have been regarded by us without it.

A good will is good not because of what it effects or accomplishes, nor because of its fitness to attain some proposed end; it is good only through its willing, i.e., it is good in itself. When it is considered in itself, then it is to be esteemed very much higher than anything which it might ever bring about merely in order to favor some inclination, or even the sum total of all inclinations. Even if, by some especially unfortunate fate or by the niggardly provision of stepmotherly nature, this will should be wholly lacking in the power to accomplish its purpose; if with the greatest effort it should yet achieve nothing, and only the good will should remain (not, to be sure, as a mere wish but as the summoning of all the means in our power), yet would it, like a jewel, still shine by its own light as something which has its full value in itself. Its usefulness or fruitlessness can neither augment nor diminish this value. Its usefulness would be, as it were, only the setting to enable us to handle it in ordinary dealings or to attract to it the attention of those who are not yet experts, but not to recommend it to real experts or to determine its value.

But there is something so strange in this idea of the absolute value of a mere will, in which no account is taken of any useful results, that in spite of all the agreement received even from ordinary reason, yet there must arise the suspicion that such an idea may perhaps have as its hidden basis merely some high-flown fancy, and that we may have misunderstood the purpose of nature in assigning to reason the governing of our will. Therefore, this idea will be examined from this point of view.

395

In the natural constitution of an organized being, i.e., one suitably adapted to the purpose of life, let there be taken as a principle that in such a being no organ is to be found for any end unless it be the most fit and the best adapted for that end. Now if that being's preservation, welfare, or in a word its happiness, were the real end of nature in the case of a being having reason and will, then nature would have hit upon a very poor arrangement in having the reason of the creature carry out this purpose. For all the actions which such a creature has to perform with this purpose in view, and the whole rule of his conduct would have been prescribed much more exactly by instinct; and the purpose in question could have been attained much more certainly by instinct than it ever can be by reason. And if in addition reason had been imparted to this favored creature, then it would have had to serve him only to contemplate the happy constitution of his nature, to admire that nature, to rejoice in it, and to feel grateful to the cause that bestowed it; but reason would not have served him to subject his faculty of desire to its weak and delusive guidance nor would it have served him to meddle incompetently with the purpose of nature. In a word, nature would have taken care that reason did not strike out into a practical use nor presume, with its weak insight, to think out for itself a plan for happiness and the means for attaining it. Nature would have taken upon herself not only the choice of ends but also that of the means, and would with wise foresight have entrusted both to instinct alone.

true

And, in fact, we find that the more a cultivated reason devotes itself to the aim of enjoying life and happiness, the further does man get away from true contentment. Because of this there arises in many persons, if only they are candid enough to admit it, a certain degree of misology, i.e., hatred of reason. This is especially so in the case of those who are the most experienced in the use of reason, because after calculating all the advantages they derive, I say not from the invention of all the arts of common luxury, but even from the sciences (which in the end seem to them to be also a luxury of the understanding), they yet find that they have in fact only brought more trouble on their heads than they have gained in happiness. Therefore, they come to envy, rather than despise, the more common run of men who are closer to the guidance of mere natural instinct and who do not allow their reason much influence on their conduct. And we must admit that the judgment of those who would temper, or even reduce below zero, the boastful eulogies on behalf of the advantages which reason is supposed to provide as regards the happiness and contentment of life is by no means morose or ungrateful to the goodness with which the world is governed. There lies at the root of such judgments, rather, the idea that existence has another and much more worthy purpose, for which, and not for happiness, reason is quite properly intended, and which must, therefore, be regarded as the supreme condition to which the private purpose of men must, for the most part, defer.

Reason, however, is not competent enough to guide the will safely as regards its objects and the satisfaction of all our needs (which it in part even multiplies); to this end would an implanted natural instinct have led much more certainly. But inasmuch as reason has been imparted to us as a practical faculty, i.e., as one which is to have influence on the will, its true function must be to produce a will which is not merely good as a means to some further end, but is good in itself. To produce a will good in itself reason was absolutely necessary, inasmuch as nature in distributing her capacities has everywhere gone to work in a purposive manner. While such a will may not indeed be the sole and complete good, it must, nevertheless, be the highest good and the condition of all the rest, even of the desire for happiness. In this case there is nothing inconsistent with the wisdom of nature that the cultivation of reason, which is requisite for the first and unconditioned purpose, may in many ways restrict, at least in this life, the attainment of the second purpose, viz., happiness, which is always conditioned. Indeed happiness can even be reduced to less than nothing, without nature's failing thereby in her purpose; for reason recognizes as its highest practical function the establishment of a good will, whereby in the attainment of this end reason is capable only of its own kind of satisfaction, viz., that of fulfilling a purpose which is in turn determined only by reason, even though such fulfilment were often to interfere with the purposes of inclination.

The concept of a will estimable in itself and good without regard to any further end must now be developed. This concept already dwells in the natural sound understanding and needs not so much to be taught as merely to be elucidated. It always holds first place in estimating the total worth of our actions and constitutes the condition of all the rest. Therefore, we shall take up the concept of *duty*, which includes that of a good will, though with certain subjective restrictions and hindrances, which far from hiding a good will or rendering it unrecognizable, rather bring it out by contrast and make it shine forth more brightly.

I here omit all actions already recognized as contrary to duty, even though they may be useful for this or that end; for in the case of these the question does not arise at all as to whether they might be done from duty, since they even conflict with duty. I also set aside those actions which are really in accordance with duty, yet to which men have no immediate inclination, but perform them because they are impelled thereto by some other inclination. For in this [second] case to decide whether the action which is in accord with duty has been done from duty or from some selfish purpose is easy. This difference is far more difficult to note in the [third] case where the action accords with duty and the subject has in addition an immediate inclination to do the action. For example,[1] that a dealer should not overcharge an inexperienced purchaser certainly accords with duty; and where there is much commerce, the prudent merchant does not overcharge but keeps to a fixed price for everyone in general, so that a child may buy from him just as well as everyone else may. Thus customers are honestly served, but this is not nearly enough for making us believe that the merchant has acted this way from duty and from principles of honesty; his own advantage required him to do it. He cannot, however, be assumed to have in addition [as in the third case] an immediate inclination toward his buyers, causing him, as it were, out of love to give no one as far as price is concerned any advantage over another. Hence the action was done neither from duty nor from immediate inclination, but merely for a selfish purpose.

On the other hand,[2] to preserve one's life is a duty; and, furthermore, everyone has also an immediate inclination to do so. But on this account 398 the often anxious care taken by most men for it has no intrinsic worth, and the maxim of their action has no moral content. They preserve their lives, to be sure, in accordance with duty, but not from duty. On the other hand,[3] if adversity and hopeless sorrow have completely taken away the taste for life, if an unfortunate man, strong in soul and more indignant at his fate than despondent or dejected, wishes for death and yet preserves his life without loving it—not from inclination or fear, but from duty— then his maxim indeed has a moral content.[4]

1. [The ensuing example provides an illustration of the second case.]

2. [This next example illustrates the third case.]

3. [The ensuing example illustrates the fourth case.]

4. [Four different cases have been distinguished in the two foregoing paragraphs. Case 1 involves those actions which are contrary to duty (lying, cheating, stealing, etc.). Case 2 involves those which accord with duty but for which a person perhaps has no immediate inclination, though he does have a mediate inclination thereto (one pays his taxes not because he likes to but in order to avoid the penalties set for delinquents, one treats his fellows well not because he really likes them but because he wants their votes when at some future time he runs for public office, etc.). A vast number of so-called "morally good" actions actually belong to this case 2—they accord with duty because of self-seeking inclinations. Case 3 involves those which accord with duty and for which a person does have an immediate inclination (one does not commit suicide because all is going well with him, one does not commit adultery because he considers his wife to be the most desirable creature in the whole world,

To be beneficent where one can is a duty; and besides this, there are many persons who are so sympathetically constituted that, without any further motive of vanity or self-interest, they find an inner pleasure in spreading joy around them and can rejoice in the satisfaction of others as their own work. But I maintain that in such a case an action of this kind, however dutiful and amiable it may be, has nevertheless no true moral worth.[5] It is on a level with such actions as arise from other inclinations, e.g., the inclination for honor, which if fortunately directed to what is in fact beneficial and accords with duty and is thus honorable, deserves praise and encouragement, but not esteem; for its maxim lacks the moral content of an action done not from inclination but from duty. Suppose then the mind of this friend of mankind to be clouded over with his own sorrow so that all sympathy with the lot of others is extinguished, and suppose him still to have the power to benefit others in distress, even though he is not touched by their trouble because he is sufficiently absorbed with his own; and now suppose that, even though no inclination moves him any longer, he nevertheless tears himself from this deadly insensibility and performs the action without any inclination at all, but solely from duty— then for the first time his action has genuine moral worth.[6] Further still, if nature has put little sympathy in this or that man's heart, if (while being an honest man in other respects) he is by temperament cold and indifferent to the sufferings of others, perhaps because as regards his own sufferings he is endowed with the special gift of patience and fortitude and expects or even requires that others should have the same; if such a man (who would truly not be nature's worst product) had not been exactly fashioned by her to be a philanthropist, would he not yet find in himself a source from which he might give himself a worth far higher than any that a good-natured temperament might have? By all means, because just here

---

etc.). Case 4 involves those actions which accord with duty but are contary to some immediate inclination (one does not commit suicide even when he is in dire distress, one does not commit adultery even though his wife has turned out to be an impossible shrew, etc.). Now case 4 is the crucial test case of the will's possible goodness—but Kant does not claim that one should lead his life in such a way as to encounter as many such cases as possible in order constantly to test his virtue (deliberately marry a shrew so as to be able to resist the temptation to commit adultery). Life itself forces enough such cases upon a person without his seeking them out. But when there is a conflict between duty and inclination, duty should always be followed. Case 3 makes for the easiest living and the greatest contentment, and anyone would wish that life might present him with far more of these cases than with cases 2 or 4. But yet one should not arrange his life in such a way as to avoid case 4 at all costs and to seek out case 3 as much as possible (become a recluse so as to avoid the possible rough and tumble involved with frequent association with one's fellows, avoid places where one might encounter the sick and the poor so as to spare oneself the pangs of sympathy and the need to exercise the virtue of benefiting those in distress, etc.). For the purpose of philosophical analysis Kant emphasizes case 4 as being the test case of the will's possible goodness, but he is not thereby advocating puritanism.]

5. [This is an example of case 3.]

6. [This is an example of case 4.]

399 does the worth of the character come out; this worth is moral and incomparably the highest of all, viz., that he is beneficent, not from inclination, but from duty.[7]

To secure one's own happiness is a duty (at least indirectly); for discontent with one's condition under many pressing cares and amid unsatisfied wants might easily become a great temptation to transgress one's duties. But here also do men of themselves already have, irrespective of duty, the strongest and deepest inclination toward happiness, because just in this idea are all inclinations combined into a sum total.[8] But the precept of happiness is often so constituted as greatly to interfere with some inclinations, and yet men cannot form any definite and certain concept of the sum of satisfaction of all inclinations that is called happiness. Hence there is no wonder that a single inclination which is determinate both as to what it promises and as to the time within which it can be satisfied may outweigh a fluctuating idea; and there is no wonder that a man, e.g., a gouty patient, can choose to enjoy what he likes and to suffer what he may, since by his calculation he has here at least not sacrificed the enjoyment of the present moment to some possibly groundless expectations of the good fortune that is supposed to be found in health. But even in this case, if the universal inclination to happiness did not determine his will and if health, at least for him, did not figure as so necessary an element in his calculations, there still remains here, as in all other cases, a law, viz., that he should promote his happiness not from inclination but from duty, and thereby for the first time does his conduct have real moral worth.[9]

Undoubtedly in this way also are to be understood those passages of Scripture which command us to love our neighbor and even our enemy. For love as an inclination cannot be commanded; but beneficence from duty, when no inclination impels us[10] and even when a natural and unconquerable aversion opposes such beneficence,[11] is practical, and not pathological, love. Such love resides in the will and not in the propensities of feeling, in principles of action and not in tender sympathy; and only this practical love can be commanded.

The second proposition[12] is this: An action done from duty has its moral worth, not in the purpose that is to be attained by it, but in the maxim ac-

---

7. [This is an even more extreme example of case 4.]

8. [This is an example of case 3.]

9. [This example is a weak form of case 4; the action accords with duty but is not contrary to some immediate inclination.]

10. [This is case 4 in its weak form.]

11. [This is case 4 in its strong form.]

12. [The first proposition of morality says that an action must be done from duty in order to have any moral worth. It is implicit in the preceding examples but was never explicitly stated.]

cording to which the action is determined. The moral worth depends, therefore, not on the realization of the object of the action, but merely on the principle of volition according to which, without regard to any objects of the faculty of desire, the action has been done. From what has gone before it is clear that the purposes which we may have in our actions, as well as their effects regarded as ends and incentives of the will, cannot give to actions any unconditioned and moral worth. Where, then, can this worth lie if it is not to be found in the will's relation to the expected effect? Nowhere but in the principle of the will, with no regard to the ends that can be brought about through such action. For the will stands, as it were, at a crossroads between its a priori principle, which is formal, and its a posteriori incentive, which is material; and since it must be determined by something, it must be determined by the formal principle of volition, if the action is done from duty—and in that case every material principle is taken away from it. 400

The third proposition, which follows from the other two, can be expressed thus: Duty is the necessity of an action done out of respect for the law. I can indeed have an inclination for an object as the effect of my proposed action; but I can never have respect for such an object, just because it is merely an effect and is not an activity of the will. Similarly, I can have no respect for inclination as such, whether my own or that of another. I can at most, if my own inclination, approve it; and, if that of another, even love it, i.e., consider it to be favorable to my own advantage. An object of respect can only be what is connected with my will solely as ground and never as effect—something that does not serve my inclination but, rather, outweighs it, or at least excludes it from consideration when some choice is made—in other words, only the law itself can be an object of respect and hence can be a command. Now an action done from duty must altogether exclude the influence of inclination and therewith every object of the will. Hence there is nothing left which can determine the will except objectively the law and subjectively pure respect for this practical law, i.e., the will can be subjectively determined by the maxim[13] that I should follow such a law even if all my inclinations are thereby thwarted. 401

Thus the moral worth of an action does not lie in the effect expected from it nor in any principle of action that needs to borrow its motive from this expected effect. For all these effects (agreeableness of one's condition and even the furtherance of other people's happiness) could have been brought about also through other causes and would not have required the will of a rational being, in which the highest and unconditioned good can alone be found. Therefore, the pre-eminent good which is called moral can consist in nothing but the representation of the law in itself, and such a representation can admittedly be found only in a rational being insofar as this representation, and not some expected effect, is the determining

---

13. A maxim is the subjective principle of volition. The objective principle (i.e., one which would serve all rational beings also subjectively as a practical principle if reason had full control over the faculty of desire) is the practical law. [See below Kant's footnote at Ak. 420–21.]

ground of the will. This good is already present in the person who acts according to this representation, and such good need not be awaited merely from the effect.[14]

402 { (But what sort of law can that be the thought of which must determine the will without reference to any expected effect, so that the will can be called absolutely good without qualification? Since I have deprived the will of every impulse that might arise for it from obeying any particular law, there is nothing left to serve the will as principle except the universal conformity of its actions to law as such, i.e., I should never act except in such a way that I can also will that my maxim should become a universal law.[15] Here mere conformity to law as such (without having as its basis any law determining particular actions) serves the will as principle and must so serve it if duty is not to be a vain delusion and a chimerical concept) The ordinary reason of mankind in its practical judgments agrees completely with this, and always has in view the aforementioned principle.

For example, take this question. When I am in distress, may I make a promise with the intention of not keeping it? I readily distinguish here the two meanings which the question may have; whether making a false promise conforms with prudence or with duty. Doubtless the former can often be the case. Indeed I clearly see that escape from some present difficulty by means of such a promise is not enough. In addition I must carefully consider whether from this lie there may later arise far greater inconvenience for me than from what I now try to escape. Furthermore, the consequences of my false promise are not easy to forsee, even with all my supposed cunning; loss of confidence in me might prove to be far more disadvantageous than the misfortune which I now try to avoid. The more

---

14. There might be brought against me here an objection that I take refuge behind the word "respect" in an obscure feeling, instead of giving a clear answer to the question by means of a concept of reason. But even though respect is a feeling, it is not one received through any outside influence but is, rather, one that is self-produced by means of a rational concept; hence it is specifically different from all feelings of the first kind, which can all be reduced to inclination or fear. What I recognize immediately as a law for me, I recognize with respect; this means merely the consciousness of the subordination of my will to a law without the mediation of other influences upon my sense. The immediate determination of the will by the law, and the consciousness thereof, is called respect, which is hence regarded as the effect of the law upon the subject and not as the cause of the law. Respect is properly the representation of a worth that thwarts my self-love. Hence respect is something that is regarded as an object of neither inclination nor fear, although it has at the same time something analogous to both. The object of respect is, therefore, nothing but the law—indeed that very law which we impose on ourselves and yet recognize as necessary in itself. As law, we are subject to it without consulting self-love; as imposed on us by ourselves, it is a consequence of our will. In the former aspect, it is analogous to fear; in the latter, to inclination. All respect for a person is properly only respect for the law (of honesty, etc.) of which the person provides an example. Since we regard the development of our talents as a duty, we think of a man of talent as being also a kind of example of the law (the law of becoming like him by practice), and that is what constitutes our respect for him. All so-called moral interest consists solely in respect for the law.

15. [This is the first time in the *Grounding* that the categorical imperative is stated.]

prudent way might be to act according to a universal maxim and to make it a habit not to promise anything without intending to keep it. But that such a maxim is, nevertheless, always based on nothing but a fear of consequences becomes clear to me at once. To be truthful from duty is, however, quite different from being truthful from fear of disadvantageous consequences; in the first case the concept of the action itself contains a law for me, while in the second I must first look around elsewhere to see what are the results for me that might be connected with the action. For to deviate from the principle of duty is quite certainly bad; but to abandon my maxim of prudence can often be very advantageous for me, though to abide by it is certainly safer. The most direct and infallible way, however, to answer the question as to whether a lying promise accords with duty is to ask myself whether I would really be content if my maxim (of extricating myself from difficulty by means of a false promise) were to hold as a universal law for myself as well as for others, and could I really say to myself that everyone may promise falsely when he finds himself in a difficulty from which he can find no other way to extricate himself. Then I immediately become aware that I can indeed will the lie but can not at all will a universal law to lie. For by such a law there would really be no promises at all, since in vain would my willing future actions be professed to other people who would not believe what I professed, or if they over-hastily did believe, then they would pay me back in like coin. Therefore, my maxim would necessarily destroy itself just as soon as it was made a universal law.[16]

Therefore, I need no far-reaching acuteness to discern what I have to do in order that my will may be morally good. Inexperienced in the course of the world and incapable of being prepared for all its contingencies, I only ask myself whether I can also will that my maxim should become a universal law. If not, then the maxim must be rejected, not because of any disadvantage accruing to me or even to others, but because it cannot be fitting as a principle in a possible legislation of universal law, and reason exacts from me immediate respect for such legislation. Indeed I have as yet no insight into the grounds of such respect (which the philosopher may investigate). But I at least understand that respect is an estimation of a worth that far outweighs any worth of what is recommended by inclination, and that the necessity of acting from pure respect for the practical law is what constitutes duty, to which every other motive must give way because duty is the condition of a will good in itself, whose worth is above all else.

Thus within the moral cognition of ordinary human reason we have arrived at its principle. To be sure, such reason does not think of this principle abstractly in its universal form, but does always have it actually in view and does use it as the standard of judgment. It would here be easy to

403

404

16. [This means that when you tell a lie, you merely take exception to the general rule that says everyone should always tell the truth and believe that what you are saying is true. When you lie, you do not thereby will that everyone else lie and not believe that what you are saying is true, because in such a case your lie would never work to get you what you want.]

show how ordinary reason, with this compass in hand, is well able to distinguish, in every case that occurs, what is good or evil, in accord with duty or contrary to duty, if we do not in the least try to teach reason anything new but only make it attend, as Socrates did, to its own principle—and thereby do we show that neither science nor philosophy is needed in order to know what one must do to be honest and good, and even wise and virtuous. Indeed we might even have conjectured beforehand that cognizance of what every man is obligated to do, and hence also to know, would be available to every man, even the most ordinary. Yet we cannot but observe with admiration how great an advantage the power of practical judgment has over the theoretical in ordinary human understanding. In the theoretical, when ordinary reason ventures to depart from the laws of experience and the perceptions of sense, it falls into sheer inconceivabilities and self-contradictions, or at least into a chaos of uncertainty, obscurity, and instability. In the practical, however, the power of judgment first begins to show itself to advantage when ordinary understanding excludes all sensuous incentives from practical laws. Such understanding then becomes even subtle, whether in quibbling with its own conscience or with other claims regarding what is to be called right, or whether in wanting to determine correctly for its own instruction the worth of various actions. And the most extraordinary thing is that ordinary understanding in this practical case may have just as good a hope of hitting the mark as that which any philosopher may promise himself. Indeed it is almost more certain in this than even a philosopher is, because he can have no principle other than what ordinary understanding has, but he may easily confuse his judgment by a multitude of foreign and irrelevant considerations and thereby cause it to swerve from the right way. Would it not, therefore, be wiser in moral matters to abide by the ordinary rational judgment or at most to bring in philosophy merely for the purpose of rendering the system of morals more complete and intelligible and of presenting its rules in a way that is more convenient for use (especially in disputation), but not for the purpose of leading ordinary human understanding away from its happy simplicity in practical matters and of bringing it by means of philosophy into a new path of inquiry and instruction?

405   Innocence is indeed a glorious thing; but, unfortunately, it does not keep very well and is easily led astray. Consequently, even wisdom—which consists more in doing and not doing than in knowing—needs science, not in order to learn from it, but in order that wisdom's precepts may gain acceptance and permanence. Man feels within himself a powerful counterweight to all the commands of duty, which are presented to him by reason as being so pre-eminently worthy of respect; this counterweight consists of his needs and inclinations, whose total satisfaction is summed up under the name of happiness. Now reason irremissibly commands its precepts, without thereby promising the inclinations anything; hence it disregards and neglects these impetuous and at the same time so seemingly plausible claims (which do not allow themselves to

be suppressed by any command). Hereby arises a natural dialectic, i.e., a propensity to quibble with these strict laws of duty, to cast doubt upon their validity, or at least upon their purity and strictness, and to make them, where possible, more compatible with our wishes and inclinations. Thereby are such laws corrupted in their very foundations and their whole dignity is destroyed—something which even ordinary practical reason cannot in the end call good.

Thus is ordinary human reason forced to go outside its sphere and take a step into the field of practical philosophy, not by any need for speculation (which never befalls such reason so long as it is content to be mere sound reason) but on practical grounds themselves. There it tries to obtain information and clear instruction regarding the source of its own principle and the correct determination of this principle in its opposition to maxims based on need and inclination, so that reason may escape from the perplexity of opposite claims and may avoid the risk of losing all genuine moral principles through the ambiguity into which it easily falls. Thus when ordinary practical reason cultivates itself, there imperceptibly arises in it a dialectic which compels it to seek help in philosophy. The same thing happens in reason's theoretical use; in this case, just as in the other, peace will be found only in a thorough critical examination of our reason.

TRANSITION FROM POPULAR MORAL PHILOSOPHY
TO A METAPHYSICS OF MORALS

If we have so far drawn our concept of duty from the ordinary use of our practical reason, one is by no means to infer that we have treated it as a concept of experience. On the contrary, when we pay attention to our experience of the way human beings act, we meet frequent and—as we ourselves admit—justified complaints that there cannot be cited a single certain example of the disposition to act from pure duty; and we meet complaints that although much may be done that is in accordance with what duty commands, yet there are always doubts as to whether what occurs has really been done from duty and so has moral worth. Hence there have always been philosophers who have absolutely denied the reality of this disposition in human actions and have ascribed everything to a more or less refined self-love. Yet in so doing they have not cast doubt upon the rightness of the concept of morality. Rather, they have spoken with sincere regret as to the frailty and impurity of human nature, which they think is noble enough to take as its precept an idea so worthy of respect but yet is too weak to follow this idea: reason, which should legislate for human nature, is used only to look after the interest of inclinations, whether singly or, at best, in their greatest possible harmony with one another.

In fact there is absolutely no possibility by means of experience to make 407 out with complete certainty a single case in which the maxim of an action that may in other respects conform to duty has rested solely on moral grounds and on the representation of one's duty. It is indeed sometimes the case that after the keenest self-examination we can find nothing except the moral ground of duty that could have been strong enough to move us to this or that good action and to such great sacrifice. But there cannot with certainty be at all inferred from this that some secret impulse of self-love, merely appearing as the idea of duty, was not the actual determining cause of the will. We like to flatter ourselves with the false claim to a more noble motive; but in fact we can never, even by the strictest examination, completely plumb the depths of the secret incentives of our actions. For when moral value is being considered, the concern is not with the actions, which are seen, but rather with their inner principles, which are not seen.

Moreover, one cannot better serve the wishes of those who ridicule all morality as being a mere phantom of human imagination getting above

itself because of self-conceit than by conceding to them that the concepts of duty must be drawn solely from experience (just as from indolence one willingly persuades himself that such is the case as regards all other concepts as well). For by so conceding, one prepares for them a sure triumph. I am willing to admit out of love for humanity that most of our actions are in accordance with duty; but if we look more closely at our planning and striving, we everywhere come upon the dear self, which is always turning up, and upon which the intent of our actions is based rather than upon the strict command of duty (which would often require self-denial). One need not be exactly an enemy of virtue, but only a cool observer who does not take the liveliest wish for the good to be straight off its realization, in order to become doubtful at times whether any true virtue is actually to be found in the world. Such is especially the case when years increase and one's power of judgment is made shrewder by experience and keener in observation. Because of these things nothing can protect us from a complete falling away from our ideas of duty and preserve in the soul a well-
408 grounded respect for duty's law except the clear conviction that even if there never have been actions springing from such pure sources, the question at issue here is not whether this or that has happened but that reason of itself and independently of all experience commands what ought to happen. Consequently, reason unrelentingly commands actions of which the world has perhaps hitherto never provided an example and whose feasibility might well be doubted by one who bases everything upon experience; for instance, even though there might never yet have been a sincere friend, still pure sincerity in friendship is nonetheless required of every man, because this duty, prior to all experience, is contained as duty in general in the idea of a reason that determines the will by means of a priori grounds.

There may be noted further that unless we want to deny to the concept of morality all truth and all reference to a possible object, we cannot but admit that the moral law is of such widespread significance that it must hold not merely for men but for all rational beings generally, and that it must be valid not merely under contingent conditions and with exceptions but must be absolutely necessary. Clearly, therefore, no experience can give occasion for inferring even the possibility of such apodeictic laws. For with what right could we bring into unlimited respect as a universal precept for every rational nature what is perhaps valid only under the contingent conditions of humanity? And how could laws for the determination of our will be regarded as laws for the determination of a rational being in general and of ourselves only insofar as we are rational beings, if these laws were merely empirical and did not have their source completely a priori in pure, but practical, reason?

Moreover, worse service cannot be rendered morality than that an attempt be made to derive it from examples. For every example of morality presented to me must itself first be judged according to principles of morality in order to see whether it is fit to serve as an original example, i.e., as a model. But in no way can it authoritatively furnish the concept of morality. Even the Holy One of the gospel must first be compared with our ideal of moral perfection before he is recognized as such. Even he says of himself, "Why do you call me (whom you see) good? None is good (the archetype of the good) except God only (whom you do not see)." But whence have we the concept of God as the highest good? Solely from the idea of moral perfection, which reason frames a priori and connects inseparably with the concept of a free will. Imitation has no place at all in moral matters. And examples serve only for encouragement, i.e., they put beyond doubt the feasibility of what the law commands and they make visible what the practical rule expresses more generally. But examples can never justify us in setting aside their true original, which lies in reason, and letting ourselves be guided by them.

If there is then no genuine supreme principle of morality that must rest merely on pure reason, independently of all experience, I think it is unnecessary even to ask whether it is a good thing to exhibit these concepts generally (*in abstracto*), which, along with the principles that belong to them, hold a priori, so far as the knowledge involved is to be distinguished from ordinary knowledge and is to be called philosophical. But in our times it may well be necessary to do so. For if one were to take a vote as to whether pure rational knowledge separated from everything empirical, i.e., metaphysics of morals, or whether popular practical philosophy is to be preferred, one can easily guess which side would be preponderant.

This descent to popular thought is certainly very commendable once the ascent to the principles of pure reason has occurred and has been satisfactorily accomplished. That would mean that the doctrine of morals has first been grounded on metaphysics and that subsequently acceptance for morals has been won by giving it a popular character after it has been firmly established. But it is quite absurd to try for popularity in the first inquiry, upon which depends the total correctness of the principles. Not only can such a procedure never lay claim to the very rare merit of a true philosophical popularity, inasmuch as there is really no art involved at all in being generally intelligible if one thereby renounces all basic insight, but such a procedure turns out a disgusting mishmash of patchwork observations and half-reasoned principles in which shallowpates revel because all this is something quite useful for the chitchat of everyday life. Persons of insight, on the other hand, feel confused by all this and turn their eyes away with a dissatisfaction which they nevertheless cannot cure. Yet philosophers, who quite see through the delusion, get little hearing when they summon people for a time from this pretended popularity in order that they may be rightfully popular only after they have attained definite insight.

One need only look at the attempts to deal with morality in the way favored by popular taste. What he will find in an amazing mixture is at one time the particular constitution of human nature (but along with this also the idea of a rational nature in general), at another time perfection, at another happiness; here moral feeling, and there the fear of God; something of this, and also something of that. But the thought never occurs to ask whether the principles of morality are to be sought at all in the knowledge of human nature (which can be had only from experience). Nor does the thought occur that if these principles are not to be sought here but to be found, rather, completely a priori and free from everything empirical in pure rational concepts only, and are to be found nowhere else even to the slightest extent—then there had better be adopted the plan of undertaking this investigation as a separate inquiry, i.e., as pure practical philosophy or (if one may use a name so much decried) as a metaphysics[1] of morals. It is better to bring this investigation to full completeness entirely by itself and to bid the public, which demands popularity, to await the outcome of this undertaking.

But such a completely isolated metaphysics of morals, not mixed with any anthropology, theology, physics, or hyperphysics, and still less with occult qualities (which might be called hypophysical), is not only an indispensable substratum of all theoretical and precisely defined knowledge of duties, but is at the same time a desideratum of the highest importance for the actual fulfillment of their precepts. For the pure thought of duty and of the moral law generally, unmixed with any extraneous addition of empirical inducements, has by the way of reason alone (which first becomes aware hereby that it can of itself be practical) an influence on the human heart so much more powerful than all other incentives[2] which may be derived from the empirical field that reason in the consciousness of its dignity despises such incentives and is able gradually to become their master. On the other hand, a mixed moral philosophy, compounded both of incentives drawn from feelings and inclinations and at the same time of rational concepts, must make the mind waver between motives that cannot be brought under any principle and that can only by accident lead to the good but often can also lead to the bad.

It is clear from the foregoing that all moral concepts have their seat and origin completely a priori in reason, and indeed in the most ordinary

411

---

1. Pure philosophy of morals (metaphysics) may be distinguished from the applied (viz., applied to human nature) just as pure mathematics is distinguished from applied mathematics and pure logic from applied logic. By this designation one is also immediately reminded that moral principles are not grounded on the peculiarities of human nature but must subsist a priori of themselves, and that from such principles practical rules must be derivable for every rational nature, and accordingly for human nature.

2. I have a letter from the late excellent Sulzer [Johann Georg Sulzer (1720–1779), an important Berlin savant, who translated Hume's *Inquiry Concerning the Principles of Morals* into German in 1755] in which he asks me why it is that moral instruction accomplishes so little, even though it contains so much that is convincing to reason. My answer was delayed so that I might make it complete. But it is just that the teachers themselves have not purified their concepts: since they try to do too well by looking everywhere for motives for being morally good, they spoil the medicine by trying to make it really strong. For the most ordinary observation shows that when a righteous act is represented as being done with a steadfast soul and sundered from all view to any advantage in this or another world, and even under the greatest temptations of need or allurement, it far surpasses and eclipses any similar action that was in the least affected by any extraneous incentive; it elevates the soul and inspires the wish to be able to act in this way. Even moderately young children feel this impression, and duties should never be represented to them in any other way.

human reason just as much as in the most highly speculative. They cannot be abstracted from any empirical, and hence merely contingent, cognition. In this purity of their origin lies their very worthiness to serve us as supreme practical principles; and to the extent that something empirical is added to them, just so much is taken away from their genuine influence and from the absolute worth of the corresponding actions. Moreover, it is not only a requirement of the greatest necessity from a theoretical point of view, when it is a question of speculation, but also of the greatest practical importance, to draw these concepts and laws from pure reason, to present them pure and unmixed, and indeed to determine the extent of this entire practical and pure rational cognition, i.e., to determine the whole faculty of pure practical reason. The principles should not be made 412 to depend on the particular nature of human reason, as speculative philosophy may permit and even sometimes finds necessary; but, rather, the principles should be derived from the universal concept of a rational being in general, since moral laws should hold for every rational being as such. In this way all morals, which require anthropology in order to be applied to humans, must be entirely expounded at first independently of anthropology as pure philosophy, i.e., as metaphysics (which can easily be done in such distinct kinds of knowledge). One knows quite well that unless one is in possession of such a metaphysics, then the attempt is futile, I shall not say to determine exactly for speculative judgment the moral element of duty in all that accords with duty, but that the attempt is impossible, even in ordinary and practical usage, especially in that of moral instruction, to ground morals on their genuine principles and thereby to produce pure moral dispositions and engraft them on men's minds for the promotion of the highest good in the world.

In this study we must advance by natural stages not merely from ordinary moral judgment (which is here ever so worthy of respect) to philosophical judgment, as has already been done, but also from popular philosophy, which goes no further than it can get by groping about with the help of examples, to metaphysics (which does not permit itself to be held back any longer by what is empirical, and which, inasmuch as it must survey the whole extent of rational knowledge of this kind, goes right up to ideas, where examples themselves fail us). In order to make such an advance, we must follow and clearly present the practical faculty of reason from its universal rules of determination to the point where the concept of duty springs from it.

Everything in nature works according to laws. Only a rational being has the power to act according to his conception of laws, i.e., according to principles, and thereby has he a will. Since the derivation of actions from laws requires reason, the will is nothing but practical reason. If reason infallibly determines the will, then in the case of such a being actions which are recognized to be objectively necessary are also subjectively necessary, i.e., the will is a faculty of choosing only that which reason, independently of inclination, recognizes as being practically necessary, i.e., as good. But if reason of itself does not sufficiently determine the will, and if the

413 will submits also to subjective conditions (certain incentives) which do not always agree with objective conditions; in a word, if the will does not in itself completely accord with reason (as is actually the case with men), then actions which are recognized as objectively necessary are subjectively contingent, and the determination of such a will according to objective laws is necessitation. That is to say that the relation of objective laws to a will not thoroughly good is represented as the determination of the will of a rational being by principles of reason which the will does not necessarily follow because of its own nature.

The representation of an objective principle insofar as it necessitates the will is called a command (of reason), and the formula of the command is called an imperative.

All imperatives are expressed by an *ought* and thereby indicate the relation of an objective law of reason to a will that is not necessarily determined by this law because of its subjective constitution (the relation of necessitation). Imperatives say that something would be good to do or to refrain from doing, but they say it to a will that does not always therefore do something simply because it has been represented to the will as something good to do. That is practically good which determines the will by means of representations of reason and hence not by subjective causes, but objectively, i.e., on grounds valid for every rational being as such. It is distinguished from the pleasant as that which influences the will only by means of sensation from merely subjective causes, which hold only for this or that person's senses but do not hold as a principle of reason valid for everyone.

414 A perfectly good will would thus be quite as much subject to objective laws (of the good), but could not be conceived as thereby necessitated to act in conformity with law, inasmuch as it can of itself, according to its subjective constitution, be determined only by the representation of the good. Therefore no imperatives hold for the divine will, and in general for a holy will; the *ought* is here out of place, because the *would* is already of itself necessarily in agreement with the law. Consequently, imperatives are only formulas for expressing the relation of objective laws of willing in general to the subjective imperfection of the will of this or that rational being, e.g., the human will.

---

3. The dependence of the faculty of desire on sensations is called inclination, which accordingly always indicates a need. The dependence of a contingently determinable will on principles of reason, however, is called interest. Therefore an interest is found only in a dependent will which is not of itself always in accord with reason; in the divine will no interest can be thought. But even the human will can take an interest in something without thereby acting from interest. The former signifies practical interest in the action, while the latter signifies pathological interest in the object of the action. The former indicates only dependence of the will on principles of reason by itself, while the latter indicates the will's dependence on principles of reason for the sake of inclination, i.e., reason merely gives the practical rule for meeting the need of inclination. In the former case the action interests me, while in the latter case what interests me is the object of the action (so far as this object is pleasant for me). In the First Section we have seen that in the case of an action done from duty regard must be given not to the interest in the object, but only to interest in the action itself and in its rational principle (viz., the law).

Now all imperatives command either hypothetically or categorically. The former represent the practical necessity of a possible action as a means for attaining something else that one wants (or may possibly want). The categorical imperative would be one which represented an action as objectively necessary in itself, without reference to another end.

Every practical law represents a possible action as good and hence as necessary for a subject who is practically determinable by reason; therefore all imperatives are formulas for determining an action which is necessary according to the principle of a will that is good in some way. Now if the action would be good merely as a means to something else, so is the imperative hypothetical. But if the action is represented as good in itself, and hence as necessary in a will which of itself conforms to reason as the principle of the will, then the imperative is categorical.

An imperative thus says what action possible by me would be good, and it presents the practical rule in relation to a will which does not forthwith perform an action simply because it is good, partly because the subject does not always know that the action is good and partly because (even if he does know it is good) his maxims might yet be opposed to the objective principles of practical reason.

A hypothetical imperative thus says only that an action is good for some purpose, either possible or actual. In the first case it is a problematic prac-   415 tical principle; in the second case an assertoric one. A categorical imperative, which declares an action to be of itself objectively necessary without reference to any purpose, i.e., without any other end, holds as an apodeictic practical principle.

Whatever is possible only through the powers of some rational being can be thought of as a possible purpose of some will. Consequently, there are in fact infinitely many principles of action insofar as they are represented as necessary for attaining a possible purpose achievable by them. All sciences have a practical part consisting of problems saying that some end is possible for us and of imperatives telling us how it can be attained. These can, therefore, be called in general imperatives of skill. Here there is no question at all whether the end is reasonable and good, but there is only a question as to what must be done to attain it. The prescriptions needed by a doctor in order to make his patient thoroughly healthy and by a poisoner in order to make sure of killing his victim are of equal value so far as each serves to bring about its purpose perfectly. Since there cannot be known in early youth what ends may be presented to us in the course of life, parents especially seek to have their children learn many different kinds of things, and they provide for skill in the use of means to all sorts of arbitrary ends, among which they cannot determine whether any one of them could in the future become an actual purpose for their ward, though there is always the possibility that he might adopt it. Their concern is so great that they commonly neglect to form and correct their children's judgment regarding the worth of things which might be chosen as ends.

There is, however, one end that can be presupposed as actual for all rational beings (so far as they are dependent beings to whom imperatives apply); and thus there is one purpose which they not merely can have but which can certainly be assumed to be such that they all do have by a natural necessity, and this is happiness. A hypothetical imperative which represents the practical necessity of an action as means for the promotion of happiness is assertoric. It may be expounded not simply as necessary to an uncertain, merely possible purpose, but as necessary to a purpose which can be presupposed a priori and with certainty as being present in everyone because it belongs to his essence. Now skill in the choice of means to one's own greatest well-being can be called prudence[4] in the narrowest sense. And thus the imperative that refers to the choice of means to one's own happiness, i.e., the precept of prudence, still remains hypothetical; the action is commanded not absolutely but only as a means to a further purpose.

Finally, there is one imperative which immediately commands a certain conduct without having as its condition any other purpose to be attained by it. This imperative is categorical. It is not concerned with the matter of the action and its intended result, but rather with the form of the action and the principle from which it follows; what is essentially good in the action consists in the mental disposition, let the consequences be what they may. This imperative may be called that of morality.

Willing according to these three kinds of principles is also clearly distinguished by dissimilarity in the necessitation of the will. To make this dissimilarity clear I think that they are most suitably named in their order when they are said to be either *rules of skill, counsels of prudence*, or *commands (laws) of morality*. For law alone involves the concept of a necessity that is unconditioned and indeed objective and hence universally valid, and commands are laws which must be obeyed, i.e., must be followed even in opposition to inclination. Counsel does indeed involve necessity, but involves such necessity as is valid only under a subjectively contingent condition, viz., whether this or that man counts this or that as belonging to his happiness. On the other hand, the categorical imperative is limited by no condition, and can quite properly be called a command since it is absolutely, though practically, necessary. The first kind of imperatives might also be called technical (belonging to art), the second kind pragmatic[5]

---

4. The word "prudence" is used in a double sense: firstly, it can mean worldly wisdom, and, secondly, private wisdom. The former is the skill of someone in influencing others so as to use them for his own purposes. The latter is the sagacity to combine all these purposes for his own lasting advantage. The value of the former is properly reduced to the latter, and it might better be said of one who is prudent in the former sense but not in the latter that he is clever and cunning, but on the whole imprudent.

5. It seems to me that the proper meaning of the word "pragmatic" could be defined most accurately in this way. For those sanctions are called pragmatic which properly flow not from the law of states as necessary enactments but from provision for the general welfare. A history is pragmatically written when it teaches prudence, i.e., instructs the world how it can provide for its interests better than, or at least as well as, has been done in former times.

(belonging to welfare), the third kind moral (belonging to free conduct as such, i.e., to morals).

The question now arises: how are all of these imperatives possible?[6] This question does not seek to know how the fulfillment of the action commanded by the imperative can be conceived, but merely how the necessitation of the will expressed by the imperative in setting a task can be conceived. How an imperative of skill is possible requires no special discussion. Whoever wills the end, wills (so far as reason has decisive influence on his actions) also the means that are indispensably necessary to his actions and that lie in his power. This proposition, as far as willing is concerned, is analytic. For in willing an object as my effect there is already thought the causality of myself as an acting cause, i.e., the use of means. The imperative derives the concept of actions necessary to this end from the concept of willing this end. (Synthetic propositions are indeed required for determining the means to a proposed end; but such propositions are concerned not with the ground, i.e., the act of the will, but only with the way to realize the object of the will.) Mathematics teaches by nothing but synthetic propositions that in order to bisect a line according to a sure principle I must from each of its extremities draw arcs such that they intersect. But when I know that the proposed result can come about only by means of such an action, then the proposition (if I fully will the effect, then I also will the action required for it) is analytic. For it is one and the same thing to conceive of something as an effect that is possible in a certain way through me and to conceive of myself as acting in the same way with regard to the aforesaid effect.

If it were only as easy to give a determinate concept of happiness, then the imperatives of prudence would exactly correspond to those of skill and would be likewise analytic. For there could be said in this case just as in the former that whoever wills the end also wills (necessarily according to reason) the sole means thereto which are in his power. But, unfortunately, the concept of happiness is such an indeterminate one that even though everyone wishes to attain happiness, yet he can never say definitely and consistently what it is that he really wishes and wills. The reason for this is that all the elements belonging to the concept of happiness are unexceptionally empirical, i.e., they must be borrowed from experience, while for the idea of happiness there is required an absolute whole, a maximum of well-being in my present and in every future condition. Now it is impossible for the most insightful and at the same time most powerful, but nonetheless finite, being to frame here a determinate concept of what it is that he really wills. Does he want riches? How much anxiety, envy, and intrigue might he not thereby bring down upon his own head! Or knowledge and insight? Perhaps these might only give him an eye that much sharper for revealing that much more dreadfully evils which are at present hidden but are yet unavoidable, or such an eye

418

---

6. [That is, why should one let his actions be determined at various times by one or the other of these three kinds of imperatives?]

might burden him with still further needs for the desires which already
concern him enough. Or long life? Who guarantees that it would not be a
long misery? Or health at least? How often has infirmity of the body kept
one from excesses into which perfect health would have allowed him to
fall, and so on? In brief, he is not able on any principle to determine with
complete certainty what will make him truly happy, because to do so
would require omniscience. Therefore, one cannot act according to
determinate principles in order to be happy, but only according to empirical counsels, e.g., of diet, frugality, politeness, reserve, etc., which
are shown by experience to contribute on the average the most to well-
being. There follows from this that imperatives of prudence, strictly
speaking, cannot command at all, i.e., present actions objectively as
practically necessary. They are to be taken as counsels (*consilia*) rather
than as commands (*praecepta*) of reason. The problem of determining
certainly and universally what action will promote the happiness of a rational being is completely insoluble. Therefore, regarding such action no
imperative that in the strictest sense could command what is to be done
to make one happy is possible, inasmuch as happiness is not an ideal of
419   reason but of imagination. Such an ideal rests merely on empirical
grounds; in vain can there be expected that such grounds should determine an action whereby the totality of an infinite series of consequences
could be attained. This imperative of prudence would, nevertheless, be
an analytic practical proposition if one assumes that the means to happiness could with certainty be assigned; for it differs from the imperative
of skill only in that for it the end is given while for the latter the end is
merely possible. Since both, however, command only the means to what
is assumed to be willed as an end, the imperative commanding him who
wills the end to will likewise the means thereto is in both cases analytic.
Hence there is also no difficulty regarding the possibility of an imperative
of prudence.

On the other hand, the question as to how the imperative of morality is
possible is undoubtedly the only one requiring a solution. For it is not at
all hypothetical; and hence the objective necessity which it presents cannot be based on any presupposition, as was the case with the hypothetical
imperatives. Only there must never here be forgotten that no example can
show, i.e., empirically, whether there is any such imperative at all.
Rather, care must be taken lest all imperatives which are seemingly
categorical may nevertheless be covertly hypothetical. For instance, when
it is said that you should not make a false promise, the assumption is that
the necessity of this avoidance is no mere advice for escaping some other
evil, so that it might be said that you should not make a false promise lest
you ruin your credit when the falsity comes to light. But when it is
asserted that an action of this kind must be regarded as bad in itself, then
the imperative of prohibition is therefore categorical. Nevertheless, it
cannot with certainty be shown by means of an example that the will is
here determined solely by the law without any other incentive, even

though such may seem to be the case. For it is always possible that secretly there is fear of disgrace and perhaps also obscure dread of other dangers; such fear and dread may have influenced the will. Who can prove by experience that a cause is not present? Experience only shows that a cause is not perceived. But in such a case the so-called moral imperative, which as such appears to be categorical and unconditioned, would actually be only a pragmatic precept which makes us pay attention to our own advantage and merely teaches us to take such advantage into consideration.

We shall, therefore, have to investigate the possibility of a categorical imperative entirely a priori, inasmuch as we do not here have the advantage of having its reality given in experience and consequently of thus being obligated merely to explain its possibility rather than to establish it. In the meantime so much can be seen for now: the categorical imperative alone purports to be a practical law, while all the others may be called principles of the will but not laws. The reason for this is that whatever is necessary merely in order to attain some arbitrary purpose can be regarded as in itself contingent, and the precept can always be ignored once the purpose is abandoned. Contrariwise, an unconditioned command does not leave the will free to choose the opposite at its own liking. Consequently, only such a command carries with it that necessity which is demanded from a law.

Secondly, in the case of this categorical imperative, or law of morality, the reason for the difficulty (of discerning its possibility) is quite serious. The categorical imperative is an a priori synthetic practical proposition;[7] and since discerning the possibility of propositions of this sort involves so much difficulty in theoretic knowledge, there may readily be gathered that there will be no less difficulty in practical knowledge.

In solving this problem, we want first to inquire whether perhaps the mere concept of a categorical imperative may not also supply us with the formula containing the proposition that can alone be a categorical imperative. For even when we know the purport of such an absolute command, the question as to how it is possible will still require a special and difficult effort, which we postpone to the last section.[8]

If I think of a hypothetical imperative in general, I do not know beforehand what it will contain until its condition is given. But if I think of a categorical imperative, I know immediately what it contains. For since, besides the law, the imperative contains only the necessity that the

420

---

7. I connect a priori, and therefore necessarily, the act with the will without presupposing any condition taken from some inclination (though I make such a connection only objectively, i.e., under the idea of a reason having full power over all subjective motives). Hence this is a practical proposition which does not analytically derive the willing of an action from some other willing already presupposed (for we possess no such perfect will) but which connects the willing of an action immediately with the concept of the will of a rational being as something which is not contained in this concept.

8. [See below Ak. 446–63.]

421 maxim[9] should accord with this law, while the law contains no condition
to restrict it, there remains nothing but the universality of a law as such
with which the maxim of the action should conform. This conformity
alone is properly what is represented as necessary by the imperative.

Hence there is only one categorical imperative and it is this: Act only
according to that maxim whereby you can at the same time will that it
should become a universal law.[10]

Now if all imperatives of duty can be derived from this one imperative
as their principle, then there can at least be shown what is understood by
the concept of duty and what it means, even though there is left
undecided whether what is called duty may not be an empty concept.

The universality of law according to which effects are produced constitutes what is properly called nature in the most general sense (as to
form), i.e., the existence of things as far as determined by universal laws.
Accordingly, the universal imperative of duty may be expressed thus: Act
as if the maxim of your action were to become through your will a universal law of nature.[11]

We shall now enumerate some duties, following the usual division of them
into duties to ourselves and to others and into perfect and imperfect duties.[12]

422 1. A man reduced to despair by a series of misfortunes feels sick of life
but is still so far in possession of his reason that he can ask himself whether
taking his own life would not be contrary to his duty to himself.[13] Now he
asks whether the maxim of his action could become a universal law of
nature. But his maxim is this: from self-love I make as my principle to
shorten my life when its continued duration threatens more evil than it
promises satisfaction. There only remains the question as to whether this

9. A maxim is the subjective principle of acting and must be distinguished from the objective principle, viz., the practical law. A maxim contains the practical rule which reason determines in accordance with the conditions of the subject (often his ignorance or his inclinations)
and is thus the principle according to which the subject does act. But the law is the objective
principle valid for every rational being, and it is the principle according to which he ought to
act, i.e., an imperative.

10. [This formulation of the categorical imperative is often referred to as the formula of
universal law.]

11. [This is often called the formula of the law of nature.]

12. There should be noted here that I reserve the division of duties for a future *Metaphysics
of Morals* [in Part II of the *Metaphysics of Morals*, entitled *The Metaphysical Principles of
Virtue*, Ak. 417–474]. The division presented here stands as merely an arbitrary one (in order
to arrange my examples). For the rest, I understand here by a perfect duty one which permits
no exception in the interest of inclination. Accordingly, I have perfect duties which are external [to others], while other ones are internal [to oneself]. This classification runs contrary to
the accepted usage of the schools, but I do not intend to justify it here, since there is no difference for my purpose whether this classification is accepted or not.

13. [Not committing suicide is an example of a perfect duty to oneself. See *Metaphysical
Principles of Virtue*, Ak. 422–24.]

principle of self-love can become a universal law of nature. One sees at once a contradiction in a system of nature whose law would destroy life by means of the very same feeling that acts so as to stimulate the furtherance of life, and hence there could be no existence as a system of nature. Therefore, such a maxim cannot possibly hold as a universal law of nature and is, consequently, wholly opposed to the supreme principle of all duty.

2. Another man in need finds himself forced to borrow money. He knows well that he won't be able to repay it, but he sees also that he will not get any loan unless he firmly promises to repay it within a fixed time. He wants to make such a promise, but he still has conscience enough to ask himself whether it is not permissible and is contrary to duty to get out of difficulty in this way. Suppose, however, that he decides to do so. The maxim of his action would then be expressed as follows: when I believe myself to be in need of money, I will borrow money and promise to pay it back, although I know that I can never do so. Now this principle of self-love or personal advantage may perhaps be quite compatible with one's entire future welfare, but the question is now whether it is right.[14] I then transform the requirement of self-love into a universal law and put the question thus: how would things stand if my maxim were to become a universal law? He then sees at once that such a maxim could never hold as a universal law of nature and be consistent with itself, but must necessarily be self-contradictory. For the universality of a law which says that anyone believing himself to be in difficulty could promise whatever he pleases with the intention of not keeping it would make promising itself and the end to be attained thereby quite impossible, inasmuch as no one would believe what was promised him but would merely laugh at all such utterances as being vain pretenses.

3. A third finds in himself a talent whose cultivation could make him a man useful in many respects. But he finds himself in comfortable circumstances and prefers to indulge in pleasure rather than to bother himself about broadening and improving his fortunate natural aptitudes. But he asks himself further whether his maxim of neglecting his natural gifts, besides agreeing of itself with his propensity to indulgence, might agree also with what is called duty.[15] He then sees that a system of nature could indeed always subsist according to such a universal law, even though every man (like South Sea Islanders) should let his talents rust and resolve to devote his life entirely to idleness, indulgence, propagation, and, in a word, to enjoyment. But he cannot possibly will that this should become a universal law of nature or be implanted in us as such a law by a natural instinct. For as a rational being he necessarily wills that all his faculties should be developed, inasmuch as they are given him for all sorts of possible purposes.

14. [Keeping promises is an example of a perfect duty to others. See *ibid.*, Ak. 423–31.]

15. [Cultivating one's talents is an example of an imperfect duty to oneself. See *ibid.*, Ak. 444–46.]

4. A fourth man finds things going well for himself but sees others (whom he could help) struggling with great hardships; and he thinks: what does it matter to me? Let everybody be as happy as Heaven wills or as he can make himself; I shall take nothing from him nor even envy him; but I have no desire to contribute anything to his well-being or to his assistance when in need. If such a way of thinking were to become a universal law of nature, the human race admittedly could very well subsist and doubtless could subsist even better than when everyone prates about sympathy and benevolence and even on occasion exerts himself to practice them but, on the other hand, also cheats when he can, betrays the rights of man, or otherwise violates them. But even though it is possible that a universal law of nature could subsist in accordance with that maxim, still it is impossible to will that such a principle should hold everywhere as a law of nature.[16] For a will which resolved in this way would contradict itself, inasmuch as cases might often arise in which one would have need of the love and sympathy of others and in which he would deprive himself, by such a law of nature springing from his own will, of all hope of the aid he wants for himself.

424   These are some of the many actual duties, or at least what are taken to be such, whose derivation from the single principle cited above is clear. We must be able to will that a maxim of our action become a universal law; this is the canon for morally estimating any of our actions. Some actions are so constituted that their maxims cannot without contradiction even be thought as a universal law of nature, much less be willed as what should become one. In the case of others this internal impossibility is indeed not found, but there is still no possibility of willing that their maxim should be raised to the universality of a law of nature, because such a will would contradict itself. There is no difficulty in seeing that the former kind of action conflicts with strict or narrow [perfect] (irremissible) duty, while the second kind conflicts only with broad [imperfect] (meritorious) duty.[17] By means of these examples there has thus been fully set forth how all duties depend as regards the kind of obligation (not the object of their action) upon the one principle.

If we now attend to ourselves in any transgression of a duty, we find that we actually do not will that our maxim should become a universal law—because this is impossible for us—but rather that the opposite of this maxim should remain a law universally.[18] We only take the liberty of making an exception to the law for ourselves (or just for this one time) to

16. [Benefiting others is an example of an imperfect duty to others. See *ibid.*, Ak. 452–54.]

17. [Compare *ibid.*, Ak. 390–94, 410–11, 421–51.]

18. [This is to say, for example, that when you tell a lie, you do so on the condition that others are truthful and believe that what you are saying is true, because otherwise your lie will never work to get you what you want. When you tell a lie, you simply take exception to the general rule that says everyone should always tell the truth.]

the advantage of our inclination. Consequently, if we weighed up everything from one and the same standpoint, namely, that of reason, we would find a contradiction in our own will, viz., that a certain principle be objectively necessary as a universal law and yet subjectively not hold universally but should admit of exceptions. But since we at one moment regard our action from the standpoint of a will wholly in accord with reason and then at another moment regard the very same action from the standpoint of a will affected by inclination, there is really no contradiction here. Rather, there is an opposition (*antagonismus*) of inclination to the precept of reason, whereby the universality (*universalitas*) of the principle is changed into a mere generality (*generalitas*) so that the practical principle of reason may meet the maxim halfway. Although this procedure cannot be justified in our own impartial judgment, yet it does show that we actually acknowledge the validity of the categorical imperative and (with all respect for it) merely allow ourselves a few exceptions which, as they seem to us, are unimportant and forced upon us.

We have thus at least shown that if duty is a concept which is to have significance and real legislative authority for our actions, then such duty can be expressed only in categorical imperatives but not at all in hypothetical ones. We have also—and this is already a great deal—exhibited clearly and definitely for every application what is the content of the categorical imperative, which must contain the principle of all duty (if there is such a thing at all). But we have not yet advanced far enough to prove a priori that there actually is an imperative of this kind, that there is a practical law which of itself commands absolutely and without any incentives, and that following this law is duty.

In order to attain this proof there is the utmost importance in being warned that we must not take it into our mind to derive the reality of this principle from the special characteristics of human nature. For duty has to be a practical, unconditioned necessity of action; hence it must hold for all rational beings (to whom alone an imperative is at all applicable) and for this reason only can it also be a law for all human wills. On the other hand, whatever is derived from the special natural condition of humanity, from certain feelings and propensities, or even, if such were possible, from some special tendency peculiar to human reason and not holding necessarily for the will of every rational being—all of this can indeed yield a maxim valid for us, but not a law. This is to say that such can yield a subjective principle according to which we might act if we happen to have the propensity and inclination, but cannot yield an objective principle according to which we would be directed to act even though our every propensity, inclination, and natural tendency were opposed to it. In fact, the sublimity and inner worth of the command are so much the more evident in a duty, the fewer subjective causes there are for it and the more they oppose it; such causes do not in the least weaken the necessitation exerted by the law or take away anything from its validity.

morality not based on human nature but a priori laws applying to all rational beings

34 * *sentiments vs*

SECOND SECTION

morality – cloud purity of a priori princ,

Here philosophy is seen in fact to be put in a precarious position, which should be firm even though there is neither in heaven nor on earth anything upon which it depends or is based. Here philosophy must show its purity as author of its laws, and not as the herald of such laws as are whispered to it by an implanted sense or by who knows what tutelary nature. Such laws may be better than nothing at all, but they can never give us principles dictated by reason. These principles must have an origin that is completely a priori and must at the same time derive from such origin their authority to command. They expect nothing from the inclination of men but, rather, expect everything from the supremacy of the law and from the respect owed to the law. Without the latter expectation, these principles condemn man to self-contempt and inward abhorrence.

Hence everything empirical is not only quite unsuitable as a contribution to the principle of morality, but is even highly detrimental to the purity of morals. For the proper and inestimable worth of an absolutely good will consists precisely in the fact that the principle of action is free of all influences from contingent grounds, which only experience can furnish. This lax or even mean way of thinking which seeks its principle among empirical motives and laws cannot too much or too often be warned against, for human reason in its weariness is glad to rest upon this pillow. In a dream of sweet illusions (in which not Juno but a cloud is embraced) there is substituted for morality some bastard patched up from limbs of quite varied ancestry and looking like anything one wants to see in it but not looking like virtue to him who has once beheld her in her true form.[19]

Therefore, the question is this: is it a necessary law for all rational beings always to judge their actions according to such maxims as they can themselves will that such should serve as universal laws? If there is such a law, then it must already be connected (completely a priori) with the concept of the will of a rational being in general. But in order to discover this connection we must, however reluctantly, take a step into metaphysics, although into a region of it different from speculative philosophy, i.e., we must enter the metaphysics of morals. In practical philosophy the concern is not with accepting grounds for what happens but with accepting laws of what ought to happen, even though it never does happen—that is, the concern is with objectively practical laws. Here there is no need to inquire into the grounds as to why something pleases or displeases, how the pleasure of mere sensation differs from taste, and whether taste differs from a general satisfaction of reason, upon what does the feeling of pleasure and displeasure rest, and how from this feeling desires and inclinations arise, and how, finally, from these there arise maxims through the cooperation

---

19. To behold virtue in her proper form is nothing other than to present morality stripped of all admixture of what is sensuous and of every spurious adornment of reward or self-love. How much she then eclipses all else that appears attractive to the inclinations can be easily seen by everyone with the least effort of his reason, if it be not entirely ruined for all abstraction.

objectivism not subjectivism
not empiricalism

of reason. All of this belongs to an empirical psychology, which would constitute the second part of the doctrine of nature, if this doctrine is regarded as the philosophy of nature insofar as this philosophy is grounded on empirical laws. But here the concern is with objectively practical laws, and hence with the relation of a will to itself insofar as it is determined solely by reason. In this case everything related to what is empirical falls away of itself, because if reason entirely by itself determines conduct (and the possibility of such determination we now wish to investigate), then reason must necessarily do so a priori.

The will is thought of as a faculty of determining itself to action in accordance with the representation of certain laws, and such a faculty can be found only in rational beings. Now what serves the will as the objective ground of its self-determination is an end; and if this end is given by reason alone, then it must be equally valid for all rational beings. On the other hand, what contains merely the ground of the possibility of the action, whose effect is an end, is called the means. The subjective ground of desire is the incentive; the objective ground of volition is the motive. Hence there arises the distinction between subjective ends, which rest on incentives, and objective ends, which depend on motives valid for every rational being. Practical principles are formal when they abstract from all subjective ends; they are material, however, when they are founded upon subjective ends, and hence upon certain incentives. The ends which a rational being arbitrarily proposes to himself as effects of this action (material ends) are all merely relative, for only their relation to a specially constituted faculty of desire in the subject gives them their worth. Consequently, such worth cannot provide any universal principles, which are valid and necessary for all rational beings and, furthermore, are valid for every volition, i.e., cannot provide any practical laws. Therefore, all such relative ends can be grounds only for hypothetical imperatives.

428

But let us suppose that there were something whose existence has in itself an absolute worth, something which as an end in itself could be a ground of determinate laws. In it, and in it alone, would there be the ground of a possible categorical imperative, i.e., of a practical law.

Now I say that man, and in general every rational being, exists as an end in himself and not merely as a means to be arbitrarily used by this or that will. He must in all his actions, whether directed to himself or to other rational beings, always be regarded at the same time as an end. All the objects of inclinations have only a conditioned value; for if there were not these inclinations and the needs founded on them, then their object would be without value. But the inclinations themselves, being sources of needs, are so far from having an absolute value such as to render them desirable for their own sake that the universal wish of every rational being must be, rather, to be wholly free from them. Accordingly, the value of any object obtainable by our action is always conditioned. Beings whose existence depends not on our will but on nature have, nevertheless, if they are not rational beings, only a relative value as means and are therefore called things. On the other hand, rational beings are called persons inasmuch as their nature already marks them out as ends in themselves, i.e., as something which is not to be used merely as means and hence there is imposed thereby a limit on all arbitrary use of such beings, which are thus objects of respect. Persons are, therefore, not merely subjective ends, whose existence as an effect of our actions has a value for us; but such beings are objective ends, i.e., exist as ends in themselves. Such an end is one for which there can be substituted no other end to which such beings should serve merely as means, for otherwise nothing at all of absolute value would be found anywhere. But if all value were conditioned and hence contingent, then no supreme practical principle could be found for reason at all.

429   If then there is to be a supreme practical principle and, as far as the human will is concerned, a categorical imperative, then it must be such that from the conception of what is necessarily an end for everyone because this end is an end in itself it constitutes an objective principle of the will and can hence serve as a practical law. The ground of such a principle is this: rational nature exists as an end in itself. In this way man necessarily thinks of his own existence; thus far is it a subjective principle of human actions. But in this way also does every other rational being think of his existence on the same rational ground that holds also for me;[20] hence it is at the same time an objective principle, from which, as a supreme practical ground, all laws of the will must be able to be derived. The practical imperative will therefore be the following: Act in such a way that you treat humanity, whether in your own person or in the person of another, always at the same time as an end and never simply as a means.[21] We now want to see whether this can be carried out in practice.

Let us keep to our previous examples.[22]

First, as regards the concept of necessary duty to oneself, the man who contemplates suicide will ask himself whether his action can be consistent with the idea of humanity as an end in itself. If he destroys himself in order to escape from a difficult situation, then he is making use of his person merely as a means so as to maintain a tolerable condition till the end of his life. Man, however, is not a thing and hence is not something to be used merely as a means; he must in all his actions always be regarded as an end in himself. Therefore, I cannot dispose of man in my own person by mutilating, damaging, or killing him. (A more exact determination of this principle so as to avoid all misunderstanding, e.g., regarding the amputation of limbs in order to save oneself, or the exposure of one's life to

20. This proposition I here put forward as a postulate. The grounds for it will be found in the last section. [See below Ak. 446–63.]

21. [This oft-quoted version of the categorical imperative is usually referred to as the formula of the end in itself.]

22. [See above Ak. 422–23.]

danger in order to save it, and so on, must here be omitted; such questions belong to morals proper.)

Second, as concerns necessary or strict duty to others, the man who intends to make a false promise will immediately see that he intends to make use of another man merely as a means to an end which the latter does not likewise hold. For the man whom I want to use for my own purposes by such a promise cannot possibly concur with my way of acting toward him 430 and hence cannot himself hold the end of this action. This conflict with the principle of duty to others becomes even clearer when instances of attacks on the freedom and property of others are considered. For then it becomes clear that a transgressor of the rights of men intends to make use of the persons of others merely as a means, without taking into consideration that, as rational beings, they should always be esteemed at the same time as ends, i.e., be esteemed only as beings who must themselves be able to hold the very same action as an end.[23]

Third, with regard to contingent (meritorious) duty to oneself, it is not enough that the action does not conflict with humanity in our own person as an end in itself; the action must also harmonize with this end. Now there are in humanity capacities for greater perfection which belong to the end that nature has in view as regards humanity in our own person. To neglect these capacities might perhaps be consistent with the maintenance of humanity as an end in itself, but would not be consistent with the advancement of this end.

Fourth, concerning meritorious duty to others, the natural end that all men have is their own happiness. Now humanity might indeed subsist if nobody contributed anything to the happiness of others, provided he did not intentionally impair their happiness. But this, after all, would harmonize only negatively and not positively with humanity as an end in itself, if everyone does not also strive, as much as he can, to further the ends of others. For the ends of any subject who is an end in himself must as far as possible be my ends also, if that conception of an end in itself is to have its full effect in me.

This principle of humanity and of every rational nature generally as an end in itself is the supreme limiting condition of every man's freedom of 431 action. This principle is not borrowed from experience, first, because of its universality, inasmuch as it applies to all rational beings generally, and no experience is capable of determining anything about them; and, secondly, because in experience (subjectively) humanity is not thought of as the end of men, i.e., as an object that we of ourselves actually make our

---

23. Let it not be thought that the trivial *quod tibi non vis fieri, etc.* [do not do to others what you do not want done to yourself] can here serve as a standard or principle. For it is merely derived from our principle, although with several limitations. It cannot be a universal law, for it contains the ground neither of duties to onself nor of duties of love toward others (for many a man would gladly consent that others should not benefit him, if only he might be excused from benefiting them). Nor, finally, does it contain the ground of strict duties toward others, for the criminal would on this ground be able to dispute with the judges who punish him; and so on.

end which as a law ought to constitute the supreme limiting condition of all subjective ends (whatever they may be); and hence this principle must arise from pure reason [and not from experience]. That is to say that the ground of all practical legislation lies objectively in the rule and in the form of universality, which (according to the first principle) makes the rule capable of being a law (say, for example, a law of nature). Subjectively, however, the ground of all practical legislation lies in the end; but (according to the second principle) the subject of all ends is every rational being as an end in himself. From this there now follows the third practical principle of the will as the supreme condition of the will's conformity with universal practical reason, viz., the idea of the will of every rational being as a will that legislates universal law.²⁴

According to this principle all maxims are rejected which are not consistent with the will's own legislation of universal law. The will is thus not merely subject to the law but is subject to the law in such a way that it must be regarded also as legislating for itself and only on this account as being subject to the law (of which it can regard itself as the author).

In the previous formulations of imperatives, viz., that based on the conception of the conformity of actions to universal law in a way similar to a natural order and that based on the universal prerogative of rational beings as ends in themselves, these imperatives just because they were thought of as categorical excluded from their legislative authority all admixture of any interest as an incentive. They were, however, only assumed to be categorical because such an assumption had to be made if the concept of duty was to be explained. But that there were practical propositions which commanded categorically could not itself be proved, nor can it be proved anywhere in this section. But one thing could have been done, viz., to indicate that in willing from duty the renunciation of all interest is the specific mark distinguishing a categorical imperative 432 from a hypothetical one and that such renunciation was expressed in the imperative itself by means of some determination contained in it. This is done in the present (third) formulation of the principle, namely, in the idea of the will of every rational being as a will that legislates universal law.

When such a will is thought of, then even though a will which is subject to law may be bound to this law by means of some interest, nevertheless a will that is itself a supreme lawgiver is not able as such to depend on any interest. For a will which is so dependent would itself require yet another law restricting the interest of its self-love to the condition that such interest should itself be valid as a universal law.

Thus the principle that every human will as a will that legislates universal law in all its maxims,²⁵ provided it is otherwise correct, would be well suited to being a categorical imperative in the following respect:

24. [This is usually called the formula of autonomy.]

25. I may here be excused from citing instances to elucidate this principle inasmuch as those which were first used to elucidate the categorical imperative and its formula can all serve the same purpose here. [See above Ak. 421–23, 429–30.]

just because of the idea of legislating universal law such an imperative is not based on any interest, and therefore it alone of all possible imperatives can be unconditional. Or still better, the proposition being converted, if there is a categorical imperative (i.e., a law for the will of every rational being), then it can only command that everything be done from the maxim of such a will as could at the same time have as its object only itself regarded as legislating universal law. For only then are the practical principle and the imperative which the will obeys unconditional, inasmuch as the will can be based on no interest at all.

When we look back upon all previous attempts that have been made to discover the principle of morality, there is no reason now to wonder why they one and all had to fail. Man was viewed as bound to laws by his duty; but it was not seen that man is subject only to his own, yet universal, legislation and that he is bound only to act in accordance with his own will, which is, however, a will purposed by nature to legislate universal laws. For when man is thought as being merely subject to a law (whatever it might be), then the law had to carry with it some interest   433 functioning as an attracting stimulus or as a constraining force for obedience, inasmuch as the law did not arise as a law from his own will. Rather, in order that his will conform with law, it had to be necessitated by something else to act in a certain way. By this absolutely necessary conclusion, however, all the labor spent in finding a supreme ground for duty was irretrievably lost; duty was never discovered, but only the necessity of acting from a certain interest. This might be either one's own interest or another's, but either way the imperative had to be always conditional and could never possibly serve as a moral command. I want, therefore, to call my principle the principle of the autonomy of the will, in contrast with every other principle, which I accordingly count under heteronomy.

The concept of every rational being as one who must regard himself as legislating universal law by all his will's maxims, so that he may judge himself and his actions from this point of view, leads to another very fruitful concept, which depends on the aforementioned one, viz., that of a kingdom of ends.

By "kingdom" I understand a systematic union of different rational beings through common laws. Now laws determine ends as regards their universal validity; therefore, if one abstracts from the personal differences of rational beings and also from all content of their private ends, then it will be possible to think of a whole of all ends in systematic connection (a whole both of rational being as ends in themselves and also of the particular ends which each may set for himself); that is, one can think of a kingdom of ends that is possible on the aforesaid principles.

For all rational beings stand under the law that each of them should treat himself and all others never merely as means but always at the same time as an end in himself. Hereby arises a systematic union of rational beings through common objective laws, i.e., a kingdom that may be called a kingdom of ends (certainly only an ideal), inasmuch as these laws have in

view the very relation of such beings to one another as ends and means.[26]
A rational being belongs to the kingdom of ends as a member when he
legislates in it universal laws while also being himself subject to these
laws. He belongs to it as sovereign, when as legislator he is himself subject
to the will of no other.

434   A rational being must always regard himself as legislator in a kingdom
of ends rendered possible by freedom of the will, whether as member or as
sovereign. The position of the latter can be maintained not merely
through the maxims of his will but only if he is a completely independent
being without needs and with unlimited power adequate to his will.

Hence morality consists in the relation of all action to that legislation
whereby alone a kingdom of ends is possible. This legislation must be
found in every rational being and must be able to arise from his will,
whose principle then is never to act on any maxim except such as can also
be a universal law and hence such as the will can thereby regard itself as
at the same time the legislator of universal law. If now the maxims do not
by their very nature already necessarily conform with this objective principle of rational beings as legislating universal laws, then the necessity of
acting on that principle is called practical necessitation, i.e., duty. Duty
does not apply to the sovereign in the kingdom of ends, but it does apply
to every member and to each in the same degree.

The practical necessity of acting according to this principle, i.e., duty,
does not rest at all on feelings, impulses, and inclinations, but only on the
relation of rational beings to one anther, a relation in which the will of a
rational being must always be regarded at the same time as legislative,
because otherwise he could not be thought of as an end in himself.
Reason, therefore, relates every maxim of the will as legislating universal
laws to every other will and also to every action toward oneself; it does so
not on account of any other practical motive or future advantage but
rather from the idea of the dignity of a rational being who obeys no law
except what he at the same time enacts himself.

In the kingdom of ends everything has either a price or a dignity.
Whatever has a price can be replaced by something else as its equivalent;
on the other hand, whatever is above all price, and therefore admits of no
equivalent, has a dignity.

Whatever has reference to general human inclinations and needs has a
market price; whatever, without presupposing any need, accords with a
435 certain taste, i.e., a delight in the mere unpurposive play of our mental
powers,[27] has an affective price; but that which constitutes the condition
under which alone something can be an end in itself has not merely a
relative worth, i.e., a price, but has an intrinsic worth, i.e., dignity.

Now morality is the condition under which alone a rational being can
be an end in himself, for only thereby can he be a legislating member in
the kingdom of ends. Hence morality and humanity, insofar as it is

26. [This is usually called the formula of the kingdom of ends.]

27. [See Kant, *Critique of Aesthetic Judgment*, §'s 1–5.]

capable of morality, alone have dignity. Skill and diligence in work have a market price; wit, lively imagination, and humor have an affective price; but fidelity to promises and benevolence based on principles (not on instinct) have intrinsic worth. Neither nature nor art contain anything which in default of these could be put in their place; for their worth consists, not in the effects which arise from them, nor in the advantage and profit which they provide, but in mental dispositions, i.e., in the maxims of the will which are ready in this way to manifest themselves in action, even if they are not favored with success. Such actions also need no recommendation from any subjective disposition or taste so as to meet with immediate favor and delight; there is no need of any immediate propensity or feeling toward them. They exhibit the will performing them as an object of immediate respect; and nothing but reason is required to impose them upon the will, which is not to be cajoled into them, since in the case of duties such cajoling would be a contradiction. This estimation, therefore, lets the worth of such a disposition be recognized as dignity and puts it infinitely beyond all price, with which it cannot in the least be brought into competition or comparison without, as it were, violating its sanctity.

What then is it that entitles the morally good disposition, or virtue, to make such lofty claims? It is nothing less than the share which such a disposition affords the rational being of legislating universal laws, so that he is fit to be a member in a possible kingdom of ends, for which his own nature has already determined him as an end in himself and therefore as a legislator in the kingdom of ends. Thereby is he free as regards all laws of nature, and he obeys only those laws which he gives to himself. Accordingly, his maxims can belong to a universal legislation to which he at the same time subjects himself. For nothing can have any worth other than what the law determines. But the legislation itself which determines all worth must for that very reason have dignity, i.e., unconditional and incomparable worth; and the word "respect" alone provides a suitable expression for the esteem which a rational being must have for it. Hence autonomy is the ground of the dignity of human nature and of every rational nature.

436

The aforementioned three ways of representing the principle of morality are at bottom only so many formulas of the very same law: one of them by itself contains a combination of the other two. Nevertheless, there is a difference in them, which is subjectively rather than objectively practical, viz., it is intended to bring an idea of reason closer to intuition (in accordance with a certain analogy) and thereby closer to feeling. All maxims have, namely,

1. A form, which consists in universality; and in this respect the formula of the moral imperative is expressed thus: maxims must be so chosen as if they were to hold as universal laws of nature.

2. A matter, viz., an end; and here the formula says that a rational being, inasmuch as he is by his very nature an end and hence an end in himself, must serve in every maxim as a condition limiting all merely relative and arbitrary ends.

3. A complete determination of all maxims by the formula that all max-

ims proceeding from his own legislation ought to harmonize with a possible kingdom of ends as a kingdom of nature.[28] There is a progression here through the categories of the *unity* of the form of the will (its universality), the *plurality* of its matter (its objects, i.e., its ends), and the *totality* or completeness of its system of ends. But one does better if in moral judgment he follows the rigorous method and takes as his basis the

437 universal formula of the categorical imperative: Act according to that maxim which can at the same time make itself a universal law. But if one wants also to secure acceptance for the moral law, it is very useful to bring one and the same action under the three aforementioned concepts and thus, as far as possible, to bring the moral law nearer to intuition.

We can now end where we started in the beginning, viz., the concept of an unconditionally good will. That will is absolutely good which cannot be evil, i.e., whose maxim, when made into a universal law, can never conflict with itself. This principle is therefore also its supreme law: Act always according to that maxim whose universality as a law you can at the same time will. This is the only condition under which a will can never be in conflict with itself, and such an imperative is categorical. Inasmuch as the validity of the will as a universal law for possible actions is analogous to the universal connection of the existence of things in accordance with universal laws, which is the formal aspect of nature in general, the categorical imperative can also be expressed thus: Act according to maxims which can at the same time have for their object themselves as universal laws of nature. In this way there is provided the formula for an absolutely good will.

Rational nature is distinguished from the rest of nature by the fact that it sets itself an end. This end would be the matter of every good will. But in the idea of an absolutely good will—good without any qualifying condition (of attaining this or that end) —complete abstraction must be made from every end that has to come about as an effect (since such would make every will only relatively good). And so the end must here be conceived, not as an end to be effected, but as an independently existing end. Hence it must be conceived only negatively, i.e., as an end which should never be acted against and therefore as one which in all willing must never be regarded merely as means but must always be esteemed at the same time as an end. Now this end can be nothing but the subject of all possible ends themselves, because this subject is at the same time the subject of a possible absolutely good will; for such a will cannot without contradiction be subordinated to any other object. The principle: So act in

438 regard to every rational being (yourself and others) that he may at the same time count in your maxim as an end in himself, is thus basically the same as the principle: Act on a maxim which at the same time contains in

---

28. Teleology considers nature as a kingdom of ends; morals regards a possible kingdom of ends as a kingdom of nature. In the former the kingdom of ends is a theoretical idea for explaining what exists. In the latter it is a practical idea for bringing about what does not exist but can be made actual by our conduct, i.e., what can be actualized in accordance with this very idea.

itself its own universal validity for every rational being. That in the use of means for every end my maxim should be restricted to the condition of its universal validity as a law for every subject says just the same as that a subject of ends, i.e., a rational being himself, must be made the ground for all maxims of actions and must thus be used never merely as means but as the supreme limiting condition in the use of all means, i.e., always at the same time as an end.

Now there follows incontestably from this that every rational being as an end in himself must be able to regard himself with reference to all laws to which he may be subject as being at the same time the legislator of universal law, for just this very fitness of his maxims for the legislation of universal law distinguishes him as an end in himself. There follows also that his dignity (prerogative) of being above all the mere things of nature implies that his maxims must be taken from the viewpoint that regards himself, as well as every other rational being, as being legislative beings (and hence are they called persons). In this way there is possible a world of rational beings (*mundus intelligibilis*) as a kingdom of ends, because of the legislation belonging to all persons as members. Therefore, every rational being must so act as if he were through his maxim always a legislating member in the universal kingdom of ends. The formal principle of these maxims is this: So act as if your maxims were to serve at the same time as a universal law (for all rational beings). Thus a kingdom of ends is possible only on the analogy of a kingdom of nature; yet the former is possible only through maxims, i.e., self-imposed rules, while the latter is possible only through laws of efficient causes necessitated from without. Regardless of this difference and even though nature as a whole is viewed as a machine, yet insofar as nature stands in a relation to rational beings as its ends, it is on this account given the name of a kingdom of nature. Such a kingdom of ends would actually be realized through maxims whose rule is prescribed to all rational beings by the categorical imperative, if these maxims were universally obeyed. But even if a rational being himself strictly obeys such a maxim, he cannot for that reason count on everyone else's being true to it, nor can he expect the kingdom of nature and its purposive order to be in harmony with him as a fitting member of a kingdom of ends made possible by himself, i.e., he cannot expect the kingdom of nature to favor his expectation of happiness. 439 Nevertheless, the law: Act in accordance with the maxims of a member legislating universal laws for a merely possible kingdom of ends, remains in full force, since it commands categorically. And just in this lies the paradox that merely the dignity of humanity as rational nature without any further end or advantage to be thereby gained—and hence respect for a mere idea—should yet serve as an inflexible precept for the will; and that just this very independence of the maxims from all such incentives should constitute the sublimity of maxims and the worthiness of every rational subject to be a legislative member in the kingdom of ends, for otherwise he would have to be regarded as subject only to the natural law of his own needs. And even if the kingdom of nature as well as the kingdom of ends were thought of as both united under one sovereign so that the latter kingdom would thereby no longer remain a mere idea but would acquire true reality, then indeed the kingdom of ends would gain the addition of a strong incentive, but never any increase in its intrinsic worth. For this sole absolute legislator must, in spite of all this, always be thought of as judging the worth of rational beings solely by the disinterested conduct prescribed to themselves by means of this idea alone. The essence of things is not altered by their external relations; and whatever without reference to such relations alone constitutes the absolute worth of man is also what he must be judged by, whoever the judge may be, even the Supreme Being. Hence morality is the relation of actions to the autonomy of the will, i.e., to the possible legislation of universal law by means of the maxims of the will. That action which is compatible with the autonomy of the will is permitted; that which is not compatible is forbidden. That will whose maxims are necessarily in accord with the laws of autonomy is a holy, or absolutely good, will. The dependence of a will which is not absolutely good upon the principle of autonomy (i.e., moral necessitation) is obligation, which cannot therefore be applied to a holy will. The objective necessity of an action from obligation is called duty.

From what has just been said, there can now easily be explained how it happens that, although in the concept of duty we think of subjection to the 440 law, yet at the same time we thereby ascribe a certain dignity and sublimity to the person who fulfills all his duties. For not insofar as he is subject to the moral law does he have sublimity, but rather has it only insofar as with regard to this very same law he is at the same time legislative, and only thereby is he subject to the law. We have also shown above[29] how neither fear nor inclination, but solely respect for the law, is the incentive which can give an action moral worth. Our own will, insofar as it were to act only under the condition of its being able to legislate universal law by means of its maxims—this will, ideally possible for us, is the proper object of respect. And the dignity of humanity consists just in its capacity to legislate universal law, though with the condition of humanity's being at the same time itself subject to this very same legislation.

Autonomy of the Will
As the Supreme Principle of Morality

Autonomy of the will is the property that the will has of being a law to itself (independently of any property of the objects of volition). The principle of autonomy is this: Always choose in such a way that in the same volition the maxims of the choice are at the same time present as universal law. That this practical rule is an imperative, i.e., that the will of every rational being is necessarily bound to the rule as a condition, cannot be proved by merely analyzing the concepts contained in it, since it is a synthetic proposition. For proof one would have to go beyond cogni-

29. [Ak. 400–402.]

tion of objects to a critical examination of the subject, i.e. go to a critique of pure practical reason, since this synthetic proposition which commands apodeictically must be capable of being cognized completely a priori. This task, however, does not belong to the present section. But that the above principle of autonomy is the sole principle of morals can quite well be shown by mere analysis of the concepts of morality; for thereby the principle of morals is found to be necessarily a categorical imperative, which commands nothing more nor less than this very autonomy.

Heteronomy of the Will
As the Source of All Spurious Principles
of Morality

441

If the will seeks the law that is to determine it anywhere but in the fitness of its maxims for its own legislation of universal laws, and if it thus goes outside of itself and seeks this law in the character of any of its objects, then heteronomy always results. The will in that case does not give itself the law, but the object does so because of its relation to the will. This relation, whether it rests on inclination or on representations of reason, admits only of hypothetical imperatives: I ought to do something because I will something else. On the other hand, the moral, and hence categorical, imperative says that I ought to act in this way or that way, even though I did not will something else. For example, the former says that I ought not to lie if I would maintain my reputation; the latter says that I ought not to lie even though lying were to bring me not the slightest discredit. The moral imperative must therefore abstract from every object to such an extent that no object has any influence at all on the will, so that practical reason (the will) may not merely minister to an interest not belonging to it but may merely show its own commanding authority as the supreme legislation. Thus, for example, I ought to endeavor to promote the happiness of others, not as though its realization were any concern of mine (whether by immediate inclination or by any satisfaction indirectly gained through reason), but merely because a maxim which excludes it cannot be comprehended as a universal law in one and the same volition.

Classification of All Possible Principles of Morality
Founded upon the Assumed Fundamental Concept
of Heteronomy

Here as elsewhere human reason in its pure use, so long as it lacks a critical examination, first tried every possible wrong way before it succeeded in finding the only right way.

All principles that can be taken from this point of view are either empirical or rational. The first kind, drawn from the principle of happiness, are based upon either physical or moral feeling. The second kind, drawn from the principle of perfection, are based upon either the rational concept of perfection as a possible effect of our will or else upon the concept of an independent perfection (the will of God) as a determining cause of our will.

Empirical principles are wholly unsuited to serve as the foundation for moral laws. For the universality with which such laws ought to hold for all rational beings without exception (the unconditioned practical necessity imposed by moral laws upon such beings) is lost if the basis of these laws is taken from the particular constitution of human nature or from the accidental circumstances in which such nature is placed. But the principle of one's own happiness is the most objectionable. Such is the case not merely because this principle is false and because experience contradicts the supposition that well-being is always proportional to well-doing, nor yet merely because this principle contributes nothing to the establishment of morality, inasmuch as making a man happy is quite different from making him good and making him prudent and sharp-sighted for his own advantage quite different from making him virtuous. Rather, such is the case because this principle of one's own happiness bases morality upon incentives that undermine it rather than establish it and that totally destroy its sublimity, inasmuch as motives to virtue are put in the same class as motives to vice and inasmuch as such incentives merely teach one to become better at calculation, while the specific difference between virtue and vice is entirely obliterated. On the other hand, moral feeling, this alleged special sense,[30] remains closer to morality than does the aforementioned principle of one's own happiness. Yet the appeal to the principle of moral feeling is superficial, since men who cannot think believe that they will be helped out by feeling, even when the question is solely one of universal laws. They do so even though feelings naturally differ from one another by an infinity of degrees, so that feelings are not capable of providing a uniform measure of good and evil; furthermore, they do so even though one man cannot by his feeling judge validly at all for other men. Nevertheless, the principle of moral feeling is closer to morality and its dignity than is the principle of one's own happiness inasmuch as the former principle pays virtue the honor of ascribing to her directly the satisfaction and esteem that is held for her, and does not, as it were, tell her to her face that our attachment to her rests not on her beauty but only on our advantage.

---

30. I count the principle of moral feeling under that of happiness, because every empirical interest promises to contribute to our well-being through the amenity afforded by something, whether immediately and without any reference to advantage or with reference to advantage. Similarly, the principle of sympathy for the happiness of others must with Hutcheson be counted along with the principle of moral sense as adopted by him. [Francis Hutcheson (1694–1747) was Professor of Moral Philosophy in the University of Glasgow, Scotland. He was the main proponent of the doctrine of moral sense.]

Among the rational principles of morality (or those arising from reason rather than from feeling) there is the ontological concept of perfection. It is empty, indeterminate, and hence of no use for finding in the immeasurable field of possible reality the maximum sum suitable for us. Furthermore, in attempting to distinguish specifically between the reality just mentioned and every other, it exhibits an inevitable tendency for turning about in a circle and cannot avoid tacitly presupposing the morality that it has to explain. Nevertheless, it is better than the theological concept, whereby morality is derived from a divine and most perfect will. It is better not merely because we cannot intuit divine perfection but can only derive it from our own concepts, among which morality is foremost; but also because if it is not so derived (and being thus derived would involve a crudely circular explanation), then the only remaining concept of God's will is drawn from such characteristics as desire for glory and dominion combined with such frightful representations as those of might and vengeance. Any system of morals based on such notions would be directly opposed to morality.

But if I had to choose between the concept of moral sense and that of perfection in general (both of which at least do not weaken morality, even though they are not at all capable of serving as its foundation), I would decide for the latter because it at least withdraws the decision of the question from sensibility and brings it to the court of pure reason, though it does not even here get any decision. Furthermore, I would choose the concept of perfection in general because it preserves the indeterminate idea (of a will good in itself) free from falsity until it can be more precisely determined.

For the rest, I believe that I may be excused from a lengthy refutation of all these doctrines. Such a refutation would be merely superfluous labor, since it is so easy and is presumably so well understood even by those whose office requires them to declare themselves for one of these theories (since their hearers would not tolerate suspension of judgment). But what interests us more here is to know that these principles never lay down anything but heteronomy of the will as the first ground of morality and that they must, consequently, necessarily fail in their purpose.

In every case where an object of the will must be laid down as the foun-   444
dation for prescribing a rule to determine the will, there the rule is nothing but heteronomy. The imperative is then conditioned, viz., if or because one wills this object, one should act thus or so. Hence the imperative can never command morally, i.e., categorically. Now the object may determine the will by means of inclination, as in the case of the principle of one's own happiness, or by means of reason directed to objects of our volition in general, as in the case of the principle of perfection. Yet in both cases the will never determines itself immediately by the thought of an action, but only by the incentive that the anticipated effect of the action has upon the will: I ought to do something because I will something else. And here must yet another law be assumed in me the subject, whereby I necessarily will this something else; this other law in turn re-

quires an imperative to restrict this maxim. For the impulse which the representation of an object that is possible by means of our powers is to exert upon the will of a subject in accordance with his natural constitution belongs to the nature of the subject, whether to his sensibility (his inclination and taste) or to his understanding and reason, whose employment on an object is by the particular arrangement of their nature attended with satisfaction; consequently, the law would, properly speaking, be given by nature. This law, insofar as it is a law of nature, must be known and proved through experience and is therefore in itself contingent and hence is not fit to be an apodeictic practical rule, such as a moral rule must be. The law of nature under discussion is always merely heteronomy of the will; the will does not give itself the law, but a foreign impulse gives the law to the will by means of the subject's nature, which is adapted to receive such an impulse.

An absolutely good will, whose principle must be a categorical imperative, will therefore be indeterminate as regards all objects and will contain merely the form of willing; and indeed that form is autonomy. This is to say that the fitness of the maxims of every good will to make themselves universal laws is itself the only law that the will of every rational being imposes on itself, without needing to assume any incentive or interest as a basis.

How such a synthetic practical a priori proposition is possible and why it is necessary are problems whose solution does not lie any longer within the bounds of a metaphysics of morals. Furthermore, we have not here
445 asserted the truth of this proposition, much less professed to have within our power a proof of it. We simply showed by developing the universally accepted concept of morality that autonomy of the will is unavoidably bound up with it, or rather is its very foundation. Whoever, then, holds morality to be something real, and not a chimerical idea without any truth, must also admit the principle here put forward. Hence this section, like the first, was merely analytic. To show that morality is not a mere phantom of the brain, which morality cannot be if the categorical imperative, and with it the autonomy of the will, is true and absolutely necessary as an a priori principle, we require a possible synthetic use of pure practical reason. But we must not venture on this use without prefacing it with a critical examination of this very faculty of reason. In the last section we shall give the main outlines of this critical examination as far as sufficient for our purpose.[31]

31. [The ensuing Third Section is difficult to grasp. Kant expressed himself more clearly regarding the topics discussed there in the *Critique of Practical Reason*, Part I, Book I ("Analytic of Pure Practical Reason").]

TRANSITION FROM A METAPHYSICS OF MORALS TO A
CRITIQUE OF PURE PRACTICAL REASON

*The Concept of Freedom Is the Key for an Explanation
of the Autonomy of the Will*

The will is a kind of causality belonging to living beings insofar as they
are rational; freedom would be the property of this causality that makes it
effective independent of any determination by alien causes. Similarly,
natural necessity is the property of the causality of all non-rational beings
by which they are determined to activity through the influence of alien
causes.

The foregoing explanation of freedom is negative and is therefore un-
fruitful for attaining an insight regarding its essence; but there arises from
it a positive concept, which as such is richer and more fruitful. The concept
of causality involves that of laws according to which something that we call
cause must entail something else—namely, the effect. Therefore freedom is
certainly not lawless, even though it is not a property of will in accordance
with laws of nature. It must, rather, be a causality in accordance with im-
mutable laws, which, to be sure, is of a special kind; otherwise a free will
would be something absurd. As we have already seen [in the preceding
paragraph], natural necessity is a heteronomy of efficient causes, inasmuch
as every effect is possible only in accordance with the law that something 447
else determines the efficient cause to exercise its causality. What else, then,
can freedom of the will be but autonomy, i.e., the property that the will has
of being a law to itself? The proposition that the will is in every action a law
to itself expresses, however, nothing but the principle of acting according
to no other maxim than that which can at the same time have itself as a
universal law for its object. Now this is precisely the formula of the
categorical imperative and is the principle of morality. Thus a free will and
a will subject to moral laws are one and the same.

Therefore if freedom of the will is presupposed, morality (together with
its principle) follows by merely analyzing the concept of freedom.
However, the principle of morality is, nevertheless, a synthetic proposition: viz., an absolutely good will is one whose maxim can always have
itself as content when such maxim is regarded as a universal law; it is synthetic because this property of the will's maxim can never be found by
analyzing the concept of an absolutely good will. Now such synthetic
propositions are possible only as follows—two cognitions are bound
together through their connection with a third in which both of them are
to be found. The positive concept of freedom furnishes this third cogni-

tion, which cannot, as is the case with physical causes, be the nature of the world of sense (in whose concept is combined the concept of something as cause in relation to something else as effect). We cannot here yet show straight away what this third cognition is which freedom indicates to us and of which we have an a priori idea, nor can we as yet conceive of the deduction of the concept of freedom from pure practical reason and therewith also the possibility of a categorical imperative. Rather, we require some further preparation.

Freedom Must Be Presupposed as a Property of the Will of All Rational Beings

It is not enough to ascribe freedom to our will, on whatever ground, if we have not also sufficient reason for attributing it to all rational beings. For inasmuch as morality serves as a law for us only insofar as we are rational beings, it must also be valid for all rational beings. And since morality must be derived solely from the property of freedom, one must show that freedom is also the property of the will of all rational beings. It 448 is not enough to prove freedom from certain alleged experiences of human nature (such a proof is indeed absolutely impossible, and so freedom can be proved only a priori). Rather, one must show that freedom belongs universally to the activity of rational beings endowed with a will. Now I say that every being which cannot act in any way other than under the idea of freedom is for this very reason free from a practical point of view. This is to say that for such a being all the laws that are inseparably bound up with freedom are valid just as much as if the will of such a being could be declared to be free in itself for reasons that are valid for theoretical philosophy.[1] Now I claim that we must necessarily attribute to every rational being who has a will also the idea of freedom, under which only can such a being act. For in such a being we think of a reason that is practical, i.e., that has causality in reference to its objects. Now we cannot possibly think of a reason that consciously lets itself be directed from outside as regards its judgments; for in that case the subject would ascribe the determination of his faculty of judgment not to his reason, but to an impulse. Reason must regard itself as the author of its principles independent of foreign influences. Therefore as practical reason or as the will of a rational being must reason regard itself as free. This is to say that the will of a rational being can be a will of its own only under the idea of freedom, and that such a will must therefore, from a practical point of view, be attributed to all rational beings.

1. I adopt this method of assuming as sufficient for our purpose that freedom is presupposed merely as an idea by rational beings in their actions in order that I may avoid the necessity of having to prove freedom from a theoretical point of view as well. For even if this latter problem is left unresolved, the same laws that would bind a being who was really free are valid equally for a being who cannot act otherwise than under the idea of its own freedom. Thus we can relieve ourselves of the burden which presses on the theory.

Concerning the Interest Attached
to the Ideas of Morality

We have finally traced the determinate concept of morality back to the idea of freedom, but we could not prove freedom to be something actual in ourselves and in human nature. We saw merely that we must presuppose it if we want to think of a being as rational and as endowed with consciousness of its causality as regards actions, i.e., as endowed with a will. And so we find that on the very same ground we must attribute to every being endowed with reason and a will this property of determining itself to action under the idea of its own freedom.

449

Now there resulted from the presupposition of this idea of freedom also the consciousness of a law of action: that the subjective principles of actions, i.e., maxims, must always be so adopted that they can also be valid objectively, i.e., universally, as principles, and can therefore serve as universal laws of our own legislation. But why, then, should I subject myself to this principle simply as a rational being and by so doing also subject to this principle all other beings endowed with reason? I am willing to grant that no interest impels me to do so, because this would not give a categorical imperative. But nonetheless I must necessarily take an interest in it and discern how this comes about, for this *ought* is properly a *would* which is valid for every rational being, provided that reason is practical for such a being without hindrances. In the case of beings who, like ourselves, are also affected by sensibility, i.e., by incentives of a kind other than the purely rational, and who do not always act as reason by itself would act, this necessity of action is expressed only as an *ought*, and the subjective necessity is to be distinguished from the objective.

It therefore seems as if we have in the idea of freedom actually only presupposed the moral law, namely, the principle of the autonomy of the will, and as if we could not prove its reality and objective necessity independently. In that case we should indeed still have gained something quite considerable by at least determining the genuine principle more exactly than had previously been done. But as regards its validity and the practical necessity of subjecting oneself to it, we would have made no progress. We could give no satisfactory answer if asked the following questions: why must the universal validity of our maxim taken as a law be a condition restricting our actions; upon what do we base the worth that we assign to this way of acting—a worth that is supposed to be so great that there can be no higher interest; how does it happen that by this alone does man believe that he feels his own personal worth, in comparison with which that of an agreeable or disagreeable condition is to be regarded as nothing.

450

Indeed we do sometimes find that we can take an interest in a personal characteristic which involves no interest in any [external] condition but only makes us capable of participating in the condition in case reason were to effect the allotment. This is to say that the mere worthiness of being happy can of itself be of interest even without the motive of participating in this happiness. This judgment, however, is in fact only the result of the importance that we have already presupposed as belonging to moral laws (when by the idea of freedom we divorce ourselves from all empirical interest). However, in this way we are not as yet able to have any insight into why it is that we should divorce ourselves from such interest, i.e., that we should consider ourselves as free in action and yet hold ourselves as subject to certain laws so as to find solely in our own person a worth that can compensate us for the loss of everything that gives worth to our condition. We do not see how this is possible and hence how the moral law can obligate us.

One must frankly admit that there is here a sort of circle from which, so it seems, there is no way to escape. In the order of efficient causes we assume that we are free so that we may think of ourselves as subject to moral laws in the order of ends. And we then think of ourselves as subject to these laws because we have attributed to ourselves freedom of the will. Freedom and self-legislation of the will are both autonomy and are hence reciprocal concepts. Since they are reciprocal, one of them cannot be used to explain the other or to supply its ground, but can at most be used only for logical purposes to bring seemingly different conceptions of the same object under a single concept (just as different fractions of the same value are reduced to lowest terms).

However, one recourse still remains open to us, namely, to inquire whether we do not take one point of view when by means of freedom we think of ourselves as a priori efficient causes, and another point of view when we represent ourselves with reference to our actions as effects which we see before our eyes.

No subtle reflection is required for the following observation, which even the commonest understanding may be supposed to make, though it does so in its own fashion through some obscure discrimination of the faculty of judgment which it calls feeling: all representations that come to us without our choice (such as those of the senses) enable us to know objects only as they affect us; what they may be in themselves remains unknown to us. Therefore, even with the closest attention and the greatest clarity that the understanding can bring to such representations, we can attain to a mere knowledge of appearances but never to knowledge of things in themselves. Once this distinction is made (perhaps merely as a result of observing the difference between representations which are given to us from without and in which we are passive from those which we produce entirely from ourselves and in which we show our own activity), then there follows of itself that we must admit and assume that behind the appearances there is something else which is not appearance, namely, things in themselves. Inasmuch as we can never cognize them except as they affect us [through our senses], we must admit that we can never come any nearer to them nor ever know what they are in themselves. This must provide a distinction, however crude, between a world of sense and a world of understanding; the former can vary considerably according to the difference of sensibility [and sense impressions]

451

in various observers, while the latter, which is the basis of the former, remains always the same. Even with regard to himself, a man cannot presume to know what he is in himself by means of the acquaintance which he has through internal sensation. For since he does not, as it were, create himself and since he acquires the concept of himself not a priori but empirically, it is natural that he can attain knowledge even about himself only through inner sense and therefore only through the appearance of his nature and the way in which his consciousness is affected. But yet he must necessarily assume that beyond his own subject's constitution as composed of nothing but appearances there must be something else as basis, namely, his ego as constituted in itself. Therefore with regard to mere perception and the receptivity of sensations, he must count himself as belonging to the world of sense; but with regard to whatever there may be in him of pure activity (whatever reaches consciousness immediately and not through affecting the senses) he must count himself as belonging to the intellectual world, of which he has, however, no further knowledge.

Such a conclusion must be reached by a reflective man regarding all the things that may be presented to him. It is presumably to be found even in 452 the most ordinary understanding, which, as is well known, is quite prone to expect that behind objects of the senses there is something else invisible and acting of itself. But such understanding spoils all this by making the invisible again sensible, i.e., it wants to make the invisible an object of intuition; and thereby does it become not a bit wiser.

Now man really finds in himself a faculty which distinguishes him from all other things and even from himself insofar as he is affected by objects. That faculty is reason, which as pure spontaneity is elevated even above understanding. For although the latter is also spontaneous and does not, like sense, merely contain representations that arise only when one is affected by things (and is therefore passive), yet understanding can produce by its activity no other concepts than those which merely serve to bring sensuous representations [intuitions] under rules and thereby to unite them in one consciousness. Without this use of sensibility, understanding would think nothing at all. Reason, on the other hand, shows such a pure spontaneity in the case of what are called ideas that it goes far beyond anything that sensibility can offer and shows its highest occupation in distinguishing the world of sense from the world of understanding, thereby prescribing limits to the understanding itself.

Therefore a rational being must regard himself qua intelligence (and hence not from the side of his lower powers) as belonging not to the world of sense but to the world of understanding. Therefore he has two standpoints from which he can regard himself and know laws of the use of his powers and hence of all his actions: first, insofar as he belongs to the world of sense subject to laws of nature (heteronomy); secondly, insofar as he belongs to the intelligible world subject to laws which, independent of nature, are not empirical but are founded only on reason.

As a rational being and hence as belonging to the intelligible world, can man never think of the causality of his own will except under the idea of

freedom; for independence from the determining causes of the world of sense (an independence which reason must always attribute to itself) is freedom. Now the idea of freedom is inseparably connected with the concept of autonomy, and this in turn with the universal principle of morali-
453   ty, which ideally is the ground of all actions of rational beings, just as natural law is the ground of all appearances.

The suspicion that we raised earlier is now removed, viz., that there might be a hidden circle involved in our inference from freedom to autonomy, and from this to the moral law—this is to say that we had perhaps laid down the idea of freedom only for the sake of the moral law in order subsequently to infer this law in its turn from freedom, and that we had therefore not been able to assign any ground at all for this law but had only assumed it by begging a principle which well-disposed souls would gladly concede us but which we could never put forward as a demonstrable proposition. But now we see that when we think of ourselves as free, we transfer ourselves into the intelligible world as members and know the autonomy of the will together with its consequence, morality; whereas when we think of ourselves as obligated, we consider ourselves as belonging to the world of sense and yet at the same time to the intelligible world.

How Is a Categorical Imperative Possible?

The rational being counts himself, qua intelligence, as belonging to the intelligible world, and only insofar as he is an efficient cause belonging to the intelligible world does he call his causality a will. But on the other side, he is conscious of himself as being also a part of the world of sense, where his actions are found as mere appearances of that causality. The possibility of these actions cannot, however, be discerned through such causality, which we do not know; rather, these actions as belonging to the world of sense must be viewed as determined by other appearances, namely, desires and inclinations. Therefore, if I were solely a member of the intelligible world, then all my actions would perfectly conform to the principle of the autonomy of a pure will; if I were solely a part of the world of sense, my actions would have to be taken as in complete conformity with the natural law of desires and inclinations, i.e., with the heteronomy of nature. (My actions would in the first case rest on the supreme principle of morality, in the second case on that of happiness.) But the intelligible world contains the ground of the world of sense and therefore also the ground of its laws; consequently, the intelligible world is (and must be thought of as) directly legislative for my will (which belongs wholly to the intelligible world). Therefore, even though on the one hand I must regard myself as a being belonging to the world of sense, yet on the other hand shall I have to know myself as an intelligence and as
454   subject to the law of the intelligible world, i.e., to reason, which contains

this law in the idea of freedom, and hence to know myself as subject to the autonomy of the will. Consequently, I must regard the laws of the intelligible world as imperatives for me, and the actions conforming to this principle as duties.

And thus are categorical imperatives possible because the idea of freedom makes me a member of an intelligible world. Now if I were a member of only that world, all my actions *would* always accord with autonomy of the will. But since I intuit myself at the same time as a member of the world of sense, my actions *ought* so to accord. This categorical *ought* presents a synthetic a priori proposition, whereby in addition to my will as affected by sensuous desires there is added further the idea of the same will, but as belonging to the intelligible world, pure and practical of itself, and as containing the supreme condition of the former will insofar as reason is concerned. All this is similar to the way in which concepts [categories] of the understanding, which of themselves signify nothing but the form of law in general, are added to intuitions of the world of sense and thus make possible synthetic a priori propositions, upon which all knowledge of nature rests.

The practical use of ordinary human reason bears out the correctness of this deduction. There is no one, not even the meanest villain, provided only that he is otherwise accustomed to the use of reason, who, when presented with examples of honesty of purpose, of steadfastness in following good maxims, and of sympathy and general benevolence (even when involved with great sacrifices of advantages and comfort) does not wish that he might also possess these qualities. Yet he cannot attain these in himself only because of his inclinations and impulses; but at the same time he wishes to be free from such inclinations which are a burden to him. He thereby proves that by having a will free of sensuous impulses he transfers himself in thought into an order of things entirely different from that of his desires in the field of sensibility. Since he cannot expect to obtain by the aforementioned wish any gratification of his desires or any condition that would satisfy any of his actual or even conceivable inclinations (inasmuch as through such an expectation the very idea that elicited the wish would be deprived of its preëminence) he can only expect a greater intrinsic worth of his own person. This better person he believes himself to be when he transfers himself to the standpoint of a member of the intelligible world, to which he is involuntarily forced by the idea of freedom, i.e., of being independent of determination by causes of the world of sense. From this standpoint he is conscious of having a good will, which by his own admission constitutes the law for the bad will belonging to him as a member of the world of sense—a law whose authority he acknowledges even while he transgresses it. The moral *ought* is, therefore, a necessary *would* insofar as he is a member of the intelligible world, and is thought by him as an *ought* only insofar as he regards himself as being at the same time a member of the world of sense.

455

Concerning the Extreme Limit of All Practical Philosophy

All men think of themselves as free as far as their will is concerned. Hence arise all judgments upon actions as being such as ought to have been done, even though they were not done. But this freedom is not a concept of experience, nor can it be such, since it always holds, even though experience shows the opposite of those requirements represented as necessary under the presupposition of freedom. On the other hand, it is just as necessary that whatever happens should be determined without any exception according to laws of nature; and this necessity of nature is likewise no concept of experience, just because it involves the concept of necessity and thus of a priori knowledge. But this concept of nature is confirmed by experience and must inevitably be presupposed if there is to be possible experience, which is coherent knowledge of the objects of sense in accordance with universal laws. Freedom is, therefore, only an idea of reason whose objective reality is in itself questionable; but nature is a concept of the understanding, which proves, and necessarily must prove, its reality by examples from experience.

There arises from this a dialectic of reason, since the freedom attributed to the will seems to contradict the necessity of nature. And even though at this parting of the ways reason for speculative purposes finds the road of natural necessity much better worn and more serviceable than that of freedom, yet for practical purposes the footpath of freedom is the only one 456 upon which it is possible to make use of reason in our conduct. Therefore, it is just as impossible for the most subtle philosophy as for the most ordinary human reason to argue away freedom. Hence philosophy must assume that no real contradiction will be found between freedom and natural necessity in the same human actions, for it cannot give up the concept of nature any more than that of freedom.

Nevertheless, even though one might never be able to comprehend how freedom is possible, yet this apparent contradiction must at least be removed in a convincing manner. For if the thought of freedom contradicts itself or nature, which is equally necessary, then freedom would have to be completely given up in favor of natural necessity.

It would, however, be impossible to escape this contradiction if the subject, deeming himself free, were to think of himself in the same sense or in the very same relationship when he calls himself free as when he assumes himself subject to the law of nature regarding the same action. Therefore, an unavoidable problem of speculative philosophy is at least to show that its illusion regarding the contradiction rests on our thinking of man in a different sense and relation when we call him free from when we regard him as being a part of nature and hence as subject to the laws of nature. Hence it must show not only that both can coexist very well, but that both must be thought of as necessarily united in the same subject; for otherwise no explanation could be given as to why reason should be burdened with an idea which involves us in a perplexity that is sorely embarrassing to reason in its theoretic use, even though it may without contradiction be united with another idea that is sufficiently established. This duty, however, is incumbent solely on speculative philosophy in order that it may clear the way for practical philosophy. Thus the philosopher has no option as to whether he will remove the apparent contradiction or leave it untouched; for in the latter case the theory regarding this could be *bonum vacans*,[2] into the possession of which the fatalist can justifiably enter and chase all morality out of its supposed property as occupying it without title.

Nevertheless, one cannot here say as yet that the boundary of practical philosophy begins. For the settlement of the controversy does not belong to practical philosophy; the latter only requires speculative reason to put an end to the dissension in which it is entangled as regards theoretical 457 questions in order that practical reason may have rest and security from external attacks that might make disputable the ground upon which it wants to build.

The just claim to freedom of the will made even by ordinary human reason is founded on the consciousness and the admitted presupposition that reason is independent of mere subjective determination by causes which together make up what belongs only to sensation and comes under the general designation of sensibility. Regarding himself in this way as intelligence, man thereby puts himself into another order of things. And when he thinks of himself as intelligence endowed with a will and consequently with causality, he puts himself into relation with determining grounds of a kind altogether different from the kind when he perceives himself as a phenomenon in the world of sense (as he really is also) and subjects his causality to external determination according to laws of nature. Now he soon realizes that both can—and indeed must—hold good at the same time. For there is not the slightest contradiction involved in saying that a thing as appearance (belonging to the world of sense) is subject to certain laws, while it is independent of those laws when regarded as a thing or being in itself. That man must represent and think of himself in this two-fold way rests, on the one hand, upon the consciousness of himself as an object affected through the senses and, on the other hand, upon the consciousness of himself as intelligence, i.e., as independent of sensuous impulses in his use of reason (and hence as belonging to the intelligible world).

And hence man claims that he has a will which reckons to his account nothing that belongs merely to his desires and inclinations, and which, on the contrary, thinks of actions that can be performed only by disregarding all desires and sensuous incitements as being possible and as indeed being necessary for him. The causality of such actions lies in man as intelligence and lies in the laws of such effects and actions as are in accordance with principles of an intelligible world, of which he knows nothing more than that in such a world reason alone, and indeed pure reason independent of sensibility, gives the law. Furthermore, since he is in such a world his

2. [vacant property]

proper self only as intelligence (whereas regarded as a human being he is merely an appearance of himself), those laws apply to him immediately and categorically. Consequently, incitements from inclinations and impulses (and hence from the whole nature of the world of sense) cannot impair the laws of his willing insofar as he is intelligence. Indeed he does not even hold himself responsible for such inclinations and impulses or ascribe them to his proper self, i.e., his will, although he does ascribe to his will any indulgence which he might extend to them if he allowed them any influence on his maxims to the detriment of the rational laws of his will.

When practical reason thinks itself into an intelligible world, it does not in the least thereby transcend its limits, as it would if it tried to enter it by intuition or sensation. The thought of an intelligible world is merely negative as regards the world of sense. The latter world does not give reason any laws for determining the will and is positive only in this single point, viz., it simultaneously combines freedom as negative determination with a positive faculty and even a causality of reason. This causality is designated as a will to act in such a way that the principle of actions may accord with the essential character of a rational cause, i.e., with the condition that the maxim of these actions have universal validity as a law. But if practical reason were to bring in an object of the will, i.e., a motive of action, from the intelligible world, then it would overstep its boundaries and pretend to be acquainted with something of which it knows nothing. The concept of an intelligible world is thus only a point of view which reason sees itself compelled to take outside of appearances in order to think of itself as practical. If the influences of sensibility were determining for man, reason would not be able to take this point of view, which is nonetheless necessary if he is not to be denied the consciousness of himself as intelligence and hence as a rational cause that is active through reason, i.e., free in its operation. This thought certainly involves the idea of an order and a legislation different from that of the mechanism of nature which applies to the world of sense; and it makes necessary the concept of an intelligible world (i.e., the whole of rational beings as things in themselves). But it makes not the slightest claim to anything more than to think of such a world as regards merely its formal condition— i.e., the universality of the will's maxims as laws and thus the will's autonomy, which alone is consistent with freedom. On the contrary, all laws determined by reference to an object yield heteronomy, which can be found only in laws of nature and can apply only to the world of sense.

But reason would overstep all its bounds if it undertook to explain how pure reason can be practical. This is exactly the same problem as explaining how freedom is possible.

For we can explain nothing but what we can reduce to laws whose object can be given in some possible experience. But freedom is a mere idea, whose objective reality can in no way be shown in accordance with laws of nature and consequently not in any possible experience. Therefore, the idea of freedom can never admit of comprehension or even of insight, because it cannot by any analogy have an example falling under it. It holds only as a necessary presupposition of reason in a being who believes himself conscious of a will, i.e., of a faculty distinct from mere desire (namely, a faculty of determining himself to action as intelligence and hence in accordance with laws of reason independently of natural instincts). But where determination according to laws of nature ceases, there likewise ceases all explanation and nothing remains but defense, i.e., refutation of the objections of those who profess to have seen deeper into the essence of things and thereupon boldly declare freedom to be impossible. One can only show them that their supposed discovery of a contradiction lies nowhere but here: in order to make the law of nature applicable to human actions, they have necessarily had to regard man as an appearance; and now when they are required to think of man qua intelligence as thing in himself as well, they still persist in regarding him as appearance. In that case, to be sure, the exemption of man's causality (i.e., his will) from all the natural laws of the world of sense would, as regards one and the same subject, give rise to a contradiction. But this disappears if they would but bethink themselves and admit, as is reasonable, that behind appearances there must lie as their ground also things in themselves (though hidden) and that the laws of their operations cannot be expected to be the same as those that govern their appearances.

The subjective impossibility of explaining freedom of the will is the same as the impossibility of discovering and explaining an interest[3] which man 460 can take in moral laws. Nevertheless, he does indeed take such an interest, the basis of which in us is called moral feeling. Some people have falsely construed this feeling to be the standard of our moral judgment, whereas it must rather be regarded as the subjective effect that the law exercises upon the will, while reason alone furnishes the objective grounds of such moral feeling.

In order to will what reason alone prescribes as an *ought* for sensuously affected rational beings, there certainly must be a power of reason to infuse a feeling of pleasure or satisfaction in the fulfillment of duty, and hence there has to be a causality of reason to determine sensibility in accordance with rational principles. But it is quite impossible to discern, i.e., to make a priori conceivable, how a mere thought which itself contains nothing sensuous can produce a sensation of pleasure or displeasure. For here is a special kind of causality regarding which, as with all causali-

---

3. Interest is that by which reason becomes practical, i.e., a cause determining the will. Therefore one says of rational beings only that they take an interest in something; nonrational creatures feel only sensuous impulses. Reason takes an immediate interest in the action only when the universal validity of the maxim of the action is a sufficient determining ground of the will. Such an interest alone is pure. But when reason is able to determine the will only by means of another object of desire or under the presupposition of some special feeling in the subject, then reason takes only a mediate interest in the action. And since reason of itself alone without the help of experience can discover neither objects of the will nor a special feeling underlying the will, the latter interest would be only empirical and not a pure rational interest. The logical interest of reason (viz., to extend its insights) is never immediate, but presupposes purposes for which reason might be used.

ty, we can determine nothing a priori but must consult experience alone. However, experience can provide us with no relation of cause and effect except between two objects of experience. But in this case pure reason by means of mere ideas (which furnish no object at all for experience) is to be the cause of an effect that admittedly lies in experience. Consequently, there is for us men no possibility at all for an explanation as to how and why the universality of a maxim as a law, and hence morality, interests us. This much only is certain: the moral law is valid for us not because it interests us (for this is heteronomy and the dependence of practical reason on sensibility, viz., on an underlying feeling whereby reason could never be morally legislative); but, rather, the moral law interests us because it is valid for us as men, since it has sprung from our will as intelligence and hence from our proper self. But what belongs to mere appearance is necessarily subordinated by reason to the nature of the thing in itself.

461

Thus the question as to how a categorical imperative is possible can be answered to the extent that there can be supplied the sole presupposition under which such an imperative is alone possible—namely, the idea of freedom. The necessity of this presupposition is discernible, and this much is sufficient for the practical use of reason, i.e., for being convinced as to the validity of this imperative, and hence also of the moral law; but how this presupposition itself is possible can never be discerned by any human reason. However, on the presupposition of freedom of the will of an intelligence, there necessarily follows the will's autonomy as the formal condition under which alone the will can be determined. To presuppose this freedom of the will (without involving any contradiction with the principle of natural necessity in the connection of appearances in the world of sense) is not only quite possible (as speculative philosophy can show), but is without any further condition also necessary for a rational being conscious of his causality through reason and hence conscious of a will (which is different from desires) as he makes such freedom in practice, i.e., in idea, the underlying condition of all his voluntary actions. But how pure reason can be practical by itself without other incentives taken from whatever source—i.e., how the mere principle of the universal validity of all reason's maxims as laws (which would certainly be the form of a pure practical reason) can by itself, without any matter (object) of the will in which some antecedent interest might be taken, furnish an incentive and produce an interest which could be called purely moral; or, in other words, how pure reason could be practical: to explain all this is quite beyond the power of human reason, and all the effort and work of seeking such an explanation is wasted.

462

It is just the same as if I tried to find out how freedom itself is possible as causality of a will. For I thereby leave the philosophical basis of explanation, and I have no other basis. Now I could indeed flutter about in the world of intelligences, i.e., in the intelligible world still remaining to me. But even though I have an idea of such a world—an idea which has its own good grounds—yet I have not the slightest acquaintance with such a world and can never attain such acquaintance by all the efforts of my natural faculty of reason. This intelligible world signifies only a something that remains over when I have excluded from the determining grounds of my will everything that belongs to the world of sense, so as to restrict the principle of having all motives come from the field of sensibility. By so doing I set bounds to this field and show that it does not contain absolutely everything within itself but that beyond it there is still something more, regarding which, however, I have no further acquaintance. After the exclusion of all matter, i.e., cognition of objects, from pure reason which thinks this ideal, nothing remains over for me except such reason's form, viz., the practical law of the universal validity of maxims; and in conformity with this law I think of reason in its relation to a pure intelligible world as a possible efficient cause, i.e., as a cause determining the will. An incentive must in this case be wholly absent; this idea of an intelligible world would here have to be itself the incentive or have to be that in which reason originally took an interest. But to make this conceivable is precisely the problem that we cannot solve.

Here then is the extreme limit of all moral inquiry. To determine this limit is of great importance for the following considerations. On the one hand, reason should not, to the detriment of morals, search around in the world of sense for the supreme motive and for some interest that is conceivable but is nonetheless empirical. On the other hand, reason should not flap its wings impotently, without leaving the spot, in a space that for it is empty, namely, the space of transcendent concepts that is called the intelligible world, and thereby lose itself among mere phantoms of the brain. Furthermore, the idea of a pure intelligible world regarded as a whole of all intelligences to which we ourselves belong as rational beings (even though we are from another standpoint also members of the world of sense) remains always a useful and permissible idea for the purpose of a rational belief, although all knowledge ends at its boundary. This idea produces in us a lively interest in the moral law by means of the splendid ideal of a universal kingdom of ends in themselves (rational beings), to which we can belong as members only if we carefully conduct ourselves 463 according to maxims of freedom as if they were laws of nature.

Concluding Remark

The speculative use of reason with regard to nature leads to the absolute necessity of some supreme cause of the world. The practical use of reason with reference to freedom leads also to absolute necessity, but only to the necessity of the laws of the actions of a rational being as such. Now it is an essential principle of all use of our reason to push its knowledge to a consciousness of its necessity (for without necessity there would be no rational knowledge). But there is an equally essential restriction of the same reason that it cannot have insight into the necessity either of what is or what does happen or of what should happen, unless there is presupposed a condition under which it is or does happen or should happen. In this way, however, the satisfaction of reason is only further and further postponed by the continual inquiry after the condition. Reason, therefore, restlessly seeks the unconditionally necessary and sees itself compelled to assume this without having any means of making such necessity conceivable; reason is happy enough if only it can find a concept which is compatible with this assumption. Hence there is no fault in our deduction of the supreme principle of morality, but rather a reproach which must be made against human reason generally, involved in the fact that reason cannot render conceivable the absolute necessity of an unconditioned practical law (such as the categorical imperative must be). Reason cannot be blamed for not being willing to explain this necessity by means of a condition, namely, by basing it on some underlying interest, because in that case the law would no longer be moral, i.e., a supreme law of freedom. And so even though we do not indeed grasp the practical unconditioned necessity of the moral imperative, we do nevertheless grasp its inconceivability. This is all that can be fairly asked of a philosophy which strives in its principles to reach the very limit of human reason.

GERMAN-ENGLISH LIST OF TERMS

A

Achtung	respect
Affektionspreis	affective price
Allgemeinheit	universality
analytisch-praktische Sätze	analytic practical propositions
Angenehme, das	pleasant, the
Anschauung, sinnliche	intuition, sensuous
Anthropologie, praktische	anthropology, practical
Arbeitsteilung	division of labor
Autonomie des Willens	autonomy of the will

B

Bedürfnisse	needs
Beispiel	example
Beurteilungsvermögen	judgment, power of
Bewegungsgrund	motive

C

Charakter	character

D

Denken	thinking
Dialektik	dialectic
Ding an sich	thing in itself

E

Einheit	unity
Empfindung	sensation
Erfahrung	experience
Erklärung	explanation
Erscheinung	appearance
Ethik	ethics

F

Form	form
Formel	formula
Freiheit	freedom

G

Gefühl	feeling
Geschmack	taste
Gesetz	law
Gesetzgebung	legislation
Gesetzmässigkeit	conformity to law
Glaube	belief
Glückseligkeit	happiness
Gott	God
Grundlegung	grounding
Grundsatz	principle
Gut	good

H

Handlung	action
Heilige, der	Holy One
Heteronomie	heteronomy
Hyperphysik	hyperphysics

I

Ich, das	ego
Ideal	ideal
Idee	idea
Imperativ	imperative
Instinkt	instinct
Intelligenz	intelligence
intelligible Welt	intelligible world
Interesse	interest

K

Kanon	canon
Kategorien	categories
Kausalität	causality
Kritik der Vernunft	critique of reason

L

Liebe	love
Logik	logic
Lüge	lying

M

Marktpreis	market price
Materie	matter
Mathematik	mathematics
Maxime	maxim
Menschenvernunft	human reason
Menschenverstand	human understanding
Menschheit	humanity
Metaphysik	metaphysics

64 GERMAN-ENGLISH LIST OF TERMS

Metaphysik der Sitten	metaphysics of morals
Misologie	misology
Mittel und Zweck	means and end
Moral	morals
Moralität	morality

N

Natur	nature
Naturnotwendigkeit	natural necessity
Neigung	inclination
Nötigung	necessitation
Notwendigkeit	necessity

O

Ordnung	order

P

Person	person
Pflicht	duty
Philosophie	philosophy
Physik	physics
Popularität	popularity
pragmatisch	pragmatic
Preis	price
Prinzip	principle
Propädeutik	propaedeutic
Psychologie	psychology

Q

Qualitäten	qualities

R

Ratschläge der Klugheit	counsels of prudence
Regel	rule
Reich der Zwecke	kingdom of ends

S

Selbst	self
Selbstliebe	self-love
Selbstmord	suicide
Selbsttätigkeit	spontaneity
Sinn	sense
Sinnenwelt	world of sense
Sinnlichkeit	sensibility
Sitten	morals
sittliches Gesetz	moral law

Sittlichkeit	morality
Sollen	ought
Spiel	play
Standpunkt	standpoint
synthetisch-praktische Sätze	synthetic practical propositions

T

Tätigkeit	activity
Teilnehmung	sympathy
Teleologie	teleology
Temperament	temperament
Totalität	totality
Transcendentalphilosophie	transcendental philosophy
transcendente Begriffe	transcendent concepts
Triebfeder	incentive
Tugend	virtue

U

Unbedingte, das	unconditioned, the
Unbegreiflichkeit	inconceivability
Unschuld	innocence
Unterweisung	instruction
Urteilskraft	judgment, faculty of

V

Verbindlichkeit	obligation
Vernunft	reason
Vernunfterkenntnis	rational knowledge
Vernunftgebrauch	use of reason
Verstand	understanding
Vielheit	plurality
Vollkommenheit	perfection

W

Weisheit	wisdom
Weltweisheit	philosophy
Wert	value, worth
Wesen, vernünftiges	being, rational
Wille	will
Würde	dignity

Z

Zweck	end

INDEX

Action (*Handlung*), morally good, xxix, 3; permitted and forbidden, 44

Activity (*Tätigkeit*), pure, of the self, 52 f.

Affective price (*Affektionspreis*), 40

Analytic practical propositions (*analytisch-praktische Sätze*), 27 ff., 29 n., 48

Ancients, the, 1, 7

Anthropology, practical (*Anthropologie, praktische*), as the empirical part of ethics in contrast to the metaphysics of morals, xxxix, 2, 3, 22, 23

Appearance (*Erscheinung*), 52, 53, 54, 57, 59, 60

Autonomy of the will (*Autonomie des Willens*), is the ground for human dignity, 41, 44; is the supreme principle of morality, 44 f., 48, 51 f.; is explained by the concept of freedom, xv f., xx ff., xxxiii f., xlvii f., lv, 49 f., 52, 53 f., *see also* 55, 60

Being, rational (*Wesen, vernünftiges*), in contrast to the particular nature of human beings, 2, 20, 21, 22 n., 23, 24, 30 n., 33, 34, 35, 36, 38, 40, 43, 46, 50, 51; is an end in itself, 35–37, 41

Belief (*Glaube*), rational, 61

Canon (*Kanon*), of moral estimation of actions, 32

Categorical imperative, *see* Imperative

Categories (*Kategorien*), related to ethics, 42

Causality (*Kausalität*), practical, 27, 49, 50, 51, 53 f., 57 f., 60; in contrast to external, 57, 59 f.

Character (*Charakter*), 7, 12 f.

Conformity to law (*Gesetzmässigkeit*), universal conformity of actions in general, 14 f.

Counsels of prudence (*Ratschläge der Klugheit*), 26 ff.

Critique of reason (*Kritik der Vernunft*), of pure practical and of pure speculative, 4, 17, 48

Dialectic (*Dialektik*), natural of practical reason, 17, 56

Dignity (*Würde*), as the inner, unconditional worth of the moral law, 22, 33, 41; of a rational being, 40, 42, 43, 44

Division of labor (*Arbeitsteilung*), in industry and in philosophy, 2

Duty (*Pflicht*), 13, 15, 33, 40, 44; is no concept of experience, 19 f.; is no chimerical concept, 14; common idea of, 2; its influence, 22; its origin, 23; its pure representation, 22; *from* duty in contrast to *in accordance with* duty, 3, 9–13, 19 f., 30–32, 44

Ego (*das Ich*), in itself, 53; two-fold aspect of, 57 f.

End (*Zweck*), 35; subjective and objective, 35–38; material or relative, 35 f., 41; end in itself, xix f., 35–38; order of ends, 52; subject of all ends, 38, 42 f.; kingdom of ends, *see* kingdom

Ethics (*Ethik*), 1

Example (*Beispiel*), value (or lack thereof) for morality, 20 f., 28, 55, 58; persons as examples of the law, 14 n.

Experience (*Erfahrung*), 2, 3, 4, 19, 20, 27, 34, 37, 46, 48, 50, 56, 58, 60

Explanation (*Erklärung*), 59, 60

Feeling (*Gefühl*), 41, 46, 52; of pleasure and displeasure, 34, 59; moral and physical, 46, 59, 59 n.

Form (*Form*), of action, 26; of maxims, 41 f.; of pure practical reason, 60; of understanding and reason, 1, 55; of universality, 38, 41, 58; of the will, 41 f., 48

Formula (*Formel*), of the categorical imperative, xiv–xxi, 24, 30, 36, 38, 40, 41–44, 49

Freedom (*Freiheit*), 41; its concept explains autonomy of the will, 49 f., 52, 53 f., 58 f., 60; is not a concept of experience, 56; is only an idea, 56, 58;

positive and negative concept of, xv f., xxxiii, 49 f., 53 f., 55, 57 f.; freedom and natural necessity, xlviii, 56–58, 60 f.; its possibility is not to be comprehended, xxxiii, 56, 58 f., 60; is not to be reasoned away, 56; its deduction is difficult, 50; is a law of the intelligible world, 55; is a property of all rational beings, 49 f.; theoretical and practical, 50 n.

God (*Gott*), as the highest good, 21; his will as supreme cause of the world, 61; as sovereign in a kingdom of ends, 39 f.; and in a kingdom of nature, 44

Good (*Gut*), the, as practically necessary, 23; in distinction to the pleasant, 24; cannot conflict with itself, 42; archetype of, 21; conditioned and unconditioned, 25; its objective laws, 24; the supreme good, 9, 13 f., 21

Grounding (*Grundlegung*), for the Metaphysics of Morals, xii f., 4 f.

Happiness (*Glückseligkeit*), xxviii f., 8 f., 12, 16, 21, 26, 27 f., 37; is an indeterminate concept, 27 f.; is an ideal of the imagination, 28; as the principle of morality, 46, 51 f., 54; of others, l, lvi f., 13, 45, 46 n.; of ourselves, 12, 46

Heteronomy (*Heteronomie*), of the will, 39, 60; source of all spurious principles of morality, 45–48; heteronomy of efficient causes (in the world of sense), 49, 53, 54, 58

Holy One (*der Heilige*), of the gospel, 21

Humanity (*Menschheit*), idea of as an end in itself, 36 ff.

Human reason, human understanding (*Menschenvernunft, Menschenverstand*), 4, 8, 9, 14, 15, 16, 17, 23, 51, 53, 55, 56, 57, 58, 60, 61, 62

Hutcheson, Francis, 46 n.

Hyperphysics (*Hyperphysik*), 22

Idea (*Idee*), in contrast to knowledge, 60 f.; of an intelligible world, 60–61; of freedom, 50, 51; of humanity as an end in itself, 36–37; practical and theoretical, 42 n., common idea of duty, 2; idea of pure will, 4; of pure practical reason, 3, 60; of reason in general, 23, 53, 56

Ideal (*Ideal*), of imagination, 28; of moral perfection, 21; of the kingdom of ends, 39, 61; of an intelligible world, 61

Imperative (*Imperativ*), definition of, 24 f.; divided into hypothetical and categorical, xvii f., xx f., xxix, xliv, 24–27, 29 f., 33, 35, 38, 44 f., 47 f.; into problematic, assertoric, and apodeictic, 25; into technical, pragmatic, and moral, 26 f.; taken as a rule of skill, 25, 26, 27, 28; as a counsel of prudence, 26–28; as a law of morality, 26, 28 f.; the categorical imperative, xiv f., xl, xliii, 25, 26; called also the imperative of morality, 26, 28, 29, 45, 48; called the practical imperative, 36; called the imperative of duty, 30; only the categorical imperative is a law, 29, 35, 36; and it is an unconditional law, 39, 62; how are problematic imperatives possible, 27; how are assertoric ones possible, 27–28; how are categorical ones possible, xxii–xxxvii, xxxviii n., 28–30, 49 f., 54–55; various formulations of the categorical imperative, *see* Formula of the categorical imperative

Incentive (*Triebfeder*), as the subjective ground of desire, 24, 35; as material principles of the will, 13; as sensuous principles, 16, 51; feelings and inclinations as such sensuous principles, 22, 44, 46

Inclination (*Neigung*), 24 n.; in contrast to duty, 10–12; contrasted with the feeling of respect, 14 n.; contrasted with reason, 33; sum of, 7, 12, 16; plurality of, 9, 34, 35, 45, 48, 55, 57

Inconceivability (*Unbegreiflichkeit*), of the moral imperative, 62

Innocence (*Unschuld*), 16

Instinct (*Instinkt*), 8, 9, 59

Instruction (*Unterweisung*), moral, 22 n., 23

Intelligence (*Intelligenz*), a rational being taken as such, 53–55, 57–59, 60; world of intelligences, 60

Intelligible world (*intelligible Welt*), defined as a *mundus intelligibilis*, 52–55, 57 f., *also* 43 f.; taken as another standpoint, 58, 60 f.

Interest (*Interesse*), defined, 24 n., 59 n.; moral and empirical, 51 f., 59 n., 61; moral, 14 n., 60–62; in general, 38 f., 50–52

Intuition, sensuous (*Anschauung, sinnliche*), 53, 55

Judgment, faculty of (*Urteilskraft*), 7, 20, 50, 52

Judgment, power of (*Beurteilungsvermögen*), practical and theoretical, 16, 23; ordinary moral judgment, 23, 42

Kingdom of ends (*Reich der Zwecke*), xvi–xix, xxi, 39–41; is only an ideal, 39; sovereign of and members of, 40; as a kingdom of nature, 42, 42 n., 43

Law (*Gesetz*), concept of, xv ff., 26, 49; laws of nature and of freedom, xxix f., 1, 53–55, 61 f.; in contrast to a mere rule, 2 f., 26; in contrast to a maxim, 13 f., 13 n., 29 f., 30 n., 35 f.

Legislation (*Gesetzgebung*), universal, 15, 37–41, 49, 51

Logic (*Logik*), 1; as pure formal philosophy, 1; general logic as distinct from transcendental philosophy, 4; pure and applied, 22 n.

Love (*Liebe*), practical as distinct from that of inclination, 12; duties of, 37 n.

Lying (*Lüge*), xviii f., 14 f.; *see also* 37, 45

Market price (*Marktpreis*), 40

Mathematics (*Mathematik*), 27; pure and applied, 22 n.

Matter (*Materie*), of action, 26; of maxims, 41; of the will, 42, 60

Maxim (*Maxime*) is the subjective principle of volition, 13 n., 30 n., 33, 42–45, 51; their form, matter, and complete determination, xviii f., xxix, liii f., 41 f.

Means and end (*Mittel und Zweck*), defined, xix ff., 35 f.; *compare* 26 ff., 35 ff.

Metaphysics (*Metaphysik*), pure but not merely formal philosophy, xxvii, 1 f., 3 f., 23; division into metaphysics of nature and metaphysics of morals, 1, 2

Metaphysics of Morals (*Metaphysik der Sitten*), 1–3; in contrast to popular moral philosophy, 5, 7–8, 21–22, 34; in contrast to a critique of practical reason, 4–5, 48; the foundation of, 5; pure and applied, 22 n.; the boundaries of, 48; Kant's work by this name published in 1797, xi, xxxviii, 4, 30 n.

Misology (*Misologie*), 8

Morality (*Moralität*), supreme principle of, 5, 62; what this principle consists of, 40, 41, 43; it follows from autonomy of the

will, xv, 54 f.

Morality (*Sittlichkeit*), is not derived from examples, 20, 34; must be derived from freedom of the will, 50, 51, 54 f., 60; is valid for all rational beings, 50; only it has intrinsic worth, 40 f.; principles thereof holding in other systems, 39, 45–48; is no phantom of imagination, 19; is no chimerical idea, 48

Moral law (*sittliches Gesetz*), is the same as practical law, 3, 20, 22; is imposed by us upon ourselves, 13 n., 34 f., 42, 51 f., 60

Morals (*Moral*), as the rational part of ethics, 1 f.; the necessity of, 2 f.; pure and applied, 2–4, 23; popular, 5; its procedure in bringing an idea of reason closer to feeling, 41 f., 42 n.

Morals (*Sitten*), system of, 5, 16, 42, 47

Motive (*Bewegungsgrund*), objective ground of volition, 35; moral and empirical, xxi, 3, 4, 22, 58, 61

Natural necessity (*Naturnotwendigkeit*), 49; is a heteronomy of efficient causes, 49; is not a concept of experience, 56; compared with freedom, xxiii–xxvi, 56 ff.

Nature (*Natur*), formally as the existence of things, 30; is a concept of understanding, 56; rational nature as an end in itself, 36, 43; laws of nature, 30–32, 38, 54, 58; doctrine of nature (physics), 1, 35; philosophy of nature, 1, 35

Necessitation (*Nötigung*), of the will by the moral law, 24, 33, 40

Necessity (*Notwendigkeit*), absolute, of the moral law, 2, 26 ff., 33, 46, 61 f.; subjective and objective, 24, 51; practical, 26

Needs (*Bedürfnisse*), as the cause of inclinations, 24 n., 35, 40

Obligation (*Verbindlichkeit*), moral, its ground, xx, 2, 52; its concept, 4, 44

Order (*Ordnung*), distinction between that of efficient causes and that of ends, 52, 55, 57, 58

Ought (*Sollen*), what ought to happen in contrast to what does happen, 1, 24, 34, 51, 55, 59, 61

Perfection (*Vollkommenheit*), moral, the ideal of, liii, 21; as spurious principle of

THE METAPHYSICAL
PRINCIPLES OF VIRTUE

CONTENTS
. . . .

THE METAPHYSICS OF MORALS

I. The Elements of Ethics

Die

Metaphysik der Sitten

in zwey Theilen.

Abgefaßt

von

Immanuel Kant.

Königsberg,
bey Friedrich Nicolovius,
1797.

THE METAPHYSICS OF MORALS

Preface to Part I,
The Metaphysical Principles of Right

Introduction

Die

Metaphysik der Sitten.

Abgefaßt

von

Immanuel Kant.

Erster Theil.
Metaphysische Anfangsgründe
der
Rechtslehre.

Königsberg,
bey Friedrich Nicolovius,
1797.

PREFACE

The *Critique of Practical Reason* was to be followed by a system, *The Metaphysics of Morals*, which falls into *The Metaphysical Principles of Right* and *The Metaphysical Principles of Virtue;* [1] and this system may be regarded as the counterpart of *The Metaphysical Foundations of Natural Science*, which has already been published. The Introduction, which follows, presents and partly makes intuitive the form of this system in both its parts.

Now, the doctrine of right [*Rechtslehre*], as the first part of the doctrine of morals, is the kind of doctrine from which we demand a system derived from reason, and this system might be called the metaphysics of right. But since the concept of right is a pure concept which nevertheless involves practice (i.e., application to cases occurring in experience), a metaphysical system of the concept of right consequently must, in its division, also take account of the empirical manifold of such cases in order to make its division complete (and such completeness is an indispensable requirement of a system of reason). But completeness of the division of what is empirical is impossible; and when we attempt it (or even try to come close to it), such concepts cannot come into the system as integral parts of it but only as instances in the remarks. Thus the only appropriate expression for the first part of *The Metaphysics of Morals* will be *The Metaphysical Principles of Right*, since, regarding those cases of application, only an approximation to the system can be expected and not the system itself. Therefore, this work will be carried out just like the (earlier) *Metaphysical Foundations of Natural Science:* the discussion of right which belongs to a system drawn up a priori will appear in the text, but those rights which are related to particular

1 [See Introduction above, p. xi with n. 1.]

3

cases occuring in experience will appear in the remarks, which
are sometimes rather lengthy. Otherwise, what is here metaphysics cannot indeed be distinguished from what is empirical
juridical practice.

I cannot better anticipate or remedy the frequent reproach
of obscurity in philosophical discourse, or even of an intentional unclarity to affect the appearance of deep insight, than
by readily accepting what Mr. Garve,[2] a philosopher in the
true sense of the word, makes a duty for every writer, especially the philosophical writer. However, for my part, I limit
this claim merely to the condition that he be followed only to
the extent allowed by the nature of the science which is to be
corrected and enlarged.

This wise man (in his work entitled *Miscellaneous Essays*,
pp. 352ff.[3]) rightly demands that every philosophical doctrine
be capable of being popularized (i.e., of being made sufficiently intelligible for general communication). I concede this
gladly, with the exception only of the system of a critique of
the faculty of reason itself and of everything that depends only
on this system for its determination. I say this because the distinction between the sensible and the supersensible in our
knowledge still comes under the competence of reason. This
system can never become popular, nor can any formal metaphysics in general, although its results can be made quite clear
for the common man (who is a metaphysician without knowing
it). Here popularity (vernacular) is unthinkable; instead, scholastic precision must be insisted upon (for this is the language
of the schools), even if such precision is denounced as meticu-
losity. Only in this way can precipitate reason be brought to
understand itself before making its dogmatic assertions.

But when pedants presume to address the public (from pulpits or in popular writings) in the technical words that are
suitable only for the schools, the critical philosopher cannot
be blamed any more than the grammarian for the folly of the

2 [Christian Garve (1742-98) was professor of philosophy at Leipzig.]
3 [Garve, *Vermischte Aufsätze* (Breslau, 1796).]

206

word-picker (*logodaedalus*). The ridicule here can fall only upon a man, not upon the science.

It sounds arrogant, egotistical, and to those who have not yet renounced their old system, disparaging, to assert that before the critical philosophy arose there was no philosophy at all. Now, in order to be able to pass judgment on this apparent presumption, one must ask whether there can really be more than one philosophy. Not only have there been various ways of philosophizing and of going back to the first principles of reason in order, with more or less success, to found a system on them; but also there had to be many attempts of this kind, each of which has, moreover, rendered service to contemporary attempts. But objectively, inasmuch as there can be only one human reason, so likewise there cannot be many philosophies; that is, only one true system of philosophy based on principles is possible, however variously and often contradictorily men may have philosophized over one and the same proposition. So the moralist rightly says that there is only one virtue and one doctrine of virtue, i.e., a single system that unites all the duties of virtue by means of one principle. The chemist says that there is only one system of chemistry (that of Lavoisier [4]). The teacher of medicine says that there is only one principle for the system of classifying diseases (that of Brown [5]). The fact that the new system has disqualified all others does not detract from the merit of older men (moralists, chemists, and teachers of medicine), because without their discoveries or even their unsuccessful attempts we would not have attained the unity of the true principle of the whole of philosophy in one system. When, therefore, someone announces a system of philosophy as his own crea-

207

[4] [The French chemist Antoine Laurent Lavoisier (1743-94) refuted the phlogiston theory, that fire is a substance, and propounded the modern theory of oxidation, thereby laying the foundations for modern chemistry.]

[5] [John Brown (1735-88), a Scottish physician. His theory of medicine is contained in his *Elementa Medicinae* (1780), which for a time was widely admired.]

tion, this amounts to his saying that there has been no other prior philosophy at all; for if he were to admit there was another (and true) philosophy, then there would be two different philosophies about the same things, and this is self-contradictory. Therefore, when the critical philosophy announces that it is a philosophy prior to which there was never any philosophy at all, it is doing nothing but what anyone who constructs a philosophy according to his own plan has done, will do, and indeed must do.

Of less significance, but not entirely without any importance, might be the reproach that an essentially distinctive part of this philosophy is not the product of this philosophy but is borrowed from another philosophy (or from mathematics). An instance of this is the discovery which a reviewer from Tübingen [6] claims to have made concerning the definition of philosophy in general which the author of the *Critique of Pure Reason* gives out as his own not inconsiderable product, and which was already given many years ago by someone else in almost the same words.[7] I leave it to everyone to judge whether the words *intellectualis quaedam constructio* could have produced the thought of "presentation of a given concept in an a priori intuition," through which philosophy is once and for all quite definitely separated from mathematics. I am certain that Hausen himself would have refused to acknowledge this interpretation of his words. For the possibility of an

208

[6] [Probably Professor J. F. Flatt, who reviewed many of Kant's works in the *Tübingen Gelehrter Anzeiger.*]

[7] *Porro de actuali constructione hic non quaeritur, cum ne possint quidem sensibiles figurae ad rigorem definitionum effingi; sed requiritur cognitio eorum, quibus absolvitur formatio, quae intellectualis quaedam constructio est.* C. A. Hausen, *Elem. Mathes.* (1734), Part I. p. 86. ["Furthermore, the concern here is not with an actual construction, since sensible figures cannot be made in accordance with the rigor of definitions; rather, what is required is the knowledge of what constitutes the form of the figure, and this form is, as it were, a construction of the intellect." Kant makes seemingly similar remarks in various places in his works; see, for instance, *Critique of Pure Reason*, B 740 ff. Christian August Hausen (1693-1745) was professor of mathematics at Leipzig.]

a priori intuition, and of space's being such an intuition rather than merely (as Wolff declared [8]) the juxtaposition of a manifold of objects external to one another given in an empirical intuition (perception), would have shocked him for the simple reason that in considering such matters he would have felt himself involved in far-reaching philosophical investigations. By the words "presentation made, as it were, by the understanding," this acute mathematician meant simply that in the (empirical) drawing of a line corresponding to a concept, attention is paid merely to the rule, and one abstracts from unavoidable deviations occurring in the execution, as can be seen in the construction of congruent figures in geometry.

Of least significance with regard to the spirit of this critical philosophy is the mischief which some imitators of this philosophy make with words that in the *Critique of Pure Reason* itself are not easily replaced by other more usual ones. Any attempt to make use of such technical terms outside of the context of the *Critique* for the public exchange of ideas certainly deserves to be corrected, as Mr. Nicolai [9] has done, although he makes no judgment about wholly renouncing such terms in their proper field as if they everywhere merely concealed a poverty of thoughts. Meanwhile, it is certainly much more fun to laugh at the unpopular pedant than at the uncritical ignoramus. (Indeed, a metaphysician who rigidly adheres to his system without turning to any critique can be counted in the latter class, although he deliberately ignores what he does not want to consider because it does not fit in with his older school.) But if, according to Shaftesbury's assertion, [10] the capacity to endure ridicule is a touchstone, not to   209

[8] [Namely, in the *Ontology*, § 588, of Christian Wolff (1674-1754).]

[9] [Christoph Friedrich Nicolai (1733-1811), a German author and bookseller who ridiculed the use of Kantian terminology in everyday life. Compare Nicolai's *Geschichte eines dicken Mannes* (Berlin and Stettin, 1794) and *Beschreibung einer Reise durch Deutschland und die Schweiz* (Berlin and Stettin, 1796).]

[10] [Anthony Ashley Cooper, third Earl of Shaftesbury (1671-1713), in his *Characteristics of Men, Manners, Opinions, Times*, Treatise II, "*Sensus Communis; An Essay on the Freedom of Wit and Humour*" (1709), Part I,

be disregarded, for the truth of a doctrine (especially a practical one); then in time, when the critical philosopher sees the paper systems of those who for a long time have been the great spokesmen collapse one after another, and sees all their followers dispersed—a fate that inevitably awaits them—then, the turn of the critical philosopher will come to laugh last, and therefore best.

Toward the end of the book I have treated some sections in less detail than might be expected in comparison with the earlier ones. This is partly because they seemed to be easily inferred from the earlier sections, and partly because the topics of the later sections (concerning public right) are just now under so much discussion, and are still so important, that this certainly justifies postponing for a while any decisive judgment.[11]

Section 1, paragraph 3: "Truth . . . may bear all lights; and one of those principal lights . . . is ridicule itself. . . . So much, at least, is allowed by all who at any time appeal to this criterion."]

11 [In the first edition there followed this remark: "I hope to be able to deliver *The Metaphysical Principles of Virtue* shortly." It was published later in the same year (1797).]

INTRODUCTION

I. CONCERNING THE RELATION OF THE FACULTIES OF THE HUMAN MIND TO THE MORAL LAWS

The faculty of desire is the capacity to be by means of one's representations the cause of the objects of these representations. The capacity which a being has of acting in accordance with its representations is life.

First, desire or aversion always has pleasure or displeasure connected with it, and the susceptibility to pleasure or displeasure is called feeling. But the converse does not always hold, for there can be a pleasure which is not connected with any desire for an object but only with the mere representation which one frames for himself of an object (irrespective of whether the object of the representation actually exists or not). Secondly, the pleasure or displeasure taken in an object of desire does not always precede the desire and need not always be regarded as the cause of the desire, but can sometimes be regarded as its effect.

Now, the ability to take pleasure or displeasure in a representation is called feeling, because both pleasure and displeasure contain what is merely subjective in relation to our representation and have no relation to an object so as to contribute to the possible cognition of it [1] (not even the cognition of our

[1] Sensibility can in general be defined by means of the subjective element in our representations; for it is the understanding that first refers the representations to an object, i.e., it alone thinks something by means of them. Now, the subjective element in our representations may be either of two kinds. On the one hand, it can be referred to an object as a means toward cognizing it (with regard to either its form or its matter: in the first case it is called pure intuition, and in the second, sensation); here sensibility, as the receptivity for a representation that is thought, is sense. On the other hand, the subjective element in our representations

9

212   own state). Usually, sensations, except for their quality, which depends upon the nature of the subject (e.g., the quality of redness, of sweetness, etc.), are related to an object as part of our cognition of it; but pleasure or displeasure (in what is red or sweet) expresses absolutely nothing about the object but simply a relation to the subject. Pleasure and displeasure cannot be more exactly defined for the reason just given. One can only specify their consequences under certain circumstances in order to make them recognizable in use.

The pleasure which is necessarily connected with desire (for an object whose representation affects feeling in this way) may be called practical pleasure, whether it is the cause or the effect of the desire. On the other hand, the pleasure which is not necessarily connected with a desire for an object and which, therefore, is really not a pleasure taken in the existence of the object of the representation, but only adheres to the mere representation, can be called mere contemplative pleasure, or passive delight. The feeling of the latter kind of pleasure is called taste. Accordingly, in a practical philosophy this kind of pleasure can be treated only episodically, not as a concept properly belonging to that philosophy. But as regards practical pleasure, the determination of the faculty of desire which is caused by and, accordingly, is necessarily preceded by this pleasure is called appetite in the strict sense; habitual appetite, however, is called inclination. The connection of pleasure with the faculty of desire, insofar as this connection is judged by the understanding to be valid according to a general rule (though only for the subject), is called interest; and hence in this case the practical pleasure is an interest of inclination. On the other hand, if the pleasure can follow only upon an

_____

may be such that it cannot become a factor in cognition, inasmuch as it contains only the relation of a representation to the subject and does not contain anything that can be used for cognizing the object; and in this case the receptivity for the representation is called feeling. Now, feeling contains the effect of the representation (whether it be a sensible or an intellectual representation) on the subject and belongs to sensibility, even though the representation itself may belong to the understanding or to reason.

antecedent determination of the faculty of desire, then it is an intellectual pleasure; and the interest in the object must be called an interest of reason. For if the interest were sensible and not founded merely upon pure principles of reason, then 213 sensation would have to be joined with pleasure and so would be able to determine the faculty of desire. Although where a merely pure interest of reason must be assumed, no interest of inclination can be substituted for it, yet in order to accommodate ourselves to ordinary speech we may admit an inclination even to what can only be the object of an intellectual pleasure, that is to say, a habitual desire from a pure interest of reason. Such an inclination, however, would be not the cause but the effect of this pure interest of reason; and we could call it the sense-free inclination (*propensio intellectualis*).

Further, concupiscence (lustfulness) is to be distinguished from desire itself as being the stimulus for the determination of desire. Concupiscence is always a sensible mental state that has not yet turned into an act of the faculty of desire.

The faculty of desiring according to concepts is called the faculty of doing or forbearing as one pleases, insofar as the ground determining it to action is found in the faculty of desire itself and not in the object. Insofar as it is combined with the consciousness of the capacity of its action to produce its object, it is called choice; [2] if not so combined, its act is called a wish. The faculty of desire whose internal ground of determination and, consequently, even whose liking [*das Belieben*] is found in the reason of the subject is called the will.[3] Ac-

[2] [The word "choice" is used to render *Willkür*. *Willkür* is the broad generic term indicating that faculty of the soul which has the power to choose. *Wahl* is, generally, the narrower term indicating a particular act of choosing or a particular choice. The distinction between *Willkür* and *Wahl* is in English approximately "choice" and "a choice"; choice makes a choice, i.e., the faculty of choosing makes a particular choice. Throughout the rest of this translation "choice" always renders *Willkür*, "a choice" renders *Wahl*.]

[3] [*Wille* will be rendered as "will" in this translation. But it must be pointed out that *Wille* is used sometimes in the narrow sense to mean the rational will, which is practical reason itself, and sometimes in the

cordingly, the will is the faculty of desire regarded not (like choice) in relation to action, but rather as the ground determining choice to action. The will itself has no determining ground; on the contrary, insofar as it can determine choice, it is practical reason itself.

Choice and even mere wish may be included under will,[4] insofar as reason can determine the faculty of desire in general. That choice which can be determined by pure reason is called free choice. That choice which is determined solely by inclination (sensible impulse, *stimulus*) would be animal choice (*arbitrium brutum*). Human choice, on the other hand, is such as to be affected but not determined by impulses. Accordingly, in itself (apart from any acquired skill of reason) it is not pure; nevertheless, it can be determined to actions by pure will. The negative concept of freedom of choice is just that independence from determination by sensible impulses. The positive concept is the capacity of pure reason to be of itself practical. Now, this is possible only through the subjection of the maxim of every action to the condition of its fitness to be a universal law. For inasmuch as pure reason is applied to choice without regard to the object of choice, it is the faculty of principles (and here they are practical principles, and thus it is a legislative faculty); and since this faculty does not contain the matter of the law, there is nothing which it can make the supreme law and determining ground of choice except the form of the law, which consists in the fitness of the maxim of choice to be a universal law. And since those maxims of men which are based on subjective causes do not of themselves coincide with the aforementioned objective maxims, reason can only prescribe this law as an imperative of command or prohibition.

In contradistinction to natural laws, these laws of freedom

214

---

broad generic sense to mean the faculty of volition in general. The meaning intended is usually clear enough from the context. In this paragraph, *Wille* is used in the narrow sense; in the next one, the broad sense. Both *Willkür* and *Wille* in the narrow sense are functions of *Wille* in the broad sense, as this and the next paragraph show.]

4 [As mentioned in note 3, will in the broad sense is meant here.]

are called moral laws. Insofar as they are directed to mere external actions and the lawfulness of such actions, they are called juridical; but when they also demand that these laws themselves are to be the determining grounds of actions, then they are ethical. Accordingly, we say that agreement with juridical laws constitutes the legality of action, while agreement with ethical ones constitutes its morality. The freedom to which juridical laws refer can only be freedom in its external exercise; but the freedom to which ethical laws refer is freedom in both the internal and external exercise of choice, insofar as choice is determined by laws of reason. So in theoretical philosophy, one says that only the objects of the external senses are in space, while all objects, those of the external senses as well as those of the internal sense, are in time, inasmuch as the representations of both kinds of objects are still representations and therefore belong to internal sense. Similarly, whether we consider freedom in the external or in the internal exercise of choice, in either case freedom's laws, being pure practical laws of reason governing free choice in general, must at the same time be internal grounds of determination of choice, although these laws need not always be considered from this point of view.

II. CONCERNING THE IDEA AND THE NECESSITY OF A METAPHYSICS OF MORALS

It has been proved in another place [5] that one must have a priori principles for natural science, which has to do with the objects of the external senses, and that it is possible—indeed, even necessary—to prefix a system of these principles, under the name of a metaphysical natural science, to physics, which is natural science applied to particular experiences. The former system, if it is to be universal in the strict sense, must be deduced from a priori grounds; although the latter (at least when the question is to guard its propositions against error) may assume many principles to be universal on the testimony

215

[5][In *The Metaphysical Foundations of Natural Science* (1786).]

of experience, just as Newton adopted the principle of the equality of action and reaction in the influence of bodies upon one another as based upon experience, and yet extended that principle to all material nature. The chemists go still further and base their most universal laws of combination and dissociation of substances by their own forces entirely on experience, and yet they have such confidence in the universality and necessity of these laws that they do not worry about discovering any error in the experiments they make with them.

But it is otherwise with moral laws. These are valid as laws only insofar as they can be seen to have an a priori basis and to be necessary. Indeed, concepts and judgments concerning ourselves and our actions and omissions have no moral significance at all if they contain only what can be learned from experience. And if one let himself be so misled as to make into a moral principle anything derived from this source, he would be in danger of the grossest and most pernicious errors.

If the doctrine of morals were nothing but a doctrine of happiness, it would be absurd to look to a priori principles for help. For however plausible it might seem that reason, even before experience, could discern by what means one could attain a lasting enjoyment of the true pleasures of life, nevertheless, everything which is taught a priori on this subject is either tautological or assumed quite without foundation. Only experience can teach us what brings us joy. The natural drives toward food, sex, rest, movement, and (in the development of our natural predispositions) the urge toward honor, the enlargement of our knowledge, etc. can alone teach, and, moreover, teach each individual in his own special way, where to find those joys; and experience can also teach him the means by which he must seek them. All apparently a priori reasoning is here basically nothing but experience raised to generality by induction; this generality (*secundum principia generalia, non universalia* [6]) is so deficient that everyone must be allowed infinitely many exceptions in order to make his choice of a way of life suitable to his particular inclination and suscepti-

216

[6] ["According to general principles, but not universal ones."]

bility for pleasure; still, in the end he becomes prudent only as a result of his own or other people's misfortunes.

But it is otherwise with the doctrines of morality. They command everyone without regard to his inclinations, solely because and insofar as he is free and has practical reason. Instruction in the laws of morality is not drawn from observation of oneself and the animality within him, nor from the perception of the course of the world—how things happen and how men in fact do act (although the German word *Sitten*, like the Latin word *mores*, designates only manners and way of life). But reason commands how one ought to act, even though no instance of such action might be found; moreover, reason pays no attention to the advantage which can accrue to us from such action, which admittedly only experience could teach. For although reason allows us to seek our advantage in every way that we can and, in addition, relying on the testimony of experience, can probably promise us on the average greater advantages from obeying its commands than from transgressing them, especially if obedience is accompanied by prudence; nevertheless, the authority of reason's precepts as commands does not rest on this fact. Instead, reason uses such considerations (by way of advice) only as a counterweight to inducements to do the opposite of what is moral, in order first to correct the error of unbalanced practical judgment, and then to make sure that the scales of judgment are tipped in favor of the a priori grounds of a pure practical reason.

Therefore, if a system of a priori knowledge from mere concepts is called metaphysics, then a practical philosophy, which has for its object not nature but the freedom of choice, will presuppose and require a metaphysics of morals; i.e., to have such a metaphysics is itself a duty. Moreover, every man has such a metaphysics within himself, although commonly only in an obscure way; for without a priori principles, how could he believe that he has within himself a power of universal legislation? Just as in the metaphysics of nature there must be principles for the application of those supreme universal basic principles of nature in general to objects of experience, so like-

217 wise a metaphysics of morals cannot dispense with similar principles of application. Accordingly, we shall often have to take as our object the special nature of man, which can be known only by experience, in order to show the implications of the universal moral principles for human nature; but this will not detract from the purity of such laws nor cast any doubt on their a priori origin—that is to say, a metaphysics of morals cannot be founded on anthropology, although it can be applied to it.

The counterpart of a metaphysics of morals, as the second member of the division of practical philosophy in general, would be moral anthropology, which would, however, contain only the subjective conditions in human nature hindering as well as favoring the performance of the laws of the metaphysics of morals. It would treat of the production, propagation, and strengthening of moral principles (in education, in school and popular instruction), and other like doctrines and precepts based on experience, which cannot be dispensed with but which must by no means come before the metaphysics nor be mixed with it. Otherwise, one would run the risk of eliciting false or at least indulgent moral laws. These would represent as unattainable what merely has not yet been attained, either because the law has not been discerned and set forth in its purity (the very thing in which its strength consists), or else because spurious or impure incentives are used for what in itself is good and in accordance with duty, and such incentives leave us no certain moral principles to serve either as guides to judgment or for the discipline of the mind in its obedience to duty, whose precept must be given a priori by pure reason absolutely alone.

As for the higher division to which that just considered [7] is subordinate, namely, the division of philosophy into theoretical and practical, I have explained myself sufficiently elsewhere (in the *Critique of Judgment* [8]), and have shown that

7 [That is, the division of practical philosophy into metaphysics of morals and moral anthropology.]

8 [Cf. *Critique of Judgment*, Introduction, Sections I and II.]

the latter branch can be nothing but moral wisdom. Everything practical concerning what is possible according to laws of nature (the proper business of art [9]) depends entirely upon the theory of nature for its precept. Only that which is practical according to laws of freedom can have principles that do not depend on any theory, for there can be no theory of that which transcends the determinations of nature. Accordingly, by the practical part of philosophy (coordinate with its theoretical part) is to be understood not any technically-practical doctrine, but rather a morally-practical doctrine. And if skillful choice [*Fertigkeit der Willkür*] acting according to laws of freedom, in contrast to laws of nature, is here also to be called art, then such an art must be understood as one making possible a system of freedom that would be like a system of nature. Such art would in truth be a divine art, if by means of it we were in a position completely to enact the precepts of reason and its idea.

218

III. CONCERNING THE DIVISION OF A METAPHYSICS OF MORALS [10]

All legislation (whether it prescribes internal or external actions, and these either a priori through mere reason or through another's choice) involves two things: first, a law which objectively represents as necessary the action that is to be done, i.e., makes the action a duty; secondly, an incentive

[9] [Here and in the following sentences art (*Kunst*) means technical skill.]
[10] The deduction of the division of a system, i.e., the proof of its completeness as well as of its continuity, namely, that the transition from the concept being divided to each member of the division in the whole series of subdivisions takes place without any gaps (*divisio per saltum*), is one of the most difficult conditions for the constructor of a system to fulfill. Furthermore, it is difficult to say what is the highest divided concept of which right and wrong (*aut fas aut nefas*) are divisions. It is the act of free choice in general. Similarly, teachers of ontology begin with the concepts of something and nothing without being aware that these are already subdivisions of a concept which is not given but which can only be the concept of an object in general.

which subjectively combines the ground determining choice to this action with the representation of the law; and so this second point amounts to this, that the law makes duty the incentive. Through the first, the action is represented as a duty, and this is a mere theoretical knowledge of the possible determination of choice, i.e., a knowledge of practical rules. Through the second, the obligation so to act is connected in the subject with a determining ground of choice in general.

219 Therefore, even though one legislation may agree with another with regard to actions that are required as duties, e.g., the actions might in all cases be external ones, all legislation can nevertheless be differentiated with regard to the incentives. That legislation which makes an action a duty and at the same time makes this duty the incentive is ethical. That which does not include the latter condition in the law, and therefore admits an incentive different from the idea of duty itself, is juridical. As regards juridical legislation, it is easily seen that the incentive here, being different from the idea of duty, must be derived from the pathological grounds determining choice, i.e., from inclinations and disinclinations, and especially from disinclinations, since such juridical legislation is supposed to be one which constrains, not an allurement which invites.

The mere agreement or disagreement of an action with the law, without regard to the incentive of the action, is called legality; but when the idea of duty arising from the law is at the same time the incentive of the action, then the agreement is called the morality of the action.

Duties in accordance with juridical legislation can be only external, because such legislation does not require that the idea of this duty, which is internal, be of itself the ground determining the choice of the agent; and since such legislation nevertheless requires a suitable incentive for the law, it can connect only external incentives with the law. Ethical legislation, on the other hand, while it makes internal actions duties, does not exclude external actions but applies generally to everything that is a duty. But just because ethical legislation does include in its law the internal incentive of the action (the idea of duty), and such a determination must by no means be mixed in with external legislation, ethical legislation consequently cannot be external (not even the external legislation of a divine will), though it may adopt duties which rest on external legislation and take them, insofar as they are duties, as incentives in its own legislation.

From all this it can be seen that all duties, simply because they are duties, belong to ethics. But their legislation is not therefore always contained in ethics; in the case of many duties, it is quite outside ethics. Thus ethics commands me to fulfill my pledge given in a contract, even though the other party could not compel me to do so; but the law (*pacta sunt servanda* [11]) and the duty corresponding to it are taken by ethics from the doctrine of right. Accordingly, the legislation that promises must be kept is contained in *jus* [12] and not in ethics. Ethics teaches only that if the incentive which juridical legislation connects with that duty, namely, external constraint, were absent, the idea of duty alone would still be sufficient as an incentive. For if this were not so, and if the legislation itself were not juridical and the duty arising from it thus not properly a juridical duty [*Rechtspflicht*] (in contradistinction to a duty of virtue [*Tugendpflicht*]), then keeping faith (in accordance with one's promise in a contract) would be put in the same class with actions of benevolence and the obligation to them, and this certainly must not happen. It is not a duty of virtue to keep one's promise, but a juridical duty, one which we can be compelled to perform. Nevertheless, it is a virtuous action (proof of virtue) to do so where no constraint is to be feared. The doctrine of right and the doctrine of virtue [*Rechtslehre und Tugendlehre*] are distinguished, therefore, not so much by their different duties as by the difference in the legislation which connects the one or the other incentive with the law.

Ethical legislation is that which cannot be external (though the duties may be external); juridical legislation is that which

[11] ["Agreements ought to be kept."]
[12] ["Right," "law."]

margin: 220

can also be external. Thus, to keep one's promise in a contract is an external duty; but the command to do so merely because it is a duty, without regard to any other incentive, belongs only to internal legislation. Accordingly, this obligation is reckoned as belonging to ethics, not as being a special kind of duty (a special kind of action to which one is bound) —for in ethics as well as in right [or law] it is an external duty —but because the legislation in this case is internal and cannot have an external legislator. For the same reason, duties of benevolence, although they are external duties (obligations to external actions), are reckoned as belonging to ethics because their legislation can only be internal. To be sure, ethics also has duties peculiar to itself (e.g., duties to oneself); but it also has duties in common with right [or law], though the manner of obligation to such duties is different. For it is the peculiarity of ethical legislation that actions be performed merely because they are duties and that the very principle of duty, no matter whence the duty arises, be made the sufficient incentive of 221 choice. Hence, while there are many directly ethical duties, internal legislation also makes all the rest indirectly ethical.

IV. BASIC CONCEPTS OF THE METAPHYSICS OF MORALS
(*Philosophia practica universalis*)

The concept of freedom is a pure concept of reason. Therefore, it is transcendent for theoretical philosophy, i.e., it is a concept for which no corresponding instance can be given in any possible experience. Accordingly, it constitutes no object of any theoretic knowledge possible for us; it can by no means be valid as a constitutive principle of speculative reason but can be valid only as a regulative and, indeed, merely negative principle of speculative reason. In the practical exercise of reason, however, the concept of freedom proves its reality by practical principles. These are laws of a causality of pure reason; they determine choice independently of all empirical conditions (independently of anything sensible) and prove the existence of a pure will in us, in which moral concepts and laws have their origin.

Upon this concept of freedom, which is positive (from a practical point of view), are founded unconditional practical laws, which are called moral. For us, whose choice is sensibly affected and therefore does not of itself conform with the pure will but often opposes it, these moral laws are imperatives (commands or prohibitions), and, moreover, are categorical (unconditional) imperatives. In being unconditional, they are distinguished from technical imperatives (rules of art [13]), which always give only conditional commands. According to categorical imperatives, certain actions are permitted or not permitted, i.e., are morally possible or impossible; however, some actions or their opposites are, according to these imperatives, morally necessary, i.e., obligatory. Hence for morally necessary actions there arises the concept of a duty. Obedience to or transgression of a duty is, to be sure, connected with a pleasure or displeasure of a peculiar kind (that of a moral feeling). However, we can take no account of this pleasure or displeasure in the practical laws of reason, because these feelings do not concern the ground of the practical laws but only the subjective effect in the mind when our choice is determined by them, and because they can be very different in different persons without objectively, i.e., in the judgment of reason, adding anything to or taking anything away from the validity or influence of these laws.

222

The following concepts are common to both parts of *The Metaphysics of Morals.*

Obligation is the necessity of a free action under a categorical imperative of reason.

An imperative is a practical rule by which an action, in itself contingent, is made necessary. An imperative is distinguished from a practical law by the fact that while the latter represents the necessity of an action, it does not consider whether this necessity already resides by internal

[13] [Just as at the end of Section II above, here art (*Kunst*) means technical skill.]

necessity in the acting subject (as in the case of a holy being), or whether, as in man, it is contingent; for where the internal necessity is the case, there is no imperative. Accordingly, an imperative is a rule whose representation makes a subjectively contingent action necessary and therefore represents the subject as one who must be constrained (necessitated) to conform to this rule. The categorical (unconditional) imperative is one that does not command mediately, through the representation of an end which could be attained by an action, but immediately, through the mere representation of this action itself (its form), which is thought through the categorical imperative as objectively necessary, and is made necessary by it. Instances of an imperative of this kind can be supplied by no other practical doctrine than that one (the doctrine of morals) which prescribes obligation. All other imperatives are technical and are one and all conditional. The ground of the possibility of categorical imperatives lies in the fact that they refer to no other determination of choice (by which a purpose could be ascribed to it) than simply to the freedom of choice.

That action is allowed (*licitum*) which is not contrary to obligation; and this freedom, which is not limited by any opposed imperative, is called the authorization [14] (*facultas moralis* [15]). Hence it is obvious what is meant by unallowed (*illicitum*).

Duty is that action to which a person is bound. It is therefore the matter of the obligation. And there can be one and the same duty (as far as the action is concerned), even though we could be obligated to the action in different ways.

The categorical imperative, inasmuch as it asserts an obligation regarding certain actions, is a morally-practical law. But since obligation contains not only practical necessity (which law in general asserts) but also constraint, the imperative mentioned is a law of either command or

223

14 [*Befugnis*, which might also be rendered as "privilege."]
15 ["Moral power."]

prohibition, according to which the performance or the omission is represented as a duty. An action which is neither commanded nor prohibited is merely allowed, because for it there is no law which limits freedom (authorization) and therefore also no duty. Such an action is called morally indifferent (*indifferens, adiaphoron, res merae facultatis*). It may be asked whether there are any such actions, and if there are, whether in order to be free to do or forbear as one pleases there must be a law of permission (*lex permissiva*) in addition to the law of command (*lex praeceptiva, lex mandati*) and the law of prohibition (*lex prohibita, lex vetiti*). If this is so, then the authorization would not always concern an indifferent action (*adiaphoron*); for no special law would be required for such an action if considered according to moral laws.

An action is called a deed insofar as it stands under laws of obligation and, consequently, insofar as the subject in this action is regarded according to his freedom of choice. By such an act the agent is regarded as the author of the effect, and this effect, together with the action itself, can be imputed to him if he is previously acquainted with the law by which an obligation rests on him.

A person is the subject whose actions are capable of being imputed.[16] Accordingly, moral personality is nothing but the freedom of a rational being under moral laws (whereas psychological personality is merely the capacity to be conscious of the identity of one's self in the various conditions of one's existence). Hence it follows that a person is subject to no laws other than those which he (either alone or at least together with others) gives to himself.

A thing is that which is not capable of any imputation. Every object of free choice that itself lacks freedom is therefore called a thing (*res corporalis*).

A deed is right or wrong in general (*rectum aut minus rectum*) insofar as it is in accordance with or contrary to duty

16 [See below, pp. 27 f.]

224 (*factum licitum aut illicitum*), no matter what the content or the origin of the duty may be. A deed contrary to duty is called a transgression (*reatus*).

An unintentional transgression, which can, nevertheless, be imputed, is called a mere fault (*culpa*). An intentional transgression (i.e., one which is accompanied by the consciousness that it is a transgression) is called a crime (*dolus*). That which is right according to external laws is called just (*justum*); what is not so is unjust (*injustum*).

A conflict of duties (*collisio officiorum s. obligationum*) would be that relationship between them in which one would (wholly or partially) cancel the other. But since duty and obligation in general are concepts which express the objective practical necessity of certain actions, and since two opposite rules cannot be necessary at the same time, then if it is a duty to act in accordance with one of them, it is not only not a duty, but contrary to duty, to act in accordance with the other. It therefore follows that a conflict of duties and obligations is inconceivable (*obligationes non colliduntur*). But two grounds of obligation (*rationes obligandi*), either one or the other of which is inadequate to establish an obligation (*rationes obligandi non obligantes*), can very well be conjoined in a subject and in the rule which he prescribes to himself, for in such a case one of the grounds is not a duty. When two such grounds are in conflict, practical philosophy does not say that the stronger obligation prevails (*fortior obligatio vincit*) but that the stronger ground of obligation prevails (*fortior obligandi ratio vincit*).

In general, those binding laws for which an external legislation is possible are called external laws (*leges externae*). Those external laws whose obligation can be recognized a priori by reason without external legislation are natural laws; those, on the other hand, which without actual external legislation would neither obligate nor be laws are called positive laws. Hence it is possible to conceive of an external legislation which contains only positive laws; but, then, it would have to be preceded by a natural law providing the ground of the authority of the legislator (i.e., his authorization to obligate others by his mere choice).

The principle which makes certain actions a duty is a practical law. The rule which the agent adopts on subjective grounds as his principle is called his maxim; hence the maxims of agents may be very different with regard to the same laws.

The categorical imperative, which in general only expresses what obligation is, is this: Act according to a maxim which can at the same time be valid as a universal law! Hence you must consider your actions first of all according to their subjective principle; but whether this principle is also objectively valid can be recognized only by this, that when your reason puts this principle to the test of conceiving yourself as universally legislating by means of it, it qualifies for such a universal legislation.

The simplicity of this law, in comparison with the great and manifold consequences which can be drawn from it, must at first seem strange, as must also its authority to command without perceptibly carrying with it any incentive. But in our wonder at the capacity of our reason to determine choice by the mere idea of the fitness of a maxim for the universality of a practical law, we learn that it is just these practical (moral) laws that first make known a property of choice which speculative reason could never have arrived at, either from a priori grounds or from experience, and the possibility of which speculative reason could by no means prove even if reason had arrived at it, whereas those practical laws incontestably prove this property, namely, freedom. Consequently, we shall be less surprised to find these laws, like mathematical postulates, indemonstrable and yet apodeictic. At the same time we shall see a whole field of practical cognitions open before us, a field which is absolutely closed to reason in its theoretical use when it treats the same idea of freedom, or, indeed, any other of its ideas of the supersensible. The agreement of an action with the law of duty is its legality (*legalitas*); that of the maxim of the action with the law is its morality (*moralitas*). A maxim is a subjective principle of action which the subject

adopts as a rule for himself (namely, how he wants to act). On the other hand, a principle of duty is that which reason absolutely and, therefore, objectively commands (how he
226 should act).

The supreme principle of the doctrine of morals is therefore: Act according to a maxim that can at the same time be valid as a universal law. Any maxim which is not qualified to be a universal law is contrary to morals.

Laws proceed from the will; maxims from choice.[17] In man, choice is free. The will relates to nothing but the law. It cannot be called either free or unfree, because it deals not with actions, but immediately with legislation for the maxims of actions (and is therefore practical reason itself). Consequently, it is absolutely necessary and is even incapable of constraint. Therefore, only choice can be called free.

Freedom of choice, however, cannot be defined as the capacity for making a choice to act for or against the law (*libertas indifferentiae*), as some people have tried to define it, even though choice as a phenomenon gives frequent instances of this in experience. For freedom (as it first becomes known to us through the moral law) is known only as a negative property within us, namely, the property of not being constrained to action by any sensible determining grounds. But freedom as a noumenon, i.e., considered according to the capacity of man only as an intelligence, cannot in the least be explained theoretically according to its positive nature as it constrains sensible choice. But we can see clearly that although experience tells us that man as a sensible being exhibits a capacity to choose not only in accordance with the law but also in opposition to it, yet his freedom as an intelligible being cannot be thus defined, since appearances can never enable us to comprehend any supersensible object

[17] [This paragraph and the following one should be compared with the discussion of will and choice in Section I above, pp. 11-13. In this paragraph and the following one, "will" is meant in the narrow sense of rational will.]

(such as free choice is). Furthermore, we can see that freedom can never be located in the fact that the rational subject is able to make a choice in opposition to his (legislative) reason, even though experience proves often enough that this does happen (though we cannot comprehend how this is possible). For it is one thing to admit a tenet (of experience) and quite another to make it both the defining principle (of the concept of free choice) and the universal mark distinguishing free choice from *arbitrio bruto s. servo*,[18] since in the first case we do not assert 227 that the mark necessarily belongs to the concept, which we must do in the latter case. Only freedom in relation to the internal legislation of reason is properly a capacity; the possibility of deviating from it is an incapacity. How, then, can the former be explained by the latter? Such an explanation is a definition which adds to the practical concept the exercise of it as experience teaches it; this is a bastard explanation (*definitio hybrida*), which presents the concept in a false light.

A law (a morally-practical one) is a proposition which contains a categorical imperative (a command). He who commands (*imperans*) by a law is the lawgiver (*legislator*). He is the author (*auctor*) of the obligation imposed by the law but is not always the author of the law. If he were so, the law would be positive (contingent) and arbitrary. The law which binds us a priori and unconditionally by means of our own reason can also be expressed as proceeding from the will of a supreme lawgiver, i.e., of one who has only rights and no duties (accordingly, from the Divine Will). But this only signifies the idea of a moral being whose will is law for all, without his being conceived as the author of the law.

Imputation (*imputatio*) in the moral sense is the judgment by which someone is regarded as the author (*causa libera* [19]) of an action, which then is called a deed (*factum*) and stands under laws. If this judgment also carries with it the juridical consequences of this deed, it is a legal imputation (*imputatio*

[18] ["Brute or servile choice."]
[19] ["Free cause."]

judiciaria s. valida); otherwise it is only a criticizing imputation (*imputatio dijudicatoria*). That person (physical or moral) who is authorized to exercise legal imputation is called the judge or the court (*judex s. forum*).

What anyone does in accordance with duty beyond what he can be compelled to do by the law is meritorious (*meritum*); what he does only just in accordance with the law is debt owed (*debitum*); lastly, what he does that is less than the law demands is moral offense (*demeritum*). The juridical effect of offense is punishment (*poena*); that of a meritorious deed is reward (*praemium*), provided that the reward promised in the law was the motive for the deed. Conduct that agrees with debt owed has no juridical effect. Kindly recompense (*remuneratio s. repensio benefica*) stands in no juridical relation to the deed.

228

The good or bad consequences of an action owed, as well as the consequences of omitting a meritorious action, cannot be imputed to the subject (*modus imputationis tollens*).

The good consequences of a meritorious action as well as the bad consequences of an unlawful action can be imputed to the subject (*modus imputationis ponens*).

Subjectively considered, the degree of imputability (*imputabilitas*) of actions must be estimated by the magnitude of the hindrances which have to be overcome. The greater the natural hindrances (of sensibility) and the less the moral hindrance (of duty), the higher is the imputation of merit in a good deed, e.g., it is higher if at a considerable sacrifice I rescue from dire necessity a man who is a complete stranger to me.

On the other hand, the less the natural hindrance and the greater the hindrance from grounds of duty, so much more is transgression (as offense) imputed. Therefore, the state of mind of the subject, namely, whether he committed the deed with emotion or with cool deliberation, makes a significant difference in imputation.

THE METAPHYSICS OF MORALS

PART II
THE METAPHYSICAL PRINCIPLES
OF VIRTUE

Preface and Introduction

Die

Metaphysik der Sitten.

Abgefaßt

von

Immanuel Kant.

Zweyter Theil.
Metaphysische Anfangsgründe
der
Tugendlehre.

Königsberg,
bey Friedrich Nicolovius,
1797.

PREFACE

If there is a philosophy (a system of rational knowledge from concepts) on any subject, then there also must be for this philosophy a system of pure rational concepts, which are independent of all intuition, i.e., there must be a metaphysics. One may ask whether metaphysical principles are likewise required for every practical philosophy insofar as it is a doctrine of duties and, consequently, whether also for the doctrine of virtue (ethics), in order that the doctrine of virtue may be presented as a true science (systematically) and not merely as an aggregate of separately sought doctrines (fragmentarily). As regards the pure doctrine of right,[1] no one will call this requirement into question; for the doctrine of right is concerned only with what is formal in choice when choice is restricted in its external relations according to laws of freedom, apart from any end as the matter of choice. Accordingly, the doctrine of duties is here merely a scientific doctrine (*doctrina scientiae*).[2]

[1] [The doctrine of right (*Rechtslehre*) is the same as *The Metaphysical Principles of Right*, which, as the first part of *The Metaphysics of Morals*, precedes *The Metaphysical Principles of Virtue*. Kant usually calls the latter simply the doctrine of virtue (*Tugendlehre*). See Introduction, p. xi with n. 1.]

[2] One who is acquainted with practical philosophy is not therefore a practical philosopher. The latter makes the rational end the principle of his actions, while at the same time joining with this end the necessary knowledge. Such knowledge, since it aims at action, need not be spun out into the subtlest threads of metaphysics, unless a juridical duty is involved. In the case of a juridical duty, the mine and thine must be exactly determined on the scales of justice in accordance with the principle of the equality of action and reaction, and hence something analogous to mathematical precision is required. No such precise determination is required in the case of a mere duty of virtue. For in this case the question is not merely to know what it is a duty to do (something which can easily be declared because of the ends which all men naturally have); but it is especially important to know the internal principle of the will, namely, that

31

Now, in this philosophy (of the doctrine of virtue), it seems directly contrary to the idea of such a doctrine that one should go back to metaphysical principles in order to make the concept of duty, purified of everything empirical (of every feeling), the incentive of action. For what sort of concept can one form of the mighty power and herculean strength that would be sufficient to overcome the vice-breeding inclinations, if virtue is to borrow her weapons from the armory of metaphysics, which is a matter of speculation that only few men know how to handle? Hence all ethical teachings in lecture rooms, from pulpits, and in popular books, become ridiculous when they are decked out with fragments of metaphysics. However, it is not therefore useless, much less ridiculous, to look for the first principles of the doctrine of virtue in a metaphysics; for someone must, as philosopher, consider the first principles of this concept of duty, otherwise neither certainty nor purity in the doctrine of virtue in general is to be expected. To rely in this case upon a certain feeling, which is called moral because of the effect expected from it, may perhaps satisfy the popular teacher, provided he requires consideration of the following problem as the touchstone for determining whether or not something is a duty of virtue: "If everyone in every case made his maxim a universal law, how could this law be consistent with itself?" But if merely a feeling made it our duty to take this proposition as a touchstone, then this duty would not be dictated by reason, but would be only instinctively (and therefore blindly) accepted.

In fact, however, no moral principle is founded upon any feeling, whatever one may think; a moral principle is really nothing but a dimly conceived metaphysics, which is inherent in every man's rational constitution—as the teacher will easily find out who tries to catechize his pupil in the Socratic method concerning the imperative of duty and its application to the moral judgment of his actions. The mode of stating the im-

---

the consciousness of this duty be at the same time the incentive of the actions, in order to say of the man who joins this principle of wisdom to his knowledge that he is a practical philosopher.

perative of duty (the technique) need not always be metaphysical; and the language need not necessarily be scholastic,
unless the pupil is to be trained as a philosopher. But the
thought must go back to the elements of metaphysics, without
which neither certainty nor purity nor even moving force can
be expected in the doctrine of virtue.

If one departs from this principle, and in order to determine
duties starts out from pathological feeling, from purely sensitive [rein-ästhetisch] feeling, or even from moral feeling (from
what is subjectively practical instead of from what is objectively practical), i.e., from the matter of the will (the end) and
not from the form of the will (the law); then, certainly, there   377
are no metaphysical principles of virtue, because however it
may arise, feeling is always physical. In this case the doctrine
of virtue (whether in schools or in lecture halls, etc.) is corrupted in its source. For it is not a matter of indifference by
what incentives as means one is led to a good purpose (the
obedience to duty). However much metaphysics may disgust
those pretended teachers of wisdom who dogmatize oracularly
or even ingeniously concerning the doctrine of duties, it is,
nevertheless, an indispensable duty for those who oppose metaphysics to go back to its principles, even in the doctrine of
virtue, and to begin by going to school on its benches.

One must justly wonder how, after all the former refine-
ments of the principle of duty, as far as it is derived from
pure reason, it was still possible to reduce that principle yet
again to a doctrine of happiness; and in such a way as in the
end to think of a certain moral happiness not resting on empirical causes, a self-contradictory nonentity. When the thinking man has triumphed over temptations to vice and is conscious of having done his often difficult duty, he finds himself
in a state of satisfaction and peace of mind which can well be
called happiness and in which virtue is its own reward. Now,
says the eudaemonist, this bliss, this happiness is the real motive for his acting virtuously. It is not the concept of duty
which directly determines his will, claims the eudaemonist;

rather, he is moved to do his duty only by means of the happiness in prospect. But, since he can promise himself this reward of virtue only from his consciousness of having done his duty, it is clear that this consciousness must have preceded the reward, i.e., he must deem himself obligated to do his duty before he thinks, and without thinking, that happiness will be the consequence of observing his duty. Hence he is involved in a circle in his etiology. He can hope to be happy (or inwardly blissful) only when he is conscious of his observance of duty; however, he can be moved to observe duty only when 378 he foresees that he will thereby be happy. But there is also a contradiction in this subtilizing. For, on the one hand, he must observe his duty without asking what effect this will have upon his happiness, hence from a moral principle; but, on the other hand, he can only recognize something as his duty when he can count on the happiness which will thereby accrue to him, hence according to a pathological principle, which is the direct opposite of the moral principle.

I believe that in another place (the Berlin *Monatsschrift*) [3] I have reduced the distinction between pathological and moral pleasure to its simplest expression. That pleasure which must precede obedience to the law in order that one may act in accordance with the law is pathological, and the process follows the order of nature. That pleasure which must be preceded by the law in order that it may be felt is in the moral order. If this distinction is not observed, if eudaemonism (the principle of happiness) is set up as the principle instead of eleutheronomy (the principle of the freedom of internal legislation), the consequence is the euthanasia (quiet death) of all morality.

The cause of these mistakes is no other than the following. Those who are accustomed only to physiological explanations

3 [Vorländer suggests that *Von einem neuerdings erhobenen vornehmen Ton* etc., which appeared in the Berlin *Monatsschrift* of 1796, is meant; this essay can be found in Volume VIII of the Royal Prussian Academy of Sciences Edition of Kant's works. But T. K. Abbott and others think that Book I, "On the Radical Evil in Human Nature," of *Religion within the Limits of Reason Alone* is meant.]

will not take up the categorical imperative, from which these laws dictatorially proceed, in spite of the fact that they feel themselves irresistibly forced by it. Annoyed over not being able to explain what lies entirely beyond the physiological sphere (namely, freedom of choice)—elevating though man's privilege is, of being capable of such an idea as freedom of choice—they are stirred up by the proud claims of speculative reason, which feels its power so strongly in other fields. They are stirred up just as if they were allies, leagued in defense of the omnipotence of theoretical reason and roused by a general call to arms to resist the idea of freedom of choice and thus at present, and perhaps for a long time to come (though ultimately in vain), to attack the moral concept of freedom and, if possible, render it suspect.

INTRODUCTION

Ethics in ancient times signified the doctrine of morals (*philosophia moralis*) in general, which was also called the doctrine of duties. Subsequently it was found advisable to assign this name to a part of the doctrine of morals, namely, to the doctrine of those duties which are not subject to external laws (and for which in German the word *Tugendlehre* was found suitable). Accordingly, the system of the general doctrine of duties is divided into the doctrine of right (*jurisprudentia*), which admits of external laws, and the doctrine of virtue (*ethica*), which does not admit of such laws; and we may let this division stand.

I. DISCUSSION OF THE CONCEPT OF A DOCTRINE OF VIRTUE

The concept of duty is in itself already the concept of a necessitation (constraint) of free choice by law; this constraint may be an external one or it may be self-constraint. The moral imperative through its categorical pronouncement (the unconditioned "ought") announces this constraint, which therefore does not apply to rational beings in general (for there may also be holy beings) but applies to men as rational natural beings. The latter are unholy enough to be influenced by pleasure to transgress the moral law, although they recognize its authority. And even when they do obey it, they do so without gladness (in conflict with their inclinations); the constraint really consists in this.[1] But since man is a free (moral) being, the concept of

1 But man, insofar as he is at the same time a moral being, i.e., when he considers himself objectively according to the humanity in his own person (and he is intended by his pure practical reason to be such a moral being), finds himself holy enough not to transgress the internal law gladly. For

duty can contain no constraint except self-constraint (through the representation of the law alone), as far as the internal determination of the will (the incentive) is concerned. For only through such constraint is it possible to combine that necessitation (even if it were external) with the freedom of choice, whereby the concept of duty will then be an ethical one.

The impulses of nature contain resisting forces (some of them powerful) and hindrances to duty's fulfillment in the mind of man. He must judge himself capable of combating these and conquering them by means of reason, not in the future, but right now (simultaneously with the thought); he must judge that he can do what the law unconditionally commands he ought to do.

Now, fortitude (*fortitudo*) is the capacity and resolved purpose to resist a strong but unjust opponent; and with regard to the opponent of the moral disposition within us, such fortitude is *virtue* (*virtus, fortitudo moralis*). Hence the general doctrine of duties, in that part which brings not external, but internal freedom under laws, is a doctrine of virtue.

The doctrine of right had to do merely with the formal condition of external freedom (consistency with itself when its maxim is made into a universal law), i.e., *right*. Ethics, on the other hand, supplies in addition a matter (an object of free choice), namely, an *end* of pure reason which is at the same time represented as an objectively necessary end, i.e., as a duty for man. For since sensible inclinations may misdirect us to ends (the matter of choice) which may be contrary to duty, 381

there is no man so depraved but that he feels upon transgressing the internal law a resistance within himself and an abhorrence of himself; he must constrain himself upon such transgression. It is impossible to explain the phenomenon that at this parting of the ways (where the beautiful fable places Hercules between virtue and sensuality) man shows more propensity to listen to inclination than to the law. For we can only explain what happens by deriving it from a cause according to laws of nature; but in that case, we would not think of choice as being free. This mutual opposition involved in self-constraint and the inevitability of such opposition make us recognize the incomprehensible character of freedom itself.

legislative reason cannot guard against their influence other than, in turn, by means of an opposing moral end, which therefore must be given a priori independently of inclination.

An end is an object of choice (of a rational being); by means of the representation of such an end, choice is determined to an action to produce the object. Now, I can indeed be forced by others to actions which are directed as means to an end, but I can never be forced by others to have an end; I alone can make something an end for myself. If, however, I am also obligated to make something which lies in the concepts of practical reason an end for myself, and if, therefore, besides the formal determining ground of choice (such as right contains) I am obligated to have in addition a material determining ground, i.e., an end that can be opposed to the end derived from sensible impulses, then this would be the concept of an end which is in itself a duty. The doctrine of such an end cannot belong to the doctrine of right but only to ethics, since the latter alone contains in its concept self-constraint according to moral laws.

For this reason ethics can also be defined as the system of the ends of pure practical reason. End and duty [2] distinguish the two parts of the general doctrine of morals. That ethics contains duties which one cannot be (physically) forced by others to observe is merely the consequence of the fact that ethics is a doctrine of ends, for being forced to have ends or to determine them contradicts itself.

That ethics is a doctrine of virtue (*doctrina officiorum virtutis*) follows from the foregoing explanation of virtue in comparison with the obligation whose peculiarity has just been pointed out. There is, namely, no other determination of choice than that to an end; the very concept of this determination implies that one cannot even be physically forced by the choice of another. Another may indeed force me to do something which is not my end (but is only the means to some other's end); but he cannot force me to make it my own end,

2 [Kant substituted "duty of constraint" (*Zwangspflicht*) for "duty" (*Pflicht*) in the second edition.]

for I can have no end except of my own making. The latter
supposition [3] is a contradiction—an act of freedom which yet
at the same time is not free. But there is no contradiction in
setting for oneself an end which is at the same time a duty
for in this case I force myself, and such force is quite consistent   382
with freedom.[4] But how is such an end possible? This is now
the question. For the possibility of the concept of a thing (that
the concept does not contradict itself) is not sufficient for ad-
mitting the possibility of the thing itself (the objective reality
of the concept).

II. DISCUSSION OF THE CONCEPT OF AN END WHICH IS AT THE SAME TIME A DUTY

One can think of the relation of an end to a duty in two
ways: either starting from the end to find the maxim of the
actions which are in accordance with duty; or, conversely,
commencing with the maxim to find the end which is at the
same time a duty. The doctrine of right proceeds in the first
way. What end a person proposes for his action is left up to
his free choice. But the maxim of his action is determined a
priori, namely, so that the freedom of the agent can be consistent with the freedom of every other person according to a
universal law.

Ethics, however, takes the opposite way. It cannot start from
the ends which a man may propose to himself and accordingly
give directions as to the maxims he should adopt, i.e., as to his
duty, for that would be to take empirical grounds for his

---

[3] [Namely, being forced to make something my end.]

[4] The less man can be physically forced, and the more he can be morally forced (by the mere representation of duty), the freer he is. The man,
for instance, who is sufficiently firmly resolved and strong-minded enough
not to give up a diversion he has undertaken, regardless of how much
harm is shown to result from it, and who, when he finds out that it
would cause him to neglect an official duty or a sick father, unhesi-
tatingly though very reluctantly desists from his purpose—this man proves
his freedom in the highest degree by the very fact that he cannot oppose
the voice of duty.

maxims, and such grounds furnish no concept of duty, inasmuch as this concept (the categorical "ought") has its root in pure reason alone. If one's maxims were to be adopted according to such ends (which are all selfish), then one could not properly speak of the concept of duty at all. Thus in ethics the concept of duty will lead to ends, and the maxims regarding the ends which we ought to set before ourselves must be founded on moral principles.

383   Setting aside the questions about what sort of end that is which is in itself a duty, and how such an end is possible, it is here necessary only to show that a duty of this kind is called a duty of virtue, and to show why it is so called.

To every duty there corresponds a right, regarded as authorization (*facultas moralis generatim* [5]); but to every duty there are not corresponding rights of another (*facultas juridica* [6]) to compel anyone; those to which such rights correspond are specifically called juridical duties. Similarly, to every ethical obligation there corresponds the concept of virtue, but not all ethical duties are therefore duties of virtue. Those duties, namely, which do not concern a certain end (the matter, the object of choice) but only the formal element of the moral determination of the will (e.g., that the action which is in accordance with duty must also be done from duty) are not duties of virtue. Only an end which is at the same time a duty can be called a *duty of virtue*. Therefore, there are several duties of virtue (and also various virtues); by contrast, however, of the former kind,[7] only a virtuous disposition that is valid for all actions is conceivable.

A duty of virtue is essentially distinguished from a juridical duty in that an external constraint is morally possible to the latter, whereas the former rests on free self-constraint alone. For finite holy beings (who cannot even be tempted to violate

[5] ["Moral power in general."]

[6] ["Juridical power."]

[7] [That is, the duty (and its corresponding virtue) which does not concern a certain end but only the formal element of the moral determination of the will.]

duty) there is no doctrine of virtue, but only a doctrine of morals; this is so because the doctrine of morals is an autonomy of practical reason, while the doctrine of virtue is at the same time an autocracy of practical reason. This is to say, such autocracy contains a consciousness—although not immediately perceived, yet nevertheless rightly inferred from the moral categorical imperative—of the power to become master of one's inclinations that oppose the law. Therefore, human morality at its highest stage can still be nothing more than virtue, even if it be entirely pure (completely free from the influence of an incentive foreign to duty). Even then it is commonly personified poetically under the name "the wise man," as an ideal (which one ought constantly to approach).

Virtue is not to be defined and esteemed merely as skill and (as expressed in the prize essay of Cochius [8]) as a habit acquired by the long practice of morally good actions. For if habit is not a result of resolute and firm principles ever more and more purified, then, like any other mechanism of technically-practical reason, it is neither armed for all eventualities nor adequately secured against changes that may be brought about by new allurements.

Remark

The negative lack of virtue (moral weakness) $= 0$ is the logical contradictory (*contradictorie oppositum* [9]) of virtue $= +a$; but vice $= -a$ is virtue's contrary (*contrarie s. realiter oppositum* [10]). And it is not merely an unnecessary but also an offensive question to ask whether great crimes do not perhaps require more strength of mind than great virtues do. For by strength of mind we understand a man's strength of purpose, insofar as he is a being endowed with freedom, and, consequently, insofar as he is master of himself (in his senses) and

[8] [Leonhard Cochius (1717-79), court preacher and a member of the Berlin Academy, obtained the prize of the Academy for his essay, *Über die Neigungen* ("Concerning the Inclinations," 1769).]
[9] ["Contradictorily opposed."]
[10] ["Contrarily or really opposed."]

accordingly is in a healthy state of mind. But great crimes are paroxysms, the very sight of which makes the man of healthy mind shudder. Therefore, the question would perhaps run something like this: can a man in a fit of madness have more physical strength than when he is in his senses? And one can grant this without therefore ascribing to him more strength of mind, if by mind one understands the vital principle of man in the free use of his powers. For since those crimes have their ground merely in the force of the inclinations that weaken reason, and since this fact does not prove strength of mind, so this question would be nearly the same as that of whether a man in a fit of illness can show more strength than he can in a healthy condition. And this question can be directly answered in the negative since the want of health, which consists in the proper balance of all the bodily forces of man, is a debilitation in the system of these forces; and only by this system can unqualified health be estimated.

III. CONCERNING THE REASON FOR CONCEIVING OF AN END WHICH IS AT THE SAME TIME A DUTY

An end is an object of free choice; the representation of the end determines choice to an action whereby the object is produced. Accordingly, every action has its end; and since no one can have an end without himself making the object of his choice the end, to have some end of action is an act of freedom of the acting subject and is not an effect of nature. But since this act which determines an end is a practical principle that does not command the means (therefore, does not command conditionally) but commands the end itself (consequently, unconditionally), so it is a categorical imperative of pure practical reason and is, therefore, one which combines the concept of duty with the concept of an end in general.

Now, there must be such an end and a categorical imperative corresponding to it. For since there are free actions, there must also be ends to which, as objects, those actions are di-

385

rected. But among these ends there must be some which are at the same time (i.e., by their very concept) duties. For if there were no such ends, and since no action can be without an end, all ends for practical reason would always be valid only as means to other ends, and a categorical imperative would be impossible. Thus the doctrine of morals would be destroyed.

Therefore, we are here concerned not with the ends which man makes for himself according to the sensible impulses of his nature, but, rather, with objects of his free choice under its own laws—objects which he ought to make his end. One may call the former the technical (subjective), properly speaking pragmatic doctrine of ends containing the rule of prudence in the choice of ends; but the latter must be called the moral (objective) doctrine of ends. However, this distinction is superfluous here since the doctrine of morals is already by its very concept clearly separated from the doctrine of nature (in this case, anthropology), inasmuch as the latter rests on empirical principles, whereas the moral doctrine of ends, which treats of duties, rests on a priori principles given in pure practical reason.

IV. WHAT ARE THE ENDS WHICH ARE AT THE SAME TIME DUTIES?

They are these: one's own perfection and the happiness of others.

One cannot invert these and make, on the one hand, our own happiness and, on the other, the perfection of others, ends which should be in themselves duties for the same person.

For one's own happiness is an end which, to be sure, all men 386 do have (by virtue of the impulse of their nature), but this end can never without contradiction be regarded as a duty. What everyone of himself already inevitably wants does not belong under the concept of duty, because a duty is a constraint to an end that is not gladly adopted. It is, therefore, a contradiction to say that one is obligated to promote his own happiness with all his powers.

Just so, it is a contradiction to make the perfection of another my end and to deem myself obligated to promote his perfection. For the perfection of another man as a person consists precisely in his being able to set his end for himself according to his own concepts of duty. And it is a contradiction to require (to make it a duty for me) that I ought to do something which no one except another himself can do.

V. EXPLANATION OF THESE TWO CONCEPTS

A. ONE'S OWN PERFECTION

The word "perfection" is liable to many misconceptions. It is sometimes understood as a concept belonging to transcendental philosophy, viz., as the concept of the totality of a manifold which, taken together, constitutes a thing. But then again it is understood as belonging to teleology, meaning the harmony of the properties of a thing with an end. Perfection in the former sense might be called quantitative (material), and in the latter, qualitative (formal). The former can be one only, for the whole of that which belongs to one thing is unitary. But there can be several of the latter in one thing, and it is of the latter perfection that we here treat.

When it is said of the perfection that belongs to man in general (properly speaking, to humanity) that to make this perfection one's end is in itself a duty, such perfection must be placed in what can be the effect of one's deed and not in what is merely a gift for which he must thank nature; for otherwise such perfection would not be a duty. Therefore, it 387 can be nothing but the cultivation of one's capacities (or natural endowments). The highest of these is the understanding, since it is the faculty of concepts, including, therefore, those which concern duty. But human perfection lies not only in the cultivation of one's understanding but also in that of one's will (moral turn of mind), in order that the demands of duty in general be satisfied. First, it is one's duty to raise himself out of the crudity of his nature, out of his animality (*quoad actum* [11]) more and more to humanity, by which alone he is capable of setting himself ends. It is his duty to supply by instruction what is lacking in his knowledge, and to correct his mistakes. He is not merely advised to do all this by technically-practical reason with a view to his other purposes (of art), but morally-practical reason absolutely commands it of him and makes this end his duty in order that he may be worthy of the humanity dwelling within him. Second, it is one's duty to push the cultivation of his will up to the purest virtuous disposition, in which the law is at the same time the incentive of one's actions which are in accordance with duty, and is obeyed from duty. This disposition, which is inner morally-practical perfection, is called moral feeling because it is a feeling of the effect which the legislative will within a person exercises upon his capacity to act according to his will. Moral feeling is a special sense (*sensus moralis*) which, admittedly, is often fanatically misused, as though (like the Socratic genius) it preceded reason or could dispense with reason's judgment; but nevertheless, it is a moral perfection that makes every particular end which is at the same time a duty one's own end.

B. The Happiness of Others

It is inevitable for human nature that one should wish for and seek happiness, i.e., satisfaction with one's condition as far as he is certain of its continuance. But for this very reason happiness is not an end which is at the same time a duty. Some people still make a distinction between moral and physical happiness (the former consisting in satisfaction with one's own person and moral conduct, and thus with what one does; the other in satisfaction with what nature bestows, and hence with what one enjoys as an external gift). Without here censuring the misuse of the word (which even contains a contradiction), we must note that only the feeling of moral happiness belongs under the previous head, namely, perfection. For 388 he who feels happy in the mere consciousness of his upright-

[11] ["As far as his action is concerned."]

ness already possesses that perfection which in the preceding section [12] was defined as that end which is at the same time a duty.

If it is to be my duty to promote happiness as my end, then it must be the happiness of other men whose (permitted) end I hereby make mine too. What they count as belonging to their happiness is left up to them to decide; but I may decline many of these things which I do not regard as so belonging, if they otherwise have no right to demand them of me. A plausible objection often made against the previous division of duties (in Section IV) consists in setting up in opposition to that end (of promoting the happiness of others) a supposed obligation to take care of my own (physical) happiness and so make this, which is my natural and merely subjective end, into a duty (an objective end). This objection needs to be set right.

Adversity, pain, and want are great temptations to transgress one's duty. Thus it would seem that affluence, strength, health, and welfare in general, which are opposed to those influences, can also be regarded as ends that are at the same time duties; that is to say, it is a duty to promote one's own happiness and not merely that of others. But in that case the end is not happiness, but the morality of the subject; and happiness is merely the means of removing the hindrances to morality, permitted means, that is, since no one has a right to demand from me the sacrifice of those ends of mine that are not immoral. It is not directly a duty to seek affluence for itself; but indirectly it may very well be a duty, namely, in order to guard against poverty, which is a great temptation to vice. But then it is not my happiness, but the preservation of the integrity of my morality, that is my end and at the same time my duty.

[12] [Section IV.]

VI. ETHICS DOES NOT GIVE LAWS FOR ACTIONS (AS DOES THE DOCTRINE OF RIGHT) BUT ONLY FOR THE MAXIMS OF ACTIONS

The concept of duty stands immediately in relation to a law (even though I abstract from every end, which is the matter of the law), as is already indicated by the formal principle of duty in the categorical imperative: "Act so that the maxim of your action can become a universal law." But in ethics this law is conceived as the law of one's own will and not of the will in general, which could also be the will of others; in the latter case such a law would give rise to a juridical duty, and such a law does not belong to the field of ethics. In ethics, maxims are regarded as being such subjective principles as merely qualify for universal legislation—which is only a negative condition (not contradicting a law in general). But how, then, can there further be a law for the maxims of actions? 389

It is the concept of an end which is at the same time a duty, a concept peculiar to ethics, that alone establishes a law for the maxims of actions, inasmuch as the subjective end (that which everyone has) is subordinated to the objective end (that which everyone ought to make his own). The imperative, "You should make this or that (e.g., the happiness of others) your end," applies to the matter of choice (an object). Now, since no free action is possible unless the agent at the same time thereby aims at some end (as matter of his choice); it follows that if there is an end which is at the same time a duty, then the maxim of actions, which are the means to ends, must contain only the condition of qualifying for possible universal legislation. On the other hand, the end which is at the same time a duty can make having such a maxim a duty, while for the maxim itself the mere possibility of agreeing with universal legislation is already enough.

For maxims of actions can be arbitrary and are subordinate

only to the restrictive condition of fitness for universal legislation as the formal principle of actions. But a law abolishes the arbitrariness of actions and is by this fact different from any recommendation (since in the latter merely knowledge of the best means to an end is required).

VII. ETHICAL DUTIES ARE OF BROAD OBLIGATION; ON THE OTHER HAND, JURIDICAL DUTIES ARE OF STRICT OBLIGATION

This proposition is a consequence of the foregoing. For if the law can command only the maxim of actions and not the actions themselves, then this is a sign that the law leaves in its obedience (observance) a latitude (*latitudo*) for free choice, i.e., it cannot definitely assign in what way and to what extent something should be brought about by an action directed to an end which is at the same time a duty. But by a broad duty is not understood a permission to make exceptions to the maxim of the actions, but only the permission to limit one maxim of duty by another (e.g., the general love of one's neighbor by the love of one's parents); and this in fact broadens the field for the practice of virtue. The broader the duty, the more imperfect, therefore, is one's obligation to an action; and the closer one nevertheless brings the maxim of his observance of this broad duty (in his own mind) to the strict duty (of right), so much the more perfect is his virtuous action.

Imperfect duties are, therefore, merely duties of virtue. The fulfillment of them is merit (*meritum*) = + *a;* but their transgression is not forthwith an offense (*demeritum*) = − *a,* but merely moral unworth = *o,* unless the subject made it a principle not to conform to these duties. The strength of purpose in such fulfillment is alone properly called virtue (*virtus*); the weakness in such transgression is not so much vice (*vitium*) as mere lack of virtue, want of moral strength (*defectus mo-*

ralis). (As the word *Tugend* ["virtue"] is derived from *taugen* ["to be good for something"], so *Untugend* ["lack of virtue"] by its etymology signifies "good for nothing.") Every action contrary to duty is called transgression (*peccatum*). Deliberate transgression that has become a principle properly constitutes what is called vice (*vitium*).

Although the conformity of actions to right (i.e., being an upright man) is nothing meritorious, yet the conformity to right of the maxim of such actions regarded as duties, i.e., *respect* for right, is meritorious. For by this latter conformity a man makes the right of humanity or of men his end and thereby enlarges his concept of duty beyond that of indebtedness (*officium debiti*), since another person by his rights can, according to the law, require actions of me but cannot require that the law at the same time contain the incentive of my actions as well. The same thing is true of the universal ethical command, "Act in accordance with duty from duty." [13] To establish this disposition of itself and to quicken it is meritorious, as in the above case, because it goes beyond the law of duty for actions and makes the law in itself also the incentive.

But just for this reason, these ethical duties must also be counted as of broad obligation. With regard to such broad obligation there exists a subjective principle of ethical reward (or, rather, of susceptibility to such reward in accordance with the law of virtue) in order that this broad obligation be brought as close as possible to a strict one. This principle is that of a moral pleasure which goes beyond mere satisfaction with oneself (which may be merely negative); and it is proudly said that, in the consciousness of this moral pleasure, virtue is its own reward.

If this merit is the merit of a man with regard to other men, i.e., if it consists in his promoting their natural—and recognized by all men as natural—end, i.e., if it consists in his making their happiness his own, then one might call it sweet

391

[13] [Or, "Act dutifully from a sense of duty." The German is, *Handle pflichtmäßig aus Pflicht*.]

merit, the consciousness of which produces a moral enjoyment in which men are by sympathy inclined to revel. On the other hand, the bitter merit of promoting the true good of others when they do not recognize their true good (in the case of the ungrateful and the thankless) usually has no such effect, but engenders only satisfaction with oneself; in this latter case, however, the merit would be even greater.

VIII. EXPOSITION OF THE DUTIES OF VIRTUE AS BROAD DUTIES

1. ONE'S OWN PERFECTION AS AN END WHICH IS AT THE SAME TIME A DUTY

(a) Physical perfection, i.e., the cultivation of all our capacities in general in order to promote the ends set before us by reason. That this is a duty and therefore an end in itself, and that the effort to bring this about, even without regard to the advantage which such an effort affords us, is based not on a conditional (pragmatic) imperative but on an unconditional (moral) one, can be seen from the following consideration. The capacity to propose an end to oneself is the characteristic of humanity (as distinguished from animality). The rational will [*Vernunftwille*] is therefore bound up with the end of the humanity in our own person, as is also, consequently, the duty to deserve well of humanity by means of culture in general, and to acquire or promote the capacity of carrying out all sorts of ends, as far as this capacity is to be found in man. This is to say that cultivating the crude predispositions of one's nature is a duty, since thus the animal is first raised to man; therefore, it is a duty in itself.

But this duty is only ethical, i.e., of broad obligation. No principle of reason prescribes exactly how far one must go in this effort (in enlarging or correcting one's faculty of understanding, i.e., in knowledge or in technical ability). Besides, the variety of circumstances which men may encounter makes quite optional the choice of the kind of occupation for which

392

one should cultivate his talent. There is here, therefore, no law of reason for actions but only for the maxim of actions, viz., "Cultivate your powers of mind and body so as to be able to fulfill all the ends which may arise for you, uncertain as you may be which ends might become your own."

(b) Cultivation of morality within ourselves. The greatest moral perfection of man is to do his duty and to do it, of course, from duty (so that the law is not merely the rule, but also the incentive of his actions). Now, at first sight this certainly seems to be a strict obligation; and the principle of duty seems to command, with the exactness and strictness of a law, not merely the legality of every action but also the morality of it, i.e., the mental disposition. But in fact, even here the law commands only the maxim of the action, namely, that the ground of the obligation is to be sought not in sensible impulses (advantage or disadvantage) but wholly in the law; and so the law does not command the action itself. For it is not possible for man to look so far into the depths of his own heart as ever to be entirely certain, even in one single action, of the purity of his moral purpose and the sincerity of his mental disposition, although he has no doubt at all about its legality. Often the weakness which dissuades a man from the risk of a crime is regarded by him as virtue (which involves the concept of strength). But how many people who have lived a long and blameless life are merely fortunate to have escaped many temptations? With each deed, how much pure moral content might have been in their mental disposition remains hidden even from themselves.

393

Therefore, this duty to estimate the worth of one's actions not merely according to their legality but also according to their morality (mental disposition) is also only of broad obligation. The law does not command this internal action in the human mind itself but merely the maxim of the action, namely, that one should strive according to every capacity so that in all actions in accordance with duty the thought of duty should of itself be a sufficient incentive.

2. THE HAPPINESS OF OTHERS AS AN END WHICH IS AT THE SAME TIME A DUTY

(a) Physical welfare. Benevolence can be unlimited, for nothing need be done about it. But the case is more difficult with beneficence, especially when it is not to be done from friendly inclination (love) toward others, but from duty and with the sacrifice and mortification of many an appetite. That beneficence is a duty results from the fact that since our self-love cannot be separated from our need to be loved by others (to obtain help from them in case of need), we therefore make ourselves an end for others; and this maxim can never be obligatory except by qualifying as a universal law and, consequently, through a will to make others our ends. Hence the happiness of others is an end which is at the same time a duty.

But while I should sacrifice a part of my welfare to others without any hope of recompense because it is my duty, yet it is impossible to set definite limits on how far this is to go. Much depends upon what the true need of each one would be according to his own feelings, and it must be left to each one to determine this need for himself. For to sacrifice one's own happiness, one's true needs, in order to promote the happiness of others would be a self-contradictory maxim if made a universal law. Therefore, this duty is only a broad one; it has a latitude within which we may do more or less without being able to assign definite limits to it. The law holds only for maxims, not for definite actions.

394   (b) The moral well-being (*salus moralis*) of others also belongs to the happiness of others, which it is our duty to promote; but this duty is only negative. The pain that a man feels from remorse of conscience, though its origin is moral, is nevertheless in its operation physical, like grief, fear, and every other diseased condition. To take care that he should not deservedly encounter this inward reproach is not indeed my duty, but is, rather, his business; but it is my duty to do

nothing which, according to human nature, might tempt him to do something for which his conscience might afterward torment him, i.e., it is my duty to give him no occasion for scandal. But there are no definite limits within which this care for the moral satisfaction of others must be kept; it therefore involves only a broad obligation.

IX. WHAT IS A DUTY OF VIRTUE?

Virtue is the strength of man's maxim in obeying his duty. All strength is known only by the obstacles it can overcome; and in the case of virtue the obstacles are the natural inclinations, which can come into conflict with moral purpose. And since it is man himself who puts these obstacles in the way of his maxims, virtue is not merely self-constraint (for that might be an effort of one inclination to constrain another), but is, moreover, a constraint according to a principle of internal freedom and, consequently, by the mere representation of his duty according to its formal law.

All duties contain the concept of constraint by law. And indeed ethical duties contain a constraint for which only an internal legislation is possible; juridical duties, on the other hand, contain one for which external legislation also is possible. Both, therefore, include the concept of constraint, either self-constraint or constraint by others. The moral power of self-constraint may be called virtue, and the action springing from such a disposition (respect for the law) may be called a virtuous (ethical) action, though the law expresses a juridical duty. For it is the doctrine of virtue that commands us to consider the rights of men as holy.

But what it is virtuous to do is not on that account properly a duty of virtue. The former can only concern the formal element of the maxims; the latter, however, concerns their matter, namely, an end which is at the same time conceived as a duty. But since the ethical obligation to ends (of which there are several) is only broad, inasmuch as it contains only a law 395 for the maxim of actions, and since the end is the matter (object) of choice, so there are many duties, differing according to the variety of lawful ends. These may be called duties of virtue (*officia honestatis*) just because they are subject only to free self-constraint, not to the constraint of other men, and because they determine an end which is at the same time a duty.

Virtue insofar as it is the agreement of the will with every duty (this agreement being grounded in a firm disposition of mind) is, like everything formal, merely one and the same. But with regard to the end of actions which is at the same time a duty, i.e., with regard to that (the material) which one ought to make an end, there can be several virtues; and since the obligation to the maxim of the end is called a duty of virtue, it follows that there are likewise several duties of virtue.

The supreme principle of the doctrine of virtue is this: "Act according to a maxim whose ends are such that there can be a universal law that everyone have these ends." According to this principle a man is an end to himself as well as to others. And it is not enough that he is not authorized to use either himself or others merely as means (this latter including also the case of his being indifferent to others), but rather, making mankind in general one's end is in itself a duty of every man.

Since this principle of the doctrine of virtue is a categorical imperative, it does not admit of a proof; but it does admit of a deduction [14] from pure practical reason. Whatever can be an end in man's relation to himself and to others is an end for pure practical reason, since this latter is a faculty of ends in general. For practical reason to be indifferent to ends, i.e., to take no interest in them, would be a contradiction; for then it would not determine the maxims of actions (and the actions always contain an end) and, consequently, would not be prac-

---

14 [*Deduktion*, usually translated as "deduction," but might be better translated as "justification." See *Critique of Pure Reason*, B 116 ff.]

tical reason. Pure reason, however, cannot a priori command any ends unless it declares these ends to be at the same time duties; such duties are then called duties of virtue.

X. THE SUPREME PRINCIPLE OF THE DOCTRINE OF RIGHT WAS ANALYTIC; THAT OF THE DOCTRINE OF VIRTUE IS SYNTHETIC

It is clear from the principle of contradiction that external constraint, insofar as it resists any hindrance to external freedom in conformity with universal law (i.e., insofar as it is a hindrance to the hindrance to external freedom), can be consistent with ends generally. I need not go beyond the concept of freedom to see this, be each man's end what he will. The supreme principle of right is therefore analytic.[15]

On the other hand, the principle of the doctrine of virtue goes beyond the concept of external freedom, and according to universal laws connects with that concept an end which this principle makes a duty. This principle of the doctrine of virtue is therefore synthetic.[16] Its possibility is contained in the deduction (Section IX above).

This extension of the concept of duty beyond the concept of external freedom and of such freedom's restriction by means of the merely formal condition of its thorough harmony puts internal freedom in place of constraint from without, this internal freedom being the power of self-constraint, not with the help of other inclinations but through pure practical reason (which scorns all such help). This extension consists in the following fact, which raises this internal freedom above juridical duty: internal freedom proposes ends from which right altogether abstracts. In the case of the moral imperative

[15] [The supreme principle of the doctrine of right is found in § C of the Introduction to *The Metaphysical Principles of Right:* "Act externally so that the free use of your choice can coexist with the freedom of any man according to a universal law."]

[16] [For Kant's distinction between analytic and synthetic judgments see *Critique of Pure Reason*, B 10 ff.]

and the supposition of freedom which this imperative necessarily involves, the law, the capacity (to fulfill the law), and the will determining the maxim make up all the elements which constitute the concept of juridical duty. But in the imperative which commands the duty of virtue there is added, besides the concept of self-constraint, that of an end. This is not an end that we have, but one that we ought to have, and hence one that pure practical reason has in itself. Pure practical reason's highest, unconditional end (which, however, is always a duty) consists in this, that virtue is its own end and, because of the merit which men accord it, is also its own reward. Herein virtue shines so brightly as an ideal that in human eyes it seems to overshadow even holiness itself, which is

397   never tempted to transgression.[17] This, however, is an illusion arising from the fact that since we have no measure for degrees of strength except the magnitude of the hindrances which could have been overcome (which are the inclinations within us), we are led to mistake the subjective conditions of estimating a magnitude for the objective conditions of the magnitude itself. But compared with human ends, all of which have hindrances to be combated, it is true that the worth of virtue itself, which is its own end, far outweighs the worth of all the utility and all the empirical ends and advantages which virtue may have as consequences.

One may indeed say that man is obligated to be virtuous (to have moral strength). For although the capacity (*facultas*) to overcome all opposing sensible impulses can and must be presupposed on behalf of freedom, yet this capacity as strength (*robur*) is something that must be acquired by upholding the

---

[17] So that one might vary two well-known verses of Haller thus:

> With all his failings man is still
> Better than angels void of will.

[The actual lines from Albrecht von Haller's poem, *Über den Ursprung des Übels* ("Concerning the Origin of Evil," 1734), are:

> For God loves no constraint; the world with its failings
> Is better than a host of angels void of will.]

moral incentive (the representation of the law) both through contemplating (*contemplatione*) the dignity of the pure law of reason within us and at the same time through exercise (*exercitio*) as well.

XI

398

According to the preceding principles, the scheme of the duties of virtue can be exhibited in the following way:

the material element of the duty of virtue

	1 my own end, which is at the same time my duty (my own perfection)	2 the end of others, whose promotion is at the same time my duty (the happiness of others)	
internal duty of virtue	3 the law, which is at the same time an incentive, on which the morality	4 the end, which is at the same time an incentive, on which the legality	external duty of virtue
	of every free determination of the will rests		

the formal element of the duty of virtue

XII. SENSITIVE BASIC CONCEPTS [18] OF THE SUSCEPTIBILITY OF THE MIND TO CONCEPTS OF DUTY GENERALLY

399

These are such moral qualities that, if one does not possess them, there can be no duty to acquire them. These are moral feeling, conscience, love of one's neighbor, and respect for oneself (self-esteem). There is no obligation to have these, because they are subjective conditions of susceptibility to the concept of duty and are not objective conditions of morality. They are

[18] [*Ästhetische Vorbegriffe*.]

all sensitive [*ästhetisch*] and antecedent but natural predispositions (*praedispositio*) of being affected by concepts of duty. Though it cannot be regarded as a duty to have these predispositions, yet every man has them, and it is by means of them that he can be obligated. The consciousness of them is not of empirical origin but can only follow upon the consciousness of a moral law—upon its effect on the mind.

A) MORAL FEELING

This is the susceptibility to pleasure or displeasure merely from the consciousness of the agreement or disagreement of our action with the law of duty. Every determination of choice proceeds from the representation of the possible action, through the feeling of pleasure or displeasure in taking an interest in the action or in its effect, to the deed; and here the sensitive condition (the affection of the internal sense) is either a pathological or a moral feeling. The former is that feeling which precedes the representation of the law; the latter is that which can only follow the representation of the law.

Now, there can be no duty to have a moral feeling or to acquire it; for all consciousness of obligation presupposes this feeling in order that the constraint which lies in the concept of duty may be known. Every man (as a moral being) has this feeling originally within himself; the obligation can only extend to cultivating it and even strengthening it through 400 wonder at its inscrutable origin. This cultivation comes about through seeing how just by the mere representation of reason this feeling is excited most strongly, in its purity and apart from every pathological stimulus.

It is not proper to call this feeling a moral sense, for by the word "sense" is generally understood a theoretical faculty of perception directed to an object; on the contrary, moral feeling (like pleasure or displeasure in general) is something merely subjective, which yields no knowledge. No man is devoid of all moral feeling; for if he were totally unsusceptible to this sensation, he would be morally dead. And if (to speak in the language of physicians) the moral vital force could no longer produce any effect on this feeling, then his humanity would be dissolved (as if by chemical laws) into mere animality, and would be irretrievably mixed with the mass of other natural beings. We have no special sense for (moral) good and evil any more than for truth, although such expressions are often used. However, we do have a susceptibility of free choice for being moved by pure practical reason (and its law), and it is this that we call moral feeling.

b) CONCERNING CONSCIENCE

Just so, conscience is not something to be acquired, and there is no duty to provide oneself with a conscience; but insofar as every man is a moral being, he has it originally within him. Being bound to have a conscience would be like having a duty to recognize duties. For conscience is practical reason, holding up before a man his duty for acquittal or condemnation in every case under a law. Hence conscience does not relate to an object, but only to the subject (affecting moral feeling by its own act), and thus it is not an obligation and duty, but an inevitable fact. Therefore, when it is said that this man has no conscience, this means he does not heed its dictates. For if he really had none, he would not impute to himself anything done in accordance with duty, nor reproach himself for anything done contrary to it; and thus he would not even be able to conceive of the duty of having a conscience.

I pass by the various divisions of conscience and only take note of a consequence of what has just been said, namely, that there is no such thing as an erring conscience. In the objective judgment of whether or not something is a duty, one can indeed sometimes be mistaken; but I cannot be mistaken in my subjective judgment as to whether I have compared something with my practical (here judicially acting) reason for the sake of such a judgment; for if I were mistaken in that,

401

I would then not have exercised practical judgment at all, and in that case there is neither truth nor error. Unconscientiousness is not lack of conscience but the propensity not to heed its judgment. But when a man is aware of having acted according to his conscience, then as far as guilt or innocence is concerned, nothing more can be demanded. He is only obligated to inform his understanding of what is or is not a duty. But when it comes, or has come, to a deed, then conscience speaks involuntarily and inevitably. To act conscientiously can, therefore, not itself be a duty, since otherwise it would be necessary to have a second conscience to be aware of the act of the first.

The duty here is only to cultivate our conscience, to sharpen our attention to the voice of this internal judge, and to use every means to get it a hearing; hence such a duty is only an indirect one.

c) CONCERNING THE LOVE OF MANKIND

Love is a matter of sensation, not of willing; and I cannot love because I would, still less because I should (being obligated to love). Hence a duty to love is nonexistent. But benevolence (*amor benevolentiae*), as a mode of action, can be subject to a law of duty. Disinterested benevolence toward men is often (though very improperly) called love; indeed, love is spoken of as being at the same time our duty even where the happiness of another is not concerned, but, rather, where the complete and free surrender of all one's ends to those of another (even superhuman) being is involved. But all duty is necessitation, a constraint, even though it might be self-constraint according to a law. And what one does from constraint does not come about from love.

402   It is our duty to benefit other men according to our capacity, whether we love them or not; and this duty loses nothing of its weight even though we must make the sad remark that our species, alas! when we know it more closely, is not such as to

be found particularly worthy of love. But hatred of mankind is always odious, even though, without any active hostility, it consists merely in complete withdrawal from mankind (solitary misanthropy). For benevolence remains always a duty, even benevolence toward the hater of mankind, whom we certainly cannot love, but to whom we can nevertheless render good.

To hate vice in men is neither a duty nor contrary to duty, but is merely a feeling of abhorrence, in which the will has no influence on the feeling nor the feeling on the will. Beneficence is a duty. Whoever often exercises this and sees his beneficent purpose succeed comes at last really to love him whom he has benefited. When therefore it is said, "Thou shalt love thy neighbor as thyself," this does not mean you should directly (at first) love and through this love (subsequently) benefit him; but rather, "Do good to your neighbor," and this beneficence will produce in you the love of mankind (as a readiness of inclination toward beneficence in general).

Complaisant love [*Liebe des Wohlgefallens*] (*amor complacentiae*) would alone be direct. But for this (as pleasure immediately connected with the representation of the existence of an object) to be a duty, i.e., being forced to find pleasure in a thing, is a contradiction.

d) CONCERNING RESPECT

Respect (*reverentia*) is likewise something merely subjective; it is a feeling of a special kind and not a judgment about an object which it would be a duty to bring about or to promote. For, if considered as a duty, this feeling could only be represented by means of the respect we have for it. To have a duty to this, therefore, would amount to being obligated to have a duty. Accordingly, it is improper to say that man has a duty of self-esteem; one ought rather to say that the law within him inevitably exacts respect for his own being, and this feeling (which is of a special kind) is the ground of certain duties, i.e., of certain actions consistent with his duty

403

to himself. Thus it cannot be said that he has a duty of self-respect, for he must have respect for the law within himself in order to be able to conceive duty at all.

XIII. UNIVERSAL PRINCIPLES OF THE METAPHYSICS OF MORALS IN THE TREATMENT OF A PURE DOCTRINE OF VIRTUE

First, a duty can have only a single ground of obligation. And if two or more proofs of the ground are adduced, then this is a sure sign that either no valid proof at all has yet been given or that there are several distinct duties which have been regarded as one.

For all moral proofs can as philosophical ones only be adduced by means of rational knowledge from concepts and not, as in mathematics, through the construction of concepts. Mathematics allows a plurality of proofs for one and the same proposition, because in a priori intuition there can be several determinations of the nature of an object all of which lead back to the very same ground. If one proof of the duty of veracity, for instance, were first drawn from the harm that a lie causes other men, and then another from the worthlessness of a liar and the violation of his self-respect, what would be proved in the first argument is a duty of benevolence and not a duty of veracity, that is to say, not the duty for which a proof was required, but another duty. But if in giving a plurality of proofs for one and the same proposition one consoles himself with the thought that the plurality of reasons will make up for the lack of weight in each taken separately, then this is a very unphilosophical expedient, which betrays artifice and dishonesty; for various insufficient reasons placed beside one another do not produce certainty, or even probability. They must advance as reason and consequence in a series up to the sufficient reason, and it is only in this way they can be demonstrative. Yet the former is the usual device of rhetoric.

404

Secondly, the difference between virtue and vice can never be sought in the degree of obedience to certain maxims, but must be sought only in the specific quality of the maxims (their relation to the law). In other words, the much-praised principle (of Aristotle [19]) that places virtue in the mean between two vices is false.[20] For instance, suppose that good management is given as the mean between two vices, prodigality and avarice. Then its origin as a virtue can neither be represented as the gradual diminution of the former vice (by saving) nor as the increase of expenditure by the avaricious; also, these vices cannot be viewed as if, proceeding as it were in opposite directions, they met together in good management. But each of them has its own maxim, which necessarily contradicts that of the other.

For the same reason, no vice can be defined as an excess in the exercise of certain actions beyond what is useful (e.g., *prodigalitas est excessus in consumendis opibus* [21]) or as a

[19] [Cf. Aristotle, *Nicomachean Ethics* II. 6 ff.]

[20] The usual classical linguistic formulas of ethics—*medio tutissimus ibis; omne nimium vertitur in vitium; est modus in rebus*, etc.; *medium tenuere beati; virtus est medium vitiorum et utrinque reductum**—contain a poor sort of wisdom which has no definite principles at all. This mean between two extremes, who will give it to me? Avarice (as a vice) is not distinguished from frugality (as a virtue) by being the latter pushed too far; but it has a quite different principle (maxim), namely, putting the end of economy not in the enjoyment of one's means but in the mere possession of them, enjoyment being renounced. Similarly, the vice of prodigality is not to be sought in the excessive enjoyment of one's means, but in the bad maxim which makes the use of them, without regard to their maintenance, the sole end. [Compare Kant's note here with his note 10 in § 10, "The Elements of Ethics," below, p. 95.]

* ["You will go safest by the mean"; "everything excessive is turned into vice"; "there is a measure in things," etc.; "happy people held to the mean"; "virtue is a mean between vices and equidistant from both extremes." These verses are to be found respectively in Ovid, *Metamorphoses* II. 137; source unknown; Horace, *Sermones* I. 1. 106 (for the full quotation see below, p. 95, n. 10†); source unknown; Horace, *Epistles* I. 18. 9.]

[21] ["Prodigality is an excess in the consumption of resources."]

deficiency in the exercise of certain actions short of what is fitting (e.g., *avaritia est defectus*, etc.[22]). For since the degree is not determined at all this way, and since the question whether or not conduct accords with duty turns entirely on this determination, such an account can be of no use as a definition.

Thirdly, ethical duties must not be estimated according to the capacity attributed to man of fulfilling the law; but, conversely, the moral capacity must be estimated according to the law, which commands categorically; therefore, ethical duties are estimated not according to the empirical knowledge that
405 we have of men as they are, but according to rational knowledge of how, in conformity with the idea of humanity, they ought to be. These three maxims of the scientific treatment of a doctrine of virtue are opposed to these older apothegms:

1. There is only one virtue and there is only one vice.
2. Virtue is the observance of the middle way between two opposite vices.
3. Virtue (like prudence) must be learned from experience.

XIV. CONCERNING VIRTUE IN GENERAL

Virtue signifies a moral strength of will. But this does not yet exhaust the concept, for such strength could also belong to a holy (superhuman) being, in whom no hindering impulse counteracts the law of his will, and who therefore gladly does everything in accordance with the law. Hence virtue is the moral strength of the will of a human being in obeying his duty; the constraint involved is moral through his own legislative reason, inasmuch as virtue constitutes itself an authority executing the law. Virtue is not itself a duty, nor is there a duty to possess it (for otherwise there would be an obligation to have a duty); but it commands and accompanies its command with a moral constraint (made possible by laws of inter-

22 ["Avarice is a deficiency in the consumption of resources."]

nal freedom). But since this constraint ought to be irresistible, strength is requisite; and the degree of this strength can be estimated only by the magnitude of the hindrances which man creates for himself through his inclinations. Vices, the brood of unlawful dispositions, are the monsters which he has to combat. For this reason moral strength as fortitude (*fortitudo moralis*) constitutes the greatest and only true martial glory of man; it is also called the true wisdom, namely, the practical, because it makes the ultimate end of the existence of man on earth its own end. In its possession alone is a man free, healthy, rich, a king, etc.; and he can suffer loss neither by chance nor by fate since he possesses himself and the virtuous man cannot lose his virtue.

All the encomiums which concern the ideal of humanity in its moral perfection can lose nothing of their practical reality by counter-examples of what men now are, have been, or will probably be hereafter. Anthropology, which proceeds from 406 mere empirical knowledge, cannot impair anthroponomy, which is erected by the unconditionally legislative reason. And although virtue can now and then be called meritorious (in relation to men, not to the law) and can be worthy of reward, yet in itself, since it is its own end, it must be regarded as its own reward.

Virtue in its whole perfection is therefore to be represented not as if man possessed virtue, but as if virtue possessed man, since in the former case it would look as if he still had an option (for which he would then require another virtue in order to select virtue from all other wares offered him). To conceive a plurality of virtues (as we unavoidably must) is nothing else but to conceive various moral objects to which the will is led by the single principle of virtue, and it is the same with the opposite vices. The expression which personifies both is a device for affecting sensibility; but this device, nevertheless, points to a moral sense. Therefore, an aesthetic of morals is not a part of, but a subjective presentation of the metaphysics of morals, whereby the feelings which accompany the constraining force of the moral law make the efficacy of that force perceptible (e.g., disgust, horror, etc., which make moral antipathy perceptible) in order to win pre-eminence over merely sensible incitement.

XV. CONCERNING THE PRINCIPLE ON WHICH THE DOCTRINE OF VIRTUE IS SEPARATED FROM THE DOCTRINE OF RIGHT

This separation, on which rests the main division of the doctrine of morals in general, is grounded on the fact that the concept of *freedom,* which is common to both, makes it necessary to divide duties into those of external and those of internal freedom; only the latter are ethical. Therefore, this internal freedom, which is the condition of every duty of virtue, must be put at the head as a preliminary part (*discursus praeliminaris*), just as above the doctrine of conscience was put at the head as the condition of all duty in general.

407

Remark
CONCERNING THE DOCTRINE OF VIRTUE ACCORDING TO THE PRINCIPLE OF INTERNAL FREEDOM

Skill [23] (*habitus*) is a facility of action and a subjective perfection of choice. But not every such facility is a free skill (*habitus libertatis*); for if the skill is habit [*Angewohnheit*] (*assuetudo*), i.e., a uniformity of action which by frequent repetition has become a necessity, then it is not a skill proceeding from freedom and accordingly is not a moral skill. Therefore, virtue cannot be defined as skill in free lawful actions, unless one adds "determining itself in its action by the representation of the law." And then this skill is not a property of choice but of will. The latter is the faculty of desire, which in adopting a

23 [*Fertigkeit*, which might also be rendered as "readiness."]

rule also declares it to be a universal law. Only such a skill of will can be counted as virtue.

Two things are required for internal freedom: to be master of oneself in a given case (*animus sui compos*), and to be lord over oneself (*imperium in semitipsum*), i.e., to subdue one's emotions and to govern one's passions. With these two conditions the character (*indoles*) is noble (*erecta*); in the opposite case, however, it is ignoble (*indoles abjecta, serva*).

XVI. VIRTUE REQUIRES, FIRST OF ALL, CONTROL OVER ONESELF

Emotions and passions are essentially distinct. Emotions belong to feeling, which, preceding reflection as it does, makes reflection more difficult or even impossible. Emotion is therefore called hasty or precipitate (*animus praeceps*), and reason declares through the concept of virtue that a man should collect himself; nevertheless, this weakness in the use of one's understanding, joined with the strength of the agitation, is only a lack of virtue [*Untugend*] and, as it were, something weak and childish. It may very well be consistent with the best will, and moreover has the one good point that its storm soon subsides. A propensity to emotion (e.g., anger) is therefore not so closely related to vice as passion is. Passion is the sensible appetite grown into a lasting inclination (e.g., hatred in contrast to anger). The calmness with which one indulges passion permits reflection and allows the mind to frame principles for it. And so when inclination falls upon something unlawful, the mind is allowed to brood over it, to root itself deeply in it, and is thereby allowed to take up what is bad (intentionally) into its maxim; this, then, is specifically bad, i.e., a true vice.

Therefore, insofar as virtue is based on internal freedom, it contains a positive command for man, namely, that he should bring all his capacities and inclinations under his authority (that of reason). And this is a positive precept of control over

408

himself; it is additional to the prohibition that man should not let himself be governed by his feelings and inclinations (the duty of apathy). For unless reason takes the reins of government in its own hands, feelings and inclinations play the master over man.

XVII. VIRTUE NECESSARILY PRESUPPOSES APATHY (CONSIDERED AS STRENGTH)

The word "apathy" has come into bad repute, just as if it meant lack of feeling and therefore subjective indifference regarding the objects of choice; it is taken for a weakness. This misinterpretation can be avoided by giving the name "moral apathy" to that lack of emotion which is to be distinguished from indifference. In moral apathy the feelings arising from sensible impressions lose their influence on moral feeling only because respect for the law is more powerful than all of these feelings together. Only the apparent strength of a

409 fever patient makes the lively sympathy with good rise to an emotion, or, rather, degenerate into it. This kind of emotion is called enthusiasm, and it is with reference to this that one is to explain the moderation usually recommended for the exercise of virtue (*insani sapiens nomen ferat, aequus iniqui, ultra quam satis est virtutem si petat ipsam.* Horace [24]); for otherwise it is absurd to suppose that a man can be too wise or too virtuous. Emotion always belongs to sensibility, no matter by what kind of object it may be excited. The true strength of virtue is the mind at rest, with a deliberate and firm resolution to bring its law into practice. That is the state of health in the moral life; emotion, on the contrary, even when it is aroused by the representation of the good, is a momentarily glittering appearance which leaves one languid. That man who will admit nothing to be morally indifferent (*adiaphora*)

[24] ["Let the wise man bear the name of fool and the just man that of a wicked one, if he pursue virtue itself beyond due bounds." *Epistles* I. 6. 15.]

and strews his steps with duties, as with traps, and will not allow it to be a matter of indifference whether one eats meat or fish, drinks beer or wine, when both agree with him—a micrology which, if adopted into the doctrine of virtue, would make its dominion a tyranny—that man can be called fantastically virtuous.

Remark

Virtue is always in progress and yet always begins at the beginning. The first follows from the fact that, objectively considered, virtue is an ideal and unattainable; but yet constantly to approximate it is nevertheless a duty. The second is founded subjectively upon the nature of man, which is affected by inclinations. Under the influence of these inclinations virtue, with its maxims adopted once for all, can never settle into a state of rest and inactivity; if it is not rising, it inevitably declines. This is so because moral maxims, unlike technical ones, cannot be based on habit (for basing a maxim on habit belongs to the physical nature of the determination of the will). But even if the *exercise* of moral maxims were to become a habit, the subject would thereby lose the freedom of adopting his maxims; this freedom, however, is the character of an action done from duty.

XVIII. BASIC CONCEPTS FOR THE DIVISION OF THE DOCTRINE OF VIRTUE 410

This principle of division must, first, as far as the formal element is concerned, contain all the conditions which serve to distinguish a part of the general doctrine of morals, by its specific form, from the doctrine of right. This comes about through the following: (1) duties of virtue are such that no external legislation can exist for them; (2) since every duty must be based on a law, this law in ethics can be a law of duty given, not for actions, but only for the maxims of actions; (3)

as follows from (2), ethical duty must be conceived as broad, not as strict duty.

Secondly, as far as the material element is concerned, the doctrine of virtue must be set up not merely as a doctrine of duties but also as a doctrine of ends, so that a man is bound to conceive himself as well as every other man as his end. One is accustomed to calling these obligations, respectively, the duties of self-love and of love of one's neighbor; but these expressions are not taken here in their proper meanings, for there can be no direct duty to love, but only to act so that one makes himself and other men his end.

Thirdly, with regard to the distinction of the formal element from the material element (the distinction of the legality from the finality) in the principle of duty, it must be noted that not every obligation of virtue [*Tugendverpflichtung*] (*obligatio ethica*) is a duty of virtue [*Tugendpflicht*] (*officium ethicum s. virtutis*). In other words, respect for the law in general does not yet establish an end which is at the same time a duty; and only such a duty is a duty of virtue. Therefore, there are many duties of virtue, but only one obligation of virtue. This is so because there are many objects that are ends for us, and it is at the same time our duty to have these ends; but there is only one virtuous disposition insofar as it is the subjective ground determining one to fulfill his duty, a disposition extending also to juridical duties, which hence cannot bear the name of duties of virtue. Therefore, any division of ethics will concern only duties of virtue. The science of the kind of obligation which has no reference to any possible external legislation is ethics itself, considered according to its formal principle.

411   *Remark*

How have I come, it will be asked, to the division of ethics into an elementology and a methodology, particularly since I could be excused from such a division in the doctrine of right? The reason is that the doctrine of virtue is concerned with broad duties, while the doctrine of right is concerned with nothing but strict duties. Hence the latter, which must by its nature determine strictly (precisely), is just as little in need of a general prescription (method) for proceeding in making a judgment as pure mathematics is; it confirms its method in its act. Ethics, on the other hand, because of the latitude which it allows for its imperfect duties, inevitably leads to questions which call upon the faculty of judgment to decide how a maxim is to be applied in particular cases, and in such a way that this faculty suggests in turn a (subordinate) maxim (concerning which one may again ask for a principle for applying this maxim to cases at hand). And so ethics gets into a casuistics, of which the doctrine of right knows nothing.

Casuistics is neither a science nor a part thereof; if it were, it would be a dogmatics. It is not so much a doctrine as to how something is to be found, as an exercise in how the truth is to be sought. Accordingly, it is interwoven fragmentarily and not systematically with ethics, i.e., it is added to the system like scholia.

On the other hand, it is not so much the exercise of judgment but much more that of reason (and indeed in the theory of its duties as well as in the exercise of them) that belongs in particular to ethics as a methodology of morally-practical reason. The method of its first exercise (in the theory of duties) is called didactics. Here the mode of teaching is either acroamatic or erotematic.[25] The latter is the art of asking the pupil what he already knows about concepts of duty, and this can be either the catechistic method or the method of Socratic dialogue. In the catechistic, the questioning proceeds merely from the pupil's memory because he has already been told about concepts of duty, while in the latter the teacher assumes

[25] [Kant derived *akroamatisch* and *erotematisch* from the Greek words, *akroaomai*, "listen to," and *eromai*, "ask."]

that the knowledge of concepts of duty is already contained naturally in the pupil's reason and that this knowledge only needs to be developed.

To didactics, as the method of the theoretic exercise of morally-practical reason, there corresponds ascetics as its practical counterpart. Ascetics is that part of the methodology in which there is taught not only the concept of virtue but also how the capacity for virtue, as well as the will for it, can be put into practice and cultivated.

412

According to these principles we shall therefore set up the system in two parts: the elements of ethics and the methodology of ethics. Each part will be separated into its main divisions; in the first part the main divisions will be according to the different subjects to whom man is obligated, and in the second part, according to both the difference of the ends which reason obligates him to have and the difference in his susceptibility to these ends.

XIX

The division which practical reason lays out for the foundation of a system of its concepts in an ethics (the architectonic division) can be made according to two different principles, singly or together. The one materially represents the subjective relation of the being who is obligated to the being who obligates; the other formally represents in a system the objective relation of ethical laws to duties in general. The first division is that of beings with regard to whom an ethical obligation can be thought. The second is that of the concepts of pure ethically-practical reason pertaining to the duties of those beings; these concepts are necessary for ethics only insofar as it is to be a science, i.e., they are necessary for the methodical composition of all the propositions which were discovered in the first division.

FIRST DIVISION OF ETHICS ACCORDING TO THE DIFFERENCE OF SUBJECTS AND THEIR LAWS

It contains

duties

of man to man	of man to beings which are not human

to himself	to other men	subhuman beings	superhuman beings

SECOND DIVISION OF ETHICS ACCORDING TO PRINCIPLES OF A SYSTEM OF PURE PRACTICAL REASON

Ethical

Elements	Methodology

Dogmatics	Casuistics	Didactics	Ascetics

This second division, since it concerns the form of the science, must therefore precede the first inasmuch as it is a plan for the whole science.

I

THE ELEMENTS OF ETHICS

Metaphysische Anfangsgründe

der

Tugendlehre

von

Immanuel Kant.

———

Königsberg,
bey Friedrich Nicolovius,
1797.

CONCERNING DUTIES TO ONESELF, GENERALLY CONSIDERED

⌘ *introduction* ⌘

§ 1. At First Glance the Concept of a Duty to Oneself Contains a Contradiction

If the "I" who obligates is taken in the same sense as the "I" who is obligated, then the concept of a duty to oneself is self-contradictory. The concept of duty contains the concept of a passive constraint (I am bound); but in a duty to myself I represent myself as binding and, therefore, as actively constraining (I, the very same subject, am the one binding). Thus a proposition expressing a duty to oneself (I ought to bind myself) would contain an obligation to be bound—a passive obligation which, nevertheless, would at the same time and in the same sense of the relation be an active obligation—and so, consequently, would contain a contradiction. This contradiction can also be brought to light by pointing out that the one who binds (*auctor obligationis* [1]) could always release the one bound (*subjectum obligationis* [2]) from the obligation (*terminus obligationis* [3]). Therefore, if both are one and the same subject, then he would not be bound at all by a duty he imposes on himself, and this involves a contradiction.

[1] ["The author of the obligation."]
[2] ["The subject of the obligation."]
[3] ["The terms of the obligation."]

§ 2. Nevertheless, There Are Duties Which Man Has to Himself

Suppose there were no such duties. Then there would be no duties at all, not even external ones. For I cannot recognize myself as bound to others except insofar as I bind myself at the same time: the law by virtue of which I regard myself as bound arises in all cases from my own practical reason, through which I am constrained while being at the same time the one who constrains.[4]

418

§ 3. Resolution of This Apparent Antinomy

Man regards himself, in his consciousness of a duty to himself, as being the subject of it in a double sense: first, as a sensible being [*Sinnenwesen*], i.e., as a man (belonging to one of the species of animals); but, then, also as an intelligence [*Vernunftwesen*] (not merely as a being possessing reason [*vernüftiges Wesen*], because reason in its theoretical function might also be a quality of a living corporeal being), which no sense perceives and which can be known only in those morally-practical relations through which the attribute of freedom, which we cannot understand, manifests itself in the influence of reason upon the internally legislative will.

Now, man, insofar as he is a natural being possessing reason (*homo phaenomenon* [5]), through his reason as cause is capable of being determined to action in the world of sense; and when he is so considered, the question of his obligation does not arise. But in regard to his personality, i.e., when he is considered as a being endowed with internal freedom (*homo noumenon* [6]), he is liable to obligation and, indeed, can be obli-

---

4 Thus, for instance, if a point of honor or of self-preservation is in question, we say, "I owe it to myself." Even when it is a question of duties of less significance, not concerning the necessity but only the merit of obeying my duties, we say, "I owe it to myself to broaden my aptitude for human society, and so on (to cultivate myself)."

5 ["Man as a phenomenon."]

6 ["Man as a noumenon."]

gated to himself (as to humanity in his own person). Accordingly, man (considered in this twofold sense) can acknowledge a duty to himself without falling into self-contradiction (because the concept of man is not thought of in only one sense).

§ 4. Concerning the Principle of the Division of the Duties to Oneself

The division can be made only with reference to the object of the duty, not with reference to the subject who obligates himself. The subject who is obligated, as well as the one who obligates, is always nothing but a man. And even though we are permitted for theoretic purposes to distinguish man's body from his soul as natural characteristics, still we are not allowed to think of them as distinct substances which obligate man in order that we may be warranted in making the division of duties to the body and duties to the soul. We are not adequately informed either by experience or by inferences of reason as to whether man has a soul (taken as a substance distinct from the body, which resides in him and enables him to think independently of the body, i.e., taken as a spiritual substance), and even less as to whether life may be a property of matter. But even if man has such a soul, still no duty of man to a body (taken as a subject obligating man) would be thinkable, even though it is the human body.

419

First, the duties to oneself therefore admit of only one objective division, *formal* and *material*. Formal duties are restrictive (negative duties); material duties are ampliative (positive duties to oneself). The former forbid man to act contrary to his natural *end* and, accordingly, involve nothing but his moral self-preservation; the latter bid him make as his end a certain object of choice, and such duties involve his perfection of himself. Both of these kinds of duties belong to virtue as duties of virtue, either as duties of omission (*sustine et abstine* [7]) or as duties of commission (*viribus concessis utere* [8]).

---

[7] ["Restrain and abstain."]
[8] ["Make use of permissible powers."]

The former appertain to the moral *health* (*ad esse* [9]) of man and have as their object the well-being of his external senses as well as of his internal sense in order that his nature in its perfection (as receptivity) may be preserved; the latter duties appertain to man's moral affluence (*ad melius esse, opulentia moralis* [10]), which consists in his having a capacity adequate for realizing all ends (as far as this is attainable), and belongs to the cultivation of himself (as an active perfection). The first principle of one's duty to himself lies in the saying, "Live in accordance with nature" (*naturae convenienter vive*), i.e., keep yourself in the perfection of your nature. The second principle is contained in the proposition, "Make yourself even more perfect than nature created you" (*perfice te ut finem; perfice te ut medium* [11]).

420   But, secondly, there is a subjective division of the duties of man to himself. According to this division the subject of the duty (man) regards himself either as at once an *animal* (physical) being and a moral being, or else *as a moral being only*.

Now, the impulses of man's animal nature are threefold: that through which nature aims at (*a*) the preservation of the individual himself, (*b*) the preservation of the species, and (*c*) the preservation of the capacity for the purposive use of his powers and of the capacity for the agreeable but, nevertheless, only animal enjoyment of life. The vices which here conflict with man's duty to himself are self-murder, the unnatural use which anyone makes of his sexual inclination, and the immoderate enjoyment of food and drink that weakens one's capacity to use his powers purposively.

Man's duty to himself insofar as he is a moral being alone (without reference to his animality) is formal, and consists in the conformity of the maxims of his will with the dignity of humanity in his person. Accordingly, such virtue consists in the prohibition against depriving himself of a moral being's excellence (this excellence consisting in acting according to

9 ["For the being."]
10 ["For a better being, moral opulence."]
11 ["Perfect yourself as an end; perfect yourself as a means."]

principles of internal freedom) by so surrendering himself to the play of mere inclinations as to make himself a thing. The vices opposed to this duty are *lying, avarice,* and *false humility* (servility). These vices take for themselves such principles as directly (according to their form) contradict the character of man as a moral being, i.e., the internal freedom, the innate dignity of man. This is as much as saying that these vices make it a principle for man to have no principle at all, and so, likewise, no character, i.e., that he throw himself away and make himself an object of contempt. The virtue which opposes all these vices could be called love of honor (*honestas interna, justum sui aestimium* [12]), which is a disposition completely different from ambition (*ambitio*) (which can also be very mean). This virtue, under the title of love of honor, will be especially prominent in the sequel.[13]

[12] ["Internal honor, proper estimation of oneself."]
[13] [See below, § 40, §42, pp. 129-31.]

First Part of the Elements of Ethics

CONCERNING PERFECT DUTIES TO ONESELF

first chapter
MAN'S DUTY TO HIMSELF INSOFAR AS HE IS AN ANIMAL BEING

§ 5

The first, though not the principal, duty of man to himself as an animal being is the preservation of himself in his animal nature.

The opposite of such self-preservation is the deliberate or intentional destruction of one's animal nature, and this destruction can be thought of as either total or partial. Total destruction is called suicide (*autochiria, suicidium*); partial can be subdivided into material, as when one deprives himself of certain integral parts (organs) by dismembering or by mutilating, and into formal, as when he deprives himself (forever or for a while) of the physical (and hence indirectly also the moral) use of his powers, i.e., self-stupefaction.

Since this chapter is concerned only with negative duties, i.e., duties of omission, the articles of duty must be directed against the vices which oppose duties one has to himself.

first article of the first chapter
CONCERNING SUICIDE

§ 6

The deliberate killing of oneself can be called *self-murder* (*homocidium dolosum* [1]) only when it can be shown that the

1 ["Deceptive murder."]

killing is really a crime committed either against one's own person, or against another person through one's own suicide (e.g., when a pregnant person kills herself).

Suicide is a crime (murder). To be sure, suicide can also be held to be a transgression of one's duty to other men, as, for instance, the transgression of the duty of one of a married couple to the other, of parents to children, of a subject to his government or to his fellow citizens, and, finally, of man to God by forsaking the station entrusted to him in this world without being recalled from it. However, we are here concerned with nothing but the violation of a duty to oneself, with whether, if I set aside all the aforementioned considerations concerning one's duty to other men, a man is still obligated to preserve his life simply because he is a person and must therefore recognize a duty to himself (and a strict one at that).

It seems absurd that a man can injure himself (*volenti non fit injuria* [2]). The Stoic therefore considered it a prerogative of his personality as a wise man to walk out of this life with an undisturbed mind whenever he liked (as out of a smoke-filled room), not because he was afflicted by actual or anticipated ills, but simply because he could make use of nothing more in this life. And yet this very courage, this strength of mind— of not fearing death and of knowing of something which man can prize more highly than his life—ought to have been an ever so much greater motive for him not to destroy himself, a being having such authoritative superiority over the strongest sensible incentives; consequently, it ought to have been a motive for him not to deprive himself of life.

Man cannot deprive himself of his personality so long as one speaks of duties, thus so long as he lives. That man ought to have the authorization to withdraw himself from all obligation, i.e., to be free to act as if no authorization at all were required for this withdrawal, involves a contradiction. To de-   **423** stroy the subject of morality in his own person is tantamount to obliterating from the world, as far as he can, the very ex-

[2] ["Injury cannot happen to him who wants to be injured."]

istence of morality itself; but morality is, nevertheless, an end in itself. Accordingly, to dispose of oneself as a mere means to some end of one's own liking is to degrade the humanity in one's person (*homo noumenon*), which, after all, was entrusted to man (*homo phaenomenon*) to preserve.

To deprive oneself of an integral part or organ (to mutilate oneself), e.g., to give away or sell a tooth so that it can be planted in the jawbone of another person, or to submit oneself to castration in order to gain an easier livelihood as a singer, and so on, belongs to partial self-murder. But this is not the case with the amputation of a dead organ, or one on the verge of mortification and thus harmful to life. Also, it cannot be reckoned a crime against one's own person to cut off something which is, to be sure, a part, but not an organ of the body, e.g., the hair, although selling one's hair for gain is not entirely free from blame.

CASUISTICAL QUESTIONS

Is it self-murder to plunge oneself into certain death (like Curtius) in order to save one's country? Or is martyrdom—the deliberate sacrifice of oneself for the good of mankind—also to be regarded, like the former case, as a heroic deed?

Is committing suicide permitted in anticipation of an unjust death sentence from one's superior? Even if the sovereign permitted such a suicide (as Nero permitted of Seneca)?

Can one attribute a criminal intention to a great, recently deceased monarch [3] because he carried a fast-acting poison with him, presumably so that if he was captured in war (which he always conducted personally), he might not be forced to submit to conditions of ransom which might be harmful to his country? (For he can be credited with such a purpose without one's being required to presume that he carried the poison out of mere arrogance.)

Bitten by a mad dog, a man already felt hydrophobia coming upon him. He declared that since he had never known any-

3 [Frederick the Great.]

body cured of it, he would destroy himself in order that, as he said in his testament, he might not in his madness (which he already felt gripping him) bring misfortune to other men too. The question is whether or not he did wrong.   424

Whoever decides to let himself be inoculated against smallpox risks his life on an uncertainty, although he does it to preserve his life. Accordingly, he is in a much more doubtful position with regard to the law of duty than is the mariner, who does not in the least create the storm to which he entrusts himself. Rather, the former invites an illness which puts him in the danger of death. Consequently, is smallpox inoculation allowed?

second article
CONCERNING WANTON SELF-ABUSE

§ 7

As one's love of life is intended by nature for the preservation of his person, so is his sexual love intended for the preservation of his kind, i.e., each is a natural end. By natural end is understood that connection of cause with effect in which the cause is thought of as if it brought about the effect intentionally, in analogy with an understanding, but without attributing understanding to the cause. Now, the question arises whether the use of one's sexual capacity, as far as the person himself who uses it is concerned, stands under a restrictive law of duty; or whether, not having the end of reproduction in view, he be authorized to devote the use of his sexual attributes to mere brute pleasure and not thereby be acting contrary to a duty to himself. In the doctrine of right it is shown that a man cannot make use of another person for the pleasure of sexual gratification without special restriction through a juridical contract by which two persons are mutually bound to one another in marriage. But here the question is whether, with regard to this gratification, a duty of man to himself prevails, the violation of which is an abuse (not merely a degradation) of the humanity in his own person. The drive to such

enjoyment is called carnal desire (also simply lust). The vice
which is thereby engendered is called lewdness; the virtue with
regard to this sensible impulse is called chastity, which is to be
represented here as a duty of man to himself. A lust is called
425   unnatural when a man is stimulated not by an actual object
but by imagining it, thus creating it himself unpurposively.
For his fancy engenders a desire contrary to an end of nature
and indeed contrary to an end more important even than that
of the love of life, since it aims only at preserving the individual, while sexual love aims at the preservation of the whole
species.

That such an unnatural use (and so misuse) of one's sexual
attributes is a violation of one's duty to himself and is certainly in the highest degree opposed to morality strikes everyone upon his thinking of it. Furthermore, the thought of it is
so revolting that even calling such a vice by its proper name is
considered a kind of immorality; such is not the case with
suicide, which no one hesitates to publish to all the world with
all its horrors (as a *species facti* [4]). It is just as if mankind in
general felt ashamed of being capable of such treatment of
one's own person, which degrades him even below the beast.
Even the allowed bodily union (in itself, to be sure, only animal union) of the two sexes in marriage occasions much deli-
cacy in polite circles, and requires a veil to be drawn over the
subject whenever it happens to be mentioned.

However, it is not so easy to produce a rational demonstra-
tion of the inadmissability of that unnatural use, and even of
the mere unpurposive use, of one's sexual attributes as being a
violation of one's duty to himself (and indeed in the highest
degree where the unnatural use is concerned). The ground of
proof surely lies in the fact that a man gives up his personality (throws it away) when he uses himself merely as a means
for the gratification of an animal drive. But this does not
make evident the high degree of violation of the humanity in
one's own person by the unnaturalness of such a vice, which
seems in its very form (disposition) to transcend even the vice

4 ["Kind of deed."]

of self-murder. The obstinate throwing away of one's life as a burden is at least not a weak surrender to animal pleasure, but requires courage; and where there is courage, there is always respect for the humanity in one's own person. On the other hand, when one abandons himself entirely to an animal inclination, he makes himself an object of unnatural gratification, i.e., a loathsome thing, and thus deprives himself of all self-respect.

CASUISTICAL QUESTIONS   426

The end of nature in the cohabitation of the sexes is propagation, i.e., the preservation of the race. This end may at least not be counteracted. Nevertheless, may exception be taken to this end, may this use be set aside (even if it happen in marriage)?

Are a married couple, for instance, allowed to make use of their sexual attributes during the wife's pregnancy, or when she is sterile (because of age or illness), or when she has no desire for sexual intercourse? Is it not contrary to the end of nature and so also contrary to one's duty to himself, just as with unnatural lust, to exercise one's sexual attributes in one or the other of these cases? Or is there here a permissive law of morally-practical reason which, in the conflict of its determining grounds, allows something that is in itself certainly unallowed in order to prevent some still greater transgression (as an indulgence)? At what point can one count the restriction of a broad obligation as Puritanism (a pedantry in observing duty that has to do with the extent of such observance)? At what point can one allow animal inclinations latitude, at the risk of forsaking the law of reason?

Sexual inclination is also called love (in the narrowest sense of the word), and is truly the greatest sensuous pleasure that can be taken in an object: it is not merely sensible pleasure taken in objects that please in the mere act of contemplating them (the susceptibility to this being called taste), but pleasure from the enjoyment of another person, which accordingly belongs to the faculty of desire and indeed to the highest degree of desire, namely, passion. But passion as love can be classed neither with complaisant love nor with benevolent love (for both of the latter draw up short of carnal gratification). Rather, it is a pleasure of a special kind (*sui generis*); and such ardor has properly nothing in common with moral love, although it can enter into close relationship with the latter if practical reason comes forward with its restrictive conditions.

427

◄ *third article* ►

CONCERNING SELF-STUPEFACTION THROUGH THE IMMODERATE USE OF FOOD AND DRINK

§ 8

The vice involved in this kind of immoderation is not here judged according to the harm, bodily pains, or even diseases, which man thereby brings upon himself. For then the principle involved would be one of well-being and comfort (consequently, of happiness) by which the harm should be counteracted. Such a principle can never be the basis for a duty, at least not for a direct duty, but only for a rule of prudence.

Animal immoderation in the enjoyment of food and drink is misuse of the means of nourishment; the capacity for the intelligent use of these means is weakened through such misuse. The vices under this heading are drunkenness and gluttony: when a man is drunk, he is simply like a beast, not to be treated as a human being; when he is gorged with food, he is temporarily incapacitated for activities which require adroitness and deliberation in the use of his powers. It is obvious that to put oneself in such a state is to violate a duty to oneself. The first of these debasements, which is even beneath the nature of an animal, is usually brought about by fermented liquors, but also by other stupefying agents such as opium and other products of the plant kingdom. These agents are misleading in that they produce for a while a dreamy euphoria and freedom from care, and even an imagined strength. But they are harmful in that afterwards depression and weakness follow and, worst of all, there results a need to take these stupefying agents again and even to increase the amount. Gluttony is even further beneath sensuous animal enjoyment in that it is occupied merely with sense as a passive condition, and not even with imagination, whereby at least an active play of representations takes place, as is the case in the aforementioned enjoyment of drunkenness. Therefore, in gluttony man more closely approximates animal enjoyment.

CASUISTICAL QUESTIONS   428

May one, if not as a panegyrist then at least as an apologist, allow wine to be used almost to the point of intoxication because it arouses a company to lively conversation and thereby unites it in frankness? Or can one even concede to wine the merit of promoting what Horace praises in Cato: *Virtus eius incaluit mero?* [5] But who can determine the measure for a man whose state no longer allows clear eyes for any measure, and who is ready to overstep it anyway? The use of opium and distilled spirits for enjoyment is closer to baseness than the use of wine because the former, with the dreamy euphoria they produce, make one taciturn, withdrawn, and uncommunicative. Therefore, they are permitted only as medicines. Mohammedanism, which completely prohibits the use of wine, has thus chosen very badly in permitting the use of opium instead.

A feast, though a formal invitation to excess in the enjoyment of both food and drink, nevertheless has beyond the mere physical luxury also a moral end in view, namely, to bring many people together for a long time in mutual communication. But inasmuch as the company (where it exceeds, as Chesterfield [6] says, the number of the muses) permits only a small exchange (with one's dinner partner), so the arrangement contradicts the aforementioned moral end. Thus, a feast is always a temptation to what is immoral, namely, immoderation and the transgression of one's duty to himself, to say nothing of the physical damage of overindulgence, which

[5] ["His virtue was warmed by wine." Horace, *Odes* III. 21. 11 ff.]
[6] [Philip Dormer Stanhope, fourth Earl of Chesterfield (1694-1773), English politician, statesman, and author. Actually the expression is to be found in Gellius, *Noctes Atticae* XIII. 11.]

might perhaps be relieved by a doctor. How far does moral authorization go in giving a hearing to these invitations to excess?

◄◙ second chapter ◙►
MAN'S DUTY TO HIMSELF CONSIDERED ONLY AS A MORAL BEING

This duty is opposed to the vices of lying, avarice, and false humility (servility).

429

I. Concerning Lying

§ 9

The greatest violation of man's duty to himself considered only as a moral being (the humanity in his person) is the opposite of veracity: lying (*aliud lingua promptum, aliud pectore inclusum genere* [7]). That no intentional untruth in the expression of one's thoughts can avoid this harsh name in ethics, which derives no authorization from harmlessness, is clear of itself (although in the doctrine of right it bore the name only when it violated another's right). For dishonor (to be an object of moral contempt), which goes with lying, accompanies also the liar, like his shadow. Lying can be either external (*mendacium externum*) or internal. By the former, man makes himself an object of contempt in the eyes of others; but by the latter, which is still worse, he makes himself contemptible in his own eyes and violates the dignity of humanity in his own person. The injury to other people which can arise from lying has nothing to do with this vice (for that would be merely a violation of one's duty to others) and so does not come into consideration here, nor does even the injury one brings upon himself; for then lying, insofar as it is merely a fault of prudence, would be contrary to the pragmatic maxim but not to the moral maxim, and so could not be regarded as a violation of duty at all. Lying is the throwing away and, as it were, the

---

[7]["When what the tongue utters is different from what is in the heart." Sallust, *The War with Cataline* 10. 5. See below, Supplement, pp. 162–166.]

obliteration of one's dignity as a human being. A man who does not himself believe what he says to another (even if it be only a person existing in idea) has even less worth than if he were a mere thing; for because of the thing's property of being useful, the other person can make some use of it, since it is a thing real and given. But to communicate one's thoughts to someone by words which (intentionally) contain the opposite of what one thinks is an end directly contrary to the natural purposiveness of his capacity to communicate his thoughts. In so doing, he renounces his personality and, as a liar, manifests himself as a mere deceptive appearance of a man, not as a true man. Veracity in one's statements is called honesty, and when these statements are at the same time promises, sincerity. But veracity in general is called uprightness.

Lying (in the ethical meaning of the word), as intentional 430 untruth in general, does not need to be harmful to others in order to be declared blameworthy, for then it would be a violation of the rights of others. Its cause may be mere levity or even good nature; indeed, even a really good end may be intended by lying. Yet to lie even for these reasons is through its mere form a crime of man against his own person and a baseness which must make a man contemptible in his own eyes.

The reality of many an *internal* lie, of which men may be guilty, is easy to set forth; yet to explain its possibility seems more difficult. Since a second person is required whom one intends to deceive, deceiving oneself deliberately seems in itself to contain a contradiction.

Man insofar as he is a moral being (*homo noumenon*) cannot use himself insofar as he is a physical being (*homo phaenomenon*) as a mere means (as a talking machine) not bound to an internal purpose (the communication of thought); but he is bound to the condition of being in accord with the declaration (*declaratio*) of the moral being, and is obligated to himself to be truthful. One lies when, for instance, he professes a belief in a future World Judge though he can really find no such belief within himself, but rather by so acknowledging in thought such a Searcher of Hearts, convinces himself that it can do no harm and may even be useful, in order at all events to insinuate himself into such a one's favor. Or if he is not in doubt about this, yet he may flatter himself for having inner reverence for His law, even though he feels no other incentive than fear of punishment.

Insincerity is simply want of conscientiousness, i.e., want of candor in confessing before one's internal judge, who is thought of as another person. For instance, strictly considered, insincerity is already involved when, out of self-love, a wish is taken as a deed because the wish has an essentially good end in view; and the internal lie, although it is contrary to man's duty to himself, receives here the name of a weakness, even as the wish of a lover to find nothing but good qualities in his beloved makes him oblivious to her obvious faults. However, this insincerity in one's declarations, practiced against oneself, deserves the strongest censure; for once the highest principle of veracity has been violated, from such a rotten spot (the falsity which seems to be rooted in human nature) the evil of untruthfulness spreads itself also into one's relationships with other men.

431

Remark

It is worth noting that the Bible dates the first crime, through which evil came into the world, not from Cain's fratricide (against which nature revolts) but rather from the first lie; and it names the original liar and the father of lies as the author of all evil. Reason can assign no further ground for man's propensity to hypocrisy (*esprit fourbe*), which must still have preceded lying, because an act of freedom, even though its effect is physical, or phenomenal, cannot be deduced or explained according to any natural law of connection of an effect with its cause, both of which are appearances.

CASUISTICAL QUESTIONS

Can an untruth from mere politeness (e.g., "your most obedient servant" at the end of a letter) be taken as lying? Nobody is deceived by it. An author asks one of his readers, "How do you like my work?" To be sure, the answer might be given in an illusory way inasmuch as one might jest concerning the captiousness of such a question. But who always has his wits about him? The slightest hesitation with the answer is already a mortification for the author. May one flatter him, then?

If I utter an untruth in actual business affairs, which come to questions of mine and thine, must I answer for all the consequences that might spring from it? For instance, a householder has instructed his servant that if a certain person should ask for him, the servant should deny knowing anything about him. The servant does this, but in doing so is the occasion of the master's slipping away and committing a great crime, which would otherwise have been prevented by the watchman who was sent out to take him. Upon whom (according to ethical principles) does the blame fall? To be sure, also upon the servant, who here violated a duty to himself by lying, the consequence of which will now be imputed to him by his own conscience.

II. Concerning Avarice   432

§ 10

I understand by this word not acquisitive avarice (the propensity to extend beyond the limits of true necessity one's acquisition of the means of living well), for this kind of avarice can also be regarded as a simple violation of one's duty (of beneficence) to others. But by avarice is here meant miserly avarice, which, when it is disgraceful, is also called stinginess or niggardliness. It is not thus called insofar as it consists in neglect of one's charitable duties to others, but rather insofar as one's restricting his own enjoyment of the means of living well to a point below the measure of his true need conflicts with his duty to himself.[8]

---

8 [In the first edition this sentence reads as follows: "Also, the word avarice does not here mean miserly avarice, which, when it is disgraceful, is called stinginess or niggardliness, but which may, nevertheless, involve nothing more than one's neglecting his charitable duties to others. But

By the censure of this vice, one can make clear in one instance the incorrectness of every explanation of virtues and also vices as being mere matters of *degree*, and at the same time one can set forth the uselessness of the Aristotelian principle that virtue consists of the middle way between two vices.

Thus, if I regard good management as the mean between prodigality and avarice and think of this mean as one of degree, then a vice would not pass over into its (*contrarie*) opposite vice without going through a virtue; and hence this virtue would be nothing but a diminished or, rather, vanishing vice. Accordingly, the consequence in the present case would be that making no use at all of the means of living well would be the real moral duty.

If a vice is to be distinguished from a virtue, then not the amount of exercise of moral maxims but, rather, the objective principle of them must be recognized and expounded as distinct. The maxim of prodigal avarice is to procure all the means of living well solely with a view to enjoyment. The maxim of miserly avarice, on the other hand, is to get as well as to keep all the means of living well, whereby one makes mere possession his end and deprives himself of the enjoyment.[9]

Thus, the characteristic mark of the latter vice is the principle of possessing the means to all kinds of ends, but with the proviso of not wanting to use any of them for oneself and so of robbing oneself of the agreeable enjoyment of life; such a thing is, with regard to its end, directly opposed to one's duty

433

---

the avarice which is really meant here is that involved in one's restricting his own enjoyment of the means of living well to a point below the measure of his own true need, and such avarice conflicts with one's duty to himself."]

[9] [In the first edition these last two sentences read as follows: "The maxim of acquisitive avarice (as in the case of a prodigal person) is to procure and keep all the means of living well with a view to enjoyment. The maxim of miserly avarice, on the other hand, is to get as well as to keep all the means of living well, but without the intention of enjoyment (i.e., without this intention, but only the possession, being the end)."]

to himself.[10] Prodigality and miserliness are thus distinguished from one another not by their degree, but specifically by their opposed maxims.

[10] The proposition that one should never do too much or do too little says nothing, for it is tautological. What is it to do too much? *Answer:* More than is good. What is it to do too little? *Answer:* To do less than is good. What is meant by I ought (to do something or to forbear doing something)? *Answer:* It is not good (contrary to duty) to do more or less than is good. If this is the wisdom we are to seek by returning to the ancients (Aristotle*) as being precisely those who were nearer the source of wisdom (*virtus consistit in medio; medium tenuere beati; est modus in rebus, sunt certi denique fines, quos ultra citraque nequit consistere rectum* †), then we have chosen badly to turn to their oracle. There is no mean between veracity and lying (as *contradictorie oppositis*); but perhaps there is a mean between frankness and reserve (as *contrarie oppositis*), as in the case of the man who so expresses his opinion that all he says is true, yet does not tell the whole truth. Now, it is quite natural to demand of the moralist that he point out this mean to me. But he cannot do this; for both duties of virtue have a latitude (*latitudinem*) of application, and what is to be done can only be determined by the faculty of judgment according to rules of prudence (pragmatic rules), not rules of ethics (moral rules), i.e., not as strict duty (*officium strictum*) but only as broad duty (*officium latum*). Therefore, he who obeys the principles of virtue, but in practice does so to a greater or lesser degree as prudence prescribes, can commit a fault (*peccatum*); but he does not practice a vice (*vitium*) insofar as he adheres strictly to these principles. Horace's verse, *Insani sapiens nomen ferat, aequus iniqui, ultra quam satis est virtutem si petat ipsam,*** is fundamentally wrong if taken literally. Perhaps *sapiens* here means only a sensible man (*prudens*) who has no fantastic conception of perfect virtue. Such perfection, as an ideal, demands approximation to it as an end, but not its full achievement, for that exceeds human powers and introduces nonsense (fantasy) into the principle of perfect virtue. For to be much too virtuous, i.e., to adhere too closely to one's duty, would be like making a circle much too round or a straight line much too straight. [Compare this note with note 20 in Section XIII of the "Introduction to the Doctrine of Virtue" above, p. 63.]

* [Cf. Aristotle, *Nicomachean Ethics* II. 6 ff.]

† ["Virtue consists in the mean"; "happy people held to the mean"; "there is a measure in things, there are definite limits this side of which, or beyond which, the good cannot lie." Sources for the first two verses are unknown. The last is in Horace, *Sermones* I. 1. 106.]

** ["Let the wise man bear the name of fool and the just man that of a wicked one, if he pursue virtue itself beyond due bounds." *Epistles* I. 6. 15.]

CASUISTICAL QUESTIONS

Since we are concerned only with one's duties to himself and since acquisitive avarice (insatiability in getting) as well as niggardliness (minute exactness in spending) both have selfishness (*solipsismus*) as their basis, and since both prodigality and miserliness seem to be blamable because they lead to poverty— in the former case unexpectedly while in the latter deliberately (by wanting to live poorly); so the question is whether both should be called vices and not, rather, mere imprudence, and consequently whether they might not lie completely outside the limits of one's duty to himself. Miserliness is not mere misunderstood thrift but is the slavish resignation of oneself to the goods of fortune, rather than the mastering of them. This is a violation of one's duty to himself. It is opposed to liberality (*liberalitas moralis*) of mind in general (not to generosity, *liberalitas sumtuosa*, which is only an application of the aforementioned liberality to a particular case); this is to say that miserliness is opposed to the principle of being independent of everything else except the moral law, and it is, accordingly, a fraud which the subject commits against himself. But what kind of law is that when the internal legislator himself does not know where to apply it? Should I stint myself on food or only on its outer display? In age or already in youth? Or is thrift in general a virtue?

III. Concerning Servility

§ 11

Man in the system of nature (*homo phaenomenon, animal rationale* [11]) is a being of little significance and, along with the other animals, considered as products of the earth, has an ordinary value (*pretium vulgare*). Even the fact that he excels these in having understanding and can set up ends for himself still gives him only an external value for his usefulness (*pretium usus*), namely, the value of a man in preference to an-

[11] ["Man as a phenomenon, rational animal."]

other animal. This is to say that he has a price as a commodity in the exchange of these animals as things, in which he still has a lower value than the general medium of exchange, money, whose value is therefore called distinctive (*pretium eminens*).

But man as a person, i.e., as the subject of a morally-practical reason, is exalted above all price. For as such a one (*homo noumenon* [12]) he is not to be valued merely as a means to the ends of other people, or even to his own ends, but is to be prized as an end in himself. This is to say, he possesses a dignity (an absolute inner worth) whereby he exacts the respect of all other rational beings in the world, can measure himself against each member of his species, and can esteem himself on a footing of equality with them.

The humanity in one's person is the object of the respect which he can require of every other human being, but which he also must not forfeit. Consequently, he can and should value himself by a measure at once both small and great, according to which he regards himself as a sensible being (according to his animal nature) or as an intelligible being (according to his moral predisposition). But since he must regard himself not merely as a person in general but also as a man, i.e., as a person having duties which his own reason has imposed upon him, his insignificance as a human animal cannot injure the consciousness of his dignity as a rational man. And he should not disavow the moral self-esteem of such a being, i.e., he should pursue his end (which in itself is a duty) neither cringingly nor servilely (*animo servili* [13]) as though seeking favor, nor should he deny his dignity; but, rather, he should always pursue his end with an awareness of the sublimity of his moral nature (and such awareness is already contained in the concept of virtue). This self-esteem is a duty of man to himself.

The consciousness and feeling of the insignificance of one's moral worth in comparison with the *law* is moral humility

[12] ["Man as a noumenon."]
[13] ["In a servile spirit."]

(*humilitas moralis*). Being persuaded of the magnitude of one's moral worth, but only through want of comparison with the law, can be called moral arrogance (*arrogantia moralis*). The renunciation of all claim to any moral worth whatever for oneself, in the conviction that one might thereby acquire a borrowed value, is morally false humility (*humilitas moralis spuria*), or spiritual servility.

Humility in comparing oneself with other men (and in general with any finite being, even a seraph) is not a duty at all. On the contrary, any endeavor to equal or surpass others in such humility with the persuasion of thereby acquiring for oneself an even greater inner worth is called pride (*ambitio*), which is directly opposed to one's duty to others. But the studied disparagement of one's own moral worth merely as a means to acquire the favor of someone else (whoever he might be) by hypocrisy and flattery [*Heuchelei und Schmeichelei*] [14] is false (counterfeit) humility; and as a degradation of one's personality, it is opposed to one's duty to himself.

True humility must inevitably follow upon our sincerely and exactly comparing ourselves with the moral law (its holiness and rigor). But from the fact that one is capable of such internal legislation and that the (physical) man feels himself compelled to venerate the (moral) man in his own person, there must also follow exaltation and the highest self-esteem. This is the feeling of one's inner worth (*valor*), according to which he is above all price (*pretium*) and possesses an inalienable dignity (*dignitas interna*), which inspires him with respect (*reverentia*) for himself.

§ 12

By the following precepts one can more or less make clear this duty regarding the dignity of the humanity in us and hence this duty to ourselves.

14 "To feign" [*heucheln*] (really "to exhale" [*häuchlen*]) seems to be derived from the groaning gasp [*Hauch*] that interrupts one's speech (sigh). On the other hand, "to flatter" [*Schmeicheln*] seems to stem from "bend" or "bow" [*Schmiegen*], and as a habit it is that of fawning [*Schmiegeln*]. Finally, it has been called by the High Germans *Schmeicheln*.

Do not become the vassals of men. Do not suffer your rights to be trampled underfoot by others with impunity. Incur no debts for which you cannot provide full security. Accept no favors which you might do without. Do not be parasites nor flatterers nor (what really differs from these only in degree) beggars. Therefore, be thrifty so that you may not become destitute. Complaining and whimpering, even merely crying out in bodily pain, are unworthy of you, and most of all when you are aware that you deserve pain. This accounts for the ennoblement (mitigation of disgrace) of a delinquent's death through the stoicism with which he dies. Kneeling down or groveling on the ground, even to express your reverence for heavenly things, is contrary to human dignity; as is also invoking heavenly things in actual images, for you then humble yourselves not to an ideal which your own reason sets before 437 you, but to an idol which is your own handiwork.

CASUISTICAL QUESTIONS

Is not man's feeling of the sublimity of his definition, i.e., his elevation of spirit (*elatio animi*) as self-esteem, so closely related to self-conceit (*arrogantia*), which is directly opposed to genuine humility (*humilitas moralis*), as to make it advisable to encourage that humility not merely in comparison with the law but even in comparison with other men? Or, rather, would not this kind of self-effacement cause other people to disdain our persons and so be contrary to our duty (of respect) to ourselves? Bowing or scraping before another seems in any case to be unworthy of a man.

Are not special manifestations of respect in words and manners, e.g., curtsies, bows, compliments, and courtly phrases designating distinctions of status with scrupulous punctilio (all of which are completely different from courtesy, which is necessary for mutual respect), even toward someone who does not hold public office, evidence of a widespread tendency to servility among men? There are the thou [*Du*], he [*Er*], you [*Ihr*], and you [*Sie*] or your right noble [*Ew. Wohledlen*], noble highness [*Hochedlen*], highborn nobility [*Hochedelge-*

borenen], wellborn [*Wohlgeborenen*] (*ohe, jam satis est!* [15]), used in the forms of address, which the Germans of all the people on earth (with the possible exception of the Indian castes) have developed to the utmost pedantry. (*Hae nugae in seria ducunt.*[16]) But whoever makes himself a worm cannot complain when he is then trampled underfoot.

first section of the second chapter

CONCERNING MAN'S DUTY TO HIMSELF INSOFAR AS HE IS THE INNATE JUDGE OF HIMSELF

§ 13

Every concept of duty contains objective constraint through the law (as moral imperative restricting our freedom) and belongs to the practical understanding, which gives the rule. However, the internal imputation of a deed, as a case standing under the law (*in meritum aut demeritum* [17]), belongs to the faculty of judgment (*judicium*), which, as the subjective principle of the imputation of the action, validly judges whether or not the action has taken place as a deed (as an action standing under law). Thereupon follows the conclusion of reason (the sentence), i.e., the connection of the lawful consequence with the action (the condemnation or acquittal). All of this takes place before a tribunal (*coram judicio*) called a court of justice (*forum*), as though before a moral person who gives effect to the law. The consciousness of an internal court of justice within man ("before which his thoughts either accuse or excuse one another" [18]) is *conscience*.

Every man has a conscience and finds himself observed by an internal judge, who threatens him and keeps him in awe (respect combined with fear). This authority watching over the laws within him is not something which he himself (arbi-

438

15 ["Oh, it's already enough!" Horace, *Satires* I. 5. 12 ff.]
16 ["These trifles lead to serious matters."]
17 ["According to merit or offense."]
18 [Romans 2:15.]

trarily) creates, but is incorporated in his being. If he tries to run away, his conscience follows him like his shadow. To be sure, he can stupefy himself with pleasures and diversions or can put himself to sleep; but he cannot avoid coming to himself now and then or waking up, at which time he immediately hears its awful voice. In his utmost depravity he can at most bring himself to the point where he no longer heeds it, but he cannot avoid hearing its voice.

This original intellectual and (as a representation of duty) moral predisposition called conscience has the peculiarity that though this whole matter is an affair of man with himself, man sees himself, nevertheless, compelled to conduct this affair as though at the bidding of another person. For the business here is the conduct of a lawsuit (*causa*) before a tribunal. But if the man accused by his conscience is represented as one and the same with the judge, then such a mode of representation is absurd in a court of justice; for in that event, the accuser would certainly lose every time. Therefore, as far as all man's duties are concerned, his conscience will have to suppose someone other than himself to be the judge of his actions, if his conscience is not to contradict itself. This other may be a real person or merely an ideal one which reason creates for itself.[19]

439

[19] This double self (on the one hand, having to stand trembling at the bar of a court of justice entrusted to one, but, on the other hand, possessing the judgeship by innate authority), this twofold personality in which the man who in his conscience accuses and judges himself must think of himself, requires an explanation, lest reason fall into contradiction with itself. I, the accuser and likewise the accused, am the very same man (*numero idem**). But man as subject of moral legislation proceeding from the concept of freedom, in which he is subject to a law he gives to himself (*homo noumenon*), is to be regarded as different from the sensible man endowed with reason (*specie diversus†*); but different only from a practical point of view, for there is no theory concerning the causal relation of the intelligible to the sensible. This specific difference is that of the faculties of man (the higher and the lower) which characterize him. A counsel (legal adviser) is granted the accused to defend him against the accuser. At the conclusion of the reports the internal judge, as a person with

* ["Same in number."]

† ["Different in species."]

Such an ideal person (the authorized judge of conscience) must be a searcher of hearts, for the court of justice is set up in our inmost selves. At the same time he must also be all-obligating: he must be, or be conceived as, a person in relation to whom all duties are to be regarded as commands by him, because conscience is the internal judge of all free actions. Now, since such a moral being must at the same time possess all authority (over heaven and earth), for otherwise he could not give proper effect to his laws (something which the office of judge necessarily requires), and since such a moral being possessing power over all is called *God*, so conscience must be conceived as the subjective principle of being accountable to God for one's deeds. Indeed, this concept of accountability is always contained (even if only in an obscure way) in every moral self-consciousness.

Now, this is not to say that by the idea to which his conscience inevitably leads him, man is entitled to suppose that such a supreme being actually exists outside himself; and even less, that man is bound by his conscience to assume such existence. For this idea is not given to him objectively by theoretical reason, but only subjectively by practical reason, which obligates itself to act in keeping with this idea. Man receives guidance from this idea only when, according to the analogy of a legislator for all rational beings, he represents conscientiousness (also called *religio*) as accountability to a holy being (who is given by morally legislative reason) distinct from him but, nevertheless, most intimately present to him, and he submits himself to this being's will as the rule of righteousness. The concept of religion is here for man only "a principle of judging all his duties as divine commands."

1. In a matter of conscience (*causa conscientiam tangens*), man supposes an admonitory (*praemonens*) conscience before

authority, makes his decision about happiness or misery, taken as moral consequences of the deed in question. We cannot further comprehend the power of the judge (as universal sovereign) with our reason, but can only respect his unconditioned *jubeo*** or *veto*.‡

** ["I command."]
‡ ["I forbid."]

his decision. When a concept of duty (something in itself moral) is involved in cases where conscience is the sole judge (*casibus conscientiae*), the utmost carefulness (*scrupulositas*) is not to be deemed hairsplitting (micrology), nor is a true transgression to be deemed a trifle (*peccatillum*) that is to be turned over to conscience for arbitration (according to the principle, *Minima non curat praetor* [20]). Therefore, to ascribe a broad conscience to someone is as much as to call him unconscientious.

2. When the deed is done, the accuser first of all enters the court of conscience; but at the same time a defender (advocate) enters along with him. Accordingly, the suit cannot come to a friendly settlement (*per amicabilem compositionem*) but must be decided according to the strictness of right. And hereupon follows,

3. The rightful sentence of conscience upon the man, whether to acquit or to condemn him; and this concludes the case. It is to be noted that the sentence can never decide upon a reward (*praemium*) as the gaining of something not there before; but the sentence may contain the joy of having escaped the danger of being found culpable. Therefore, satisfaction in the comforting encouragement of one's conscience is not positive (as enjoyment) but only negative (as relief following previous anxiety). Only this satisfaction can be attributed to virtue, insofar as virtue is a struggle against the influence of the evil principle in man.

second section   441
CONCERNING THE FOREMOST COMMAND OF ALL DUTIES TO ONESELF

§ 14

This command is the following: know (search, fathom) yourself, not for the sake of your physical perfection (fitness or unfitness for all kinds of ends whether of your own liking or

[20] ["The praetor does not bother with very small things."]

ordered of you), but for your moral perfection regarding your duty; test your heart—whether it be good or bad, whether the source of your actions be pure or impure, whether the source of your actions be such as can be imputed to yourself and belong to your moral condition, either as part of the original essence of man, or as something derivative (acquired or developed).

Moral self-knowledge, which tries to fathom the scarcely penetrable depths of the heart, is the beginning of all human wisdom. For this wisdom, which consists in the accord of one's will with his ultimate end, requires a man first and foremost to remove the internal hindrances (of a bad will seated within him), and then to try and develop his inalienable original predisposition of a good will. Only descent into the hell of self-knowledge prepares the way for godliness.

§ 15

This moral self-knowledge will, first of all, dispel fanatical contempt for oneself as a man or for the whole human species in general; for this contempt contradicts itself. Only through the magnificent predisposition within us toward good, which makes man worthy of respect, can it happen that one finds the man worthy of contempt who acts contrary to this predisposition, and also finds himself worthy of such if he acts contrary to it—a contempt which can, then, always fall only upon this or that man, but never upon humanity in general. This moral self-knowledge also opposes that egotistical self-esteem of holding mere wishes to be proofs of a good heart; for even though they may occur with ever so great yearning, they are and remain in themselves not deeds. (Prayer is also only an internal wish declared before a searcher of hearts.) Impartiality in judging oneself according to the law, and uprightness in confessing one's inner moral worth or lack thereof are duties to oneself; they follow immediately from the foremost command of self-knowledge.

442

◂ episodic section ▸

CONCERNING THE AMPHIBOLY OF THE MORAL CONCEPTS OF REFLECTION: TO REGARD WHAT IS A DUTY OF MAN TO HIMSELF OR TO OTHER MEN AS A DUTY TO OTHER BEINGS

§ 16

To judge by mere reason, man has no duties except to men (himself or others), for his duty to any subject at all is the moral constraint by his will. Accordingly, a subject who constrains (obligates) must, first, be a person; and he must, secondly, be given as an object of experience, because he is to influence the purpose of a man's will; and such an influence can occur only in the relationship of two existing beings (for a mere creation of thought cannot become the cause of any purposive achievement). Since in all our experience we are acquainted with no being which might be capable of obligation (active or passive) except man, man therefore can have no duty to any being other than man. And if he supposes that he has such another duty, then this happens through an amphiboly of the concepts of reflection; [21] and so his supposed duty to other beings is merely his duty to himself. He is led to this misunderstanding because he confuses his duty *regarding* other beings with a duty *toward* these beings.

Now, this supposed duty can be referred to nonpersonal objects or to objects which are personal but utterly imperceptible (not to be presented to the external senses). The former (subhuman) objects can be (1) mere physical matter, (2) that part of nature organized for reproduction but without sensation, or (3) that part of nature organized for reproduction and endowed with sensation and choice: (1) minerals, (2) plants, and (3) animals. The personal but imperceptible (superhuman) objects can be thought of as spiritual beings (angels, God). Whether or not there is a relation of duty between beings of

[21] [For Kant's meaning of an amphiboly of the concepts of reflection see *Critique of Pure Reason*, B 324 ff.]

either kind (subhuman or superhuman) and men, and what takes place between them will now be investigated.

§ 17

A propensity to the bare destruction (*spiritus destructionis*) of beautiful though lifeless things in nature is contrary to man's duty to himself. For such a propensity weakens or destroys that feeling in man which is indeed not of itself already moral, but which still does much to promote a state of sensibility favorable to morals, or at least to prepare for such a state—namely, pleasure in loving something without any intention of using it, e.g., finding a disinterested delight in beautiful crystallizations or in the indescribable beauty of the plant kingdom.

Even more intimately opposed to man's duty to himself is a savage and at the same time cruel treatment of that part of creation which is living, though lacking reason (animals). For thus is compassion for their suffering dulled in man, and thereby a natural predisposition very serviceable to morality in one's relations with other men is weakened and gradually obliterated. However, man is authorized to put animals to adroit and painless slaughter or to make them do hard work, as long as it is not beyond their strength (work such as men themselves often have to put up with). On the other hand, physical experiments involving excruciating pain for animals and conducted merely for the sake of speculative inquiry (when the end might also be achieved without such experiments) are to be abhorred. Even gratitude for the long-performed service of an old horse or dog (just as if they were members of the household) belongs indirectly to a man's duty, namely, his duty *regarding* these animals; but directly considered, such a duty is always only his duty *to* himself.

§ 18

We also have a duty regarding that which lies completely beyond the limits of our experience, but the possibility of which, nevertheless, is to be met with in our ideas, e.g., in our idea of God. This is called the duty of religion, namely, that "of recognizing all our duties as (*instar*) divine commands." But this is not the consciousness of a duty *to* God. For since this idea arises entirely out of our own reason and is made by us in order, from a theoretical standpoint, to explain the purposiveness of the universe, or, for practical purposes, to serve as an incentive in our conduct, we do not hereby have before us a given being *to* whom we are obligated; for the actuality of such a being would first have to be proved (disclosed) by experience. But it is a duty of man to himself to apply this idea, which offers itself unavoidably to reason, to the moral law within him; in such an application this idea is of the greatest moral fruitfulness. In this (*practical*) sense, to have religion can be asserted to be a duty of man to himself.

444

CONCERNING THE IMPERFECT DUTIES OF MAN TO HIMSELF (REGARDING HIS END)

first section
CONCERNING HIS DUTY TO HIMSELF TO DEVELOP AND INCREASE HIS NATURAL PERFECTION, THAT IS, FOR PRAGMATIC REASONS

§ 19

It is a duty of man to himself to cultivate his natural powers (of the spirit, of the mind, and of the body) as means to all kinds of possible ends. Man owes it to himself (an an intelligence) not to let his natural predispositions and capacities (which his reason can use some day) remain unused, and not to leave them, as it were, to rust. Let it even be supposed that he is satisfied with the inborn range of his capacities for meeting his natural needs. Nevertheless, it is his reason which, by means of principles, points out to him this satisfaction with the meager compass of his capacities; for he (as a being capable of having ends or of making objects ends for himself) must owe the use of his powers not merely to natural instinct, but also to the freedom with which he determines their scope. It 445 is thus not for the advantage which the cultivation of his capacity (for all kinds of ends) can provide that man should concern himself with such cultivation, even though, in view of the roughness of nature's requirements, this advantage would perhaps (according to Rousseau's principles) turn out to be profitable. But it is a command of morally-practical reason

108

and a duty of man to himself to build up his capacities (one more than another according to the variety of his ends), and to be a man fit (in a pragmatic sense) for the end of his existence.

Powers of the spirit are those whose exercise is possible only through reason. They are creative as far as their use is not obtained from experience but is derived a priori from principles. Such are mathematics, logic, and the metaphysics of nature. The latter two can also be counted as theoretical philosophy, which, to be sure, does not literally mean wisdom, but only science. However, philosophy can be favorable to the end of wisdom.

Powers of the mind are those which are at the disposal both of the understanding and of the rule which the understanding uses to satisfy purposes of its own liking, and in this they follow the lead of experience. Such are memory, imagination, and the like, upon which learnedness, taste (internal and external beautification), and so on can be established. These latter offer tools for many purposes.

Finally, the cultivation of the powers of the body (the true gymnastics) is care for that which constitutes the stuff (the matter) of man, without which the ends of man would remain unfulfilled. Consequently, the continual deliberate stimulation of the animal in man is a duty of man to himself.

§ 20

Which of these natural perfections may be preferable, and in what proportions, in comparison with one another, it may be man's duty to himself to make them his aim, are matters left to one's own rational reflection upon his desire for a certain mode of life, and his evaluation of the powers requisite for it. This reflection and evaluation are necessary in order to choose what his mode of life should be, e.g., a handicraft, commerce, or a learned profession. For apart from the necessity of self-preservation, which in itself can establish no duty, man owes it to himself to be a useful member of the world,   446 because being one belongs also to the worth of the humanity in his own person, which he should not degrade.

However, man's duty to himself regarding his physical perfection is only a broad and imperfect duty. This is so because such a duty contains, to be sure, a law for the maxim of actions, but determines nothing so far as the actions themselves are concerned—nothing as to their kind and degree. Rather, it allows a latitude for free choice.

✦ second section ✦
CONCERNING ONE'S DUTY TO HIMSELF TO HEIGHTEN HIS MORAL PERFECTION, THAT IS, FOR PURELY MORAL REASONS

§ 21

First of all, such perfection consists subjectively in the purity (*puritas moralis*) of one's disposition toward duty: when, without any admixture of aims taken from sensibility, the law is its own incentive, and one's actions occur not only in accordance with duty but also from duty. "Be holy" [22] is here the command. Secondly, such perfection consists objectively in doing one's full duty and in attaining the completeness of one's moral end regarding himself. "Be perfect!" [23] For man, striving for this goal is always only a progression from one stage of perfection to another. "If there is any virtue, if there is any praise, aspire to it." [24]

§ 22

This duty to oneself is in quality strict and perfect, though in degree it is broad and imperfect because of the frailty (*fragilitas*) of human nature.

Such perfection, which it is indeed a duty to strive after but not to attain (in this life)—the obedience to this duty consist-

22 [I Peter 1:16.]
23 [Matthew 5:48.]
24 [Philippians 4:8.]

ing thus only in a constant progression toward this perfection —is in reference to the object (the idea whose fulfillment one must make his end) a strict and perfect duty, but in reference to the subject, a broad and only imperfect duty to oneself.

The depths of the human heart are unfathomable. Who   447
knows himself well enough, when he feels an incentive for observing duty, to tell whether the incentive arises wholly from the representation of the law, or whether many other sensible impulses contribute to it? Such impulses aim at advantage (or aim at preventing disadvantage) and might well, on another occasion, also serve vice. But as for what concerns perfection as a moral end, there is indeed in idea (objectively) only one virtue (as moral strength of one's maxims); but in fact (subjectively) there is a multitude of virtues of heterogeneous qualities, among which, if one wanted to look for it, one might possibly discover some lack of virtue (although this would not bear the name of vice since it is in the company of many virtues). However, a sum of virtues, whose completeness or deficiency our self-knowledge never lets us adequately discern, can establish nothing but an imperfect duty to be perfect.

Thus, all the duties to oneself regarding the end of the humanity in one's own person are only imperfect duties.

CONCERNING ETHICAL DUTIES TO OTHERS

first chapter
CONCERNING DUTIES TO OTHER PEOPLE CONSIDERED SIMPLY AS MEN

first section
CONCERNING THE DUTY OF LOVE TOWARD OTHER MEN

DIVISION

§ 23

The main division can be that of duties to others in which one's performance at the same time obligates them, and duties whose observance does not entail the obligation of other people. The performance of the former duties is meritorious; that of the latter is owed. Love and respect are the feelings which accompany the exercise of these duties toward others. These feelings can be considered separately (each in itself), and they can also exist separately (love for one's neighbor, though he deserve little respect; also, necessary respect for any man, though he be judged hardly worthy of love). But they are basically, according to the law, always combined in one duty, although in such a way that sometimes the one duty and sometimes the other is the subject's principle, to which the other is joined as accessory. Thus we acknowledge ourselves obligated to be beneficent to a poor man. But this kindness also involves

112

a dependence of his welfare upon my generosity, which humiliates him. Therefore, it is a duty to spare the recipient such humiliation and to preserve his self-respect by treating this beneficence either as a mere debt that is owed him, or as a   449
small favor.

§ 24

When the laws of duty (not laws of nature) concerning the external relationships of men to one another are under consideration, we regard ourselves as being in a moral (intelligible) world in which, by analogy with the physical world, the association of rational beings (on earth) is effected through attraction and repulsion. According to the principle of *mutual love* they are directed constantly to approach one another; by the principle of *respect* which they owe one another they are directed to keep themselves at a distance. Should one of these great moral forces sink, "so then would nothingness (immorality) with gaping throat drink up the whole realm of (moral) beings like a drop of water," if I may here make use of Haller's words,[1] but in a different connection.

§ 25

Now, *love* is not understood here as feeling (sensitive [*ästhetisch*]), i.e., as pleasure in the perfection of other men, nor, accordingly, as complaisant love (for there can be no obligation to have feelings). Instead, love must be thought of practically, as the maxim of benevolence; and this maxim results in beneficence.

The same must be said about the *respect* to be shown others. By respect is understood not merely the feeling that arises when we compare our own worth with that of another (of the sort that a child feels toward his parents, a student toward his teacher, and in general, through mere habit, an inferior toward his superior), but, rather, it is to be understood as the maxim that limits our self-esteem by the dignity of humanity

---

[1] [Adapted from Albrecht von Haller's poem, *Über die Ewigkeit* ("Concerning Eternity," 1736).]

in another person; hence it is understood in the practical sense (*observantia aliis praestanda* [2]).

450

The duty of free respect to others, since it is actually only negative (not to exalt oneself above others) and is thus analogous to the juridical duty (not to encroach upon their rights), can, although it is merely a duty of virtue, be regarded as a strict duty in comparison with the broad duty to love one's fellow men.

The duty to love one's neighbor can also be expressed as the duty to make the ends of others (as long as they are not immoral) my own. The duty to respect one's neighbor is contained in the maxim, degrade no other man merely as a means to personal ends (do not require another person to throw himself away in order to pander to one's own ends).

When I exercise the duty of love toward someone, I at the same time obligate that person; I make myself deserve well from him. But when I observe the duty of respect, I obligate only myself and keep myself within my own bounds in order not to deprive another of any of the value which he as a human being is entitled to put upon himself.

CONCERNING THE DUTY OF LOVE IN PARTICULAR

§ 26

Since the love of mankind (philanthropy) is here thought of as practical and, consequently, not as complaisant love taken in men, it must be placed in active benevolence, and thus concerns the maxim of actions. He who finds satisfaction in the well-being (*salus*) of men insofar as he regards them only as human beings, and who takes pleasure when things go well with everyone, is called a friend of mankind in general (philanthropist). He who takes pleasure only when things go badly with other people is called an enemy of mankind (misanthrope in the practical sense). He who is indifferent to how things may go with other people if only they go well with himself is a self-seeker (*solipsista*). But he who shuns mankind because he can take no delight in human beings, though he wishes

2 ["Respect should be shown to others."]

them all well, would be shy of mankind (a sensitive [*ästhetisch*] misanthrope); and his withdrawal from men might be called anthropophobia.

§27

The maxim of benevolence (practical love of mankind) is a duty of all men toward one another. One may or may not find them worthy of love according to the ethical law of perfection: love thy neighbor as thyself. Every morally-practical relation 451 of men to one another is a relation of them in the representation of pure reason, i.e., of free actions according to maxims which are suitable for universal legislation and which thus cannot be selfish (*ex solipsismo prodeuntes* [3]). I want every other person to have benevolence (*benevolentiam*) for me; I should therefore be benevolent to every other person. But since every other person except me would not be everybody (and consequently the maxim would not have in itself the universality of a law, which universality is, however, necessary for an obligation), so the law of the duty of benevolence must comprise me also as an object of benevolence in the command of practical reason. But it is not as if I were thereby obligated to love myself (for such self-love occurs unavoidably, and so there is no obligation to it). Instead, legislative reason, which in its idea of humanity in general comprises me along with the whole race, also includes me, insofar as it is universally legislative, in the duty of mutual benevolence according to the principle of equality with all other men; and it permits me to be benevolent to myself under the condition that I also am benevolent to everyone else. This is because only in this way is my maxim (of beneficence) qualified for the universal legislation on which every law of duty is founded.

§28

Benevolence in the form of a general love of mankind is extensively, to be sure, the greatest possible benevolence, but intensively (in degree), the smallest possible. If I say that I

---

[3] ["Proceeding from selfishness."]

take an interest in the welfare of this man merely in accordance with the general love of mankind, the interest I take in him is the smallest that can be; to him I am merely not indifferent.

However, one person may be closer to me than another; and I am the one closest to myself as far as benevolence is concerned. Now, how does this accord with the formula, love thy neighbor (thy fellow man) as thyself? If one person is closer to me (in the duty of benevolence) than another, I am obligated to show greater benevolence to the one than to the other. But I am admittedly closer to myself (even according to duty) than to any other person. So it seems that I cannot say that I should love every man as I love myself without contradicting myself, for the measure of self-love would admit of no dif-
452 ference in degree. One soon sees that what is meant here is not mere well-wishing, which is, strictly speaking, a mere complaisant regard for the welfare of every other person without one's having to contribute anything to it (every man for himself, God for us all), but, rather, an active practical benevolence, which makes the welfare and happiness of others one's end (beneficence). For in the wishing, I may be benevolent to everyone alike; but nevertheless, in the doing, the degree may be very different according to the differences in the persons loved (of whom one may concern me more than another), without violating the universality of the maxim.

DIVISION OF THE DUTIES OF LOVE

They are the following: duties (a) of beneficence, (b) of gratitude, (c) of sympathy.

A. Concerning the Duty of Beneficence

§ 29

To do well by oneself, as far as necessary in order to find satisfaction simply in living (to take care of one's body, but not to the point of effeminacy), belongs among the duties to oneself. The opposite of this is from avarice (slavishly) to deprive oneself of the enjoyment of life's necessities, or from an exaggerated discipline of one's natural inclinations (fanatically) to take no pleasure in life's joys, both of which conflict with man's duty to himself.

But how can one, over and above our wishing other men well (which costs us nothing), further require that this benevolence become practical, i.e., how can one require as a duty that everyone who has the means show beneficence to those who are needy? Benevolence is the satisfaction one takes in the happiness (well-being) of others. But beneficence is the maxim to make the happiness of others an end for oneself, and the duty of beneficence involves the subject's being constrained by his reason to adopt this maxim as a universal law.

It is not obvious of itself that such a law lies generally in reason; rather, the maxim, "Every man for himself, God (destiny) for us all," seems far more natural.

§ 30

453

It is a duty of every man to be beneficent, i.e., to be helpful to men in need according to one's means, for the sake of their happiness and without hoping for anything thereby.

For every man who finds himself in need wishes that he might be helped by other men. But if he should make known his maxim of not wanting to give assistance in turn to others in their need—if he should make such a maxim a universal permissive law—then everyone would likewise refuse him assistance when he was in need, or at least everyone would be entitled to refuse. Thus the selfish maxim conflicts with itself when it is made a universal law, i.e., it is contrary to duty. Consequently, the altruistic maxim of beneficence toward those in need is a universal duty of men; this is so because they are to be regarded as fellow men, i.e., as needy rational beings, united by nature in one dwelling place for mutual aid.

§ 31

For a rich man (abundantly provided with the means for promoting the happiness of others, i.e., provided with means above and beyond his own needs), beneficence is hardly even to be held as his meritorious duty, though he does obligate the one he benefits. The satisfaction with which he thus provides himself, and which costs him no sacrifice, is a kind of reveling in moral feelings. Furthermore, he must carefully avoid any appearance of intending to obligate the other person, lest he not render a true benefit, inasmuch as by his act he expresses that he wants to lay an obligation upon the receiver (which always humbles the one obligated in his own eyes). Rather, the benefactor must express himself as being obligated or honored by the other's acceptance, treating the duty merely as a debt he owes, if he cannot (though it is better when he can) carry out his beneficence completely in secret. This virtue is greater when the means for beneficence are limited, and when the benefactor is strong enough to silently assume the burden which he spares the other; he then can truly be regarded as morally rich.

454   CASUISTICAL QUESTIONS

How far should one push the expenditure of his means in beneficence? Certainly not to the point where he would finally need the beneficence of others. How valuable is the benefit which one bestows impersonally (as when, in departing from this life, he leaves a will)? Can he who exercises a legal power over another deprive this other of freedom by acting according to his own option as to what will make this other person happy (a serf of his estate, for instance)? I say, can this man regard himself as a benefactor when he looks after such a person paternally, as it were, according to his own concepts of happiness? Or, rather, is not the unrighteousness of depriving someone of his freedom something so contrary to juridical duty in general, that to count upon the beneficence of one's master and to surrender oneself to it on such conditions would be the greatest throwing away of one's humanity? And, further, would not then the greatest care of the master for such a person be no beneficence at all? Or can the merit of such beneficence perhaps be so great that the rights of humanity might be outweighed by comparison with it? I can benefit no one (with the exception of minors and the mentally deranged) according to my own concepts of happiness, but only according to the concepts of him whom I think of benefiting; I actually do not benefit him when I urge a gift upon him.

The wherewithal for doing good, which depends upon the gifts of fortune, is for the most part a result of the patronage of various men owing to the injustice of government, which introduces an inequality of wealth that makes beneficence necessary. Under such circumstances, does the assistance which the rich render the needy deserve at all the name of beneficence, with which one so gladly plumes himself as merit?

B. CONCERNING THE DUTY OF GRATITUDE

Gratitude is honoring a person for a benefit rendered us. The feeling joined to this judgment is one of respect toward the benefactor who obligates us, whereas the benefactor is to be regarded as standing only in the relationship of love toward   455 the recipient. Since a merely heartfelt benevolence on the part of the benefactor, without physical results, deserves to be called a duty of virtue, this is then the ground of a distinction between active and merely affective gratitude.

§ 32

Gratitude is a duty. It is not merely a maxim of prudence by which I acknowledge my obligation for the beneficence someone has shown me in order to move him to greater beneficence (*gratiarum actio est ad plus dandum invitatio* [4]), thereby availing myself of this acknowledgement merely as a means to my further aims. But gratitude is an immediate constraint through the moral law, i.e., a duty.

Gratitude, moreover, must be regarded especially as a sacred duty, i.e., as a duty whose violation (serving as a scandalous example) can destroy the moral incentive for beneficence in its very principle. For a moral object is sacred when the obli-

[4] ["Thanking is an invitation for more giving."]

gation regarding it can never be wholly discharged by any act commensurate with it (and for this reason the one obligated always remains obligated). All else is ordinary duty. But a person can never, by any recompense, acquit himself of a benefit received, because the recipient can never wrest from the giver the priority of merit, namely, to have been the first in benevolence. But even without such an act (of beneficence), just the mere heartfelt benevolence is already a ground for the obligation to gratitude. A thankful sentiment of this kind is called gratefulness.

§ 33

Gratitude in its extensiveness involves not only contemporaries but also predecessors, even those whom one cannot name with certainty. For this reason it is considered improper not to defend so far as possible the ancients, who can be regarded as our teachers, against all attacks, accusations, and disrespect. But it is a foolish delusion to attribute to them on account of their antiquity a superiority over the moderns in talents and good will, just as if it were a law of nature that the world 456 should continually decline from its original perfection; and it is also a delusion to disdain everything new in comparison with the old.

Gratitude in its intensiveness, i.e., the degree of obligation to this virtue, is to be estimated according to the profit and advantage which the person obligated has derived from the benefit, and according to the disinterestedness with which it was bestowed. The least degree is to render equivalent services to the (still living) benefactor who is able to receive them, and if he is not, to render such services to others. However, a benefit received is not to be thought a burden, which one would rather be spared (because a person so favored stands a step lower than his patron, and this hurts one's pride), but is to be accepted as an occasion for a morally good deed, i.e., as an opportunity to combine this virtue of gratitude with that of philanthropy, which, along with the genuineness of the benevolent disposition, is at the same time the tenderness of benevolence (attention to the smallest degree of this disposition in the representation of duty), and thus is to be accepted as an opportunity to cultivate philanthropy.

C. Sympathetic Feeling in General Is a Duty

§ 34

Rejoicing with others and having pity for them (*sympathia moralis*) are, to be sure, sensible [*sinnlich*] feelings of a sensitive [*ästhetisch*] pleasure or displeasure taken in another's enjoyment or pain (compassion, sympathetic feeling), the susceptibility to which has already been placed in men by nature. But to make use of this susceptibility for furthering an active and rational benevolence is, in addition, a particular, though only conditional duty, which goes by the name of humanity, because here man is regarded not merely as a rational being but also as an animal endowed with reason. Now, this humanity may be seated in the capacity and will to share another's feelings (*humanitas practica* [5]), or merely in the susceptibility for mutual feelings of enjoyment or pain (*humanitas aesthetica* [sensitive humanity]), which nature herself provides. The first kind is free and is therefore called sympathetic (*communio sentiendi liberalis* [6]), and is based upon practical reason. The second kind is not free (*communio sentiendi illiberalis, servilis* [7]) and can be called communicable (like a susceptibility to heat or to contagious diseases); it is also called commiseration, because it spreads itself naturally among living men.[8] Obligation extends only to the first kind.

457

It was a sublime way of representing the wise man, as the Stoic conceived him, when he let the wise one say: I wish I

5 ["Practical humanity."]

6 ["Free communion of feeling."]

7 ["Communion of feeling that is not free."]

8 [Kant contrasts *Teilnehmung*, "sympathy," with *Mitleidenschaft*, "commiseration." The former is practical (active), while the latter is merely sensitive (passive).]

had a friend, not that he might give me help in poverty, sickness, captivity, and so on, but in order that I might stand by him and save a human being. But for all that, the very same wise man, when his friend is not to be saved, says to himself: What's it to me? i.e., he rejected commiseration.

Indeed, if another person suffers and I let myself (through my imagination) also become infected by his pain, which I still cannot remedy, then two people suffer, although the evil really (in nature) affects only the one. But it cannot possibly be a duty to increase the evils of the world or, therefore, to do good from pity; for this would be an insulting kind of beneficence, expressing the sort of benevolence one has for an unworthy person. Such benevolence is called softheartedness and should not occur at all among human beings, who are not to boast of their worthiness to be happy.

§ 35

But though it is not in itself a duty to feel pity and so likewise to rejoice with others, active sympathizing with their lot is a duty. To this end it accordingly is an indirect duty to cultivate our natural (sensitive) feelings for others, and to make use of them as so many means for sympathy based on moral principles and the feeling appropriate to them. Thus it is a duty not to avoid places where the poor, who lack the most necessary things, are to be found; instead, it is a duty to seek them out. It is a duty not to shun sickrooms or prisons and so on in order to avoid the pain of compassion, which one may not be able to resist. For this feeling, though painful, nevertheless is one of the impulses placed in us by nature for effecting what the representation of duty might not accomplish by itself.

CASUISTICAL QUESTIONS

Would it not be better for the world's welfare if all morality in human beings were restricted exclusively to juridical duties (but done with the greatest conscientiousness), and if benevolence were counted among things morally indifferent? It is not too easy to see what consequence such a thing might have for the happiness of human beings. But in such a case the world would, at all events, lack a great moral ornament, namely, the love of mankind. To represent the world as a beautiful moral whole in its complete perfection, this love of mankind is required for its own sake, without any advantages (of happiness) being counted upon.

Gratitude, strictly speaking, is not love of the obligated person for his benefactor, but is respect for him. For equality in duties can and must be the basis of universal love for one's neighbor, but in gratitude, the one obligated stands a step lower than his benefactor. Therefore, would not a cause of much ingratitude be a person's pride in not wanting to see anyone above him? Would there not be resentment in not being able to put oneself in complete equality (which concerns relations of duty) with one's benefactor?

CONCERNING THE VICES OF HATING MANKIND, WHICH ARE DIRECTLY OPPOSED TO LOVING MANKIND

§ 36

They make up the detestable family of envy, ingratitude, and malice. The hatred involved in these is not open and violent but secret and veiled, which adds meanness to one's unmindfulness of his duty to his neighbor, and in this way violates one's duty to himself as well.

(a) Envy (*livor*) is a propensity to view the welfare of others grudgingly, although their welfare does not damage one's own. When it breaks out in action (by impairing another's welfare), it is a special kind of envy; otherwise, it is simply jealousy (*invidentia*). Envy is only indirectly a vicious disposition, namely, vexation at seeing our own welfare overshadowed by another's, because we prize our welfare and make it tangible not according to its inner worth but only by comparing it with that of other people. For this reason one speaks of an 459 enviable harmony and happiness in a marriage or a family, and so on, just as if envying someone were allowed in many cases. Thus the agitations of envy lie in the nature of mankind, and only their eruption makes them into the abominable vice of a sullen passion that is self-tormenting and, at least in wish, destructive of the happiness of others. Therefore, this vice is opposed to a man's duty to himself as well as to his duty to others.

(b) When ingratitude to one's benefactor goes as far as hating him, it is called a special kind of ingratitude, but otherwise merely ungratefulness. Ingratitude is, to be sure, an extremely detestable vice in the public judgment, yet man is so notorious for it, that one thinks it not unlikely to make an enemy even by rendering a benefit. The basis for the possibility of such a vice lies in the misunderstood duty to oneself not to need or ask for the beneficence of others, because their beneficence puts one under an obligation to them—to bear the hardships of life oneself rather than bother others with one's difficulties and thereby become indebted (obligated) to them: all of this because one is afraid of being thought a dependent on a level below one's patron, something repugnant to genuine self-esteem (pride in the dignity of humanity in one's own person). Therefore, gratitude is freely shown to those who inevitably precede us in beneficence (to ancestors in remembrance, or to our elders), but only stingily shown to contemporaries. Yes, in order to make this relationship of inequality between the person benefited and his benefactor imperceptible, even the opposite of gratitude is shown. But this is a shocking vice, not merely because of the damage which such an example must generally cause men, scaring them away from further beneficence (for they can, with genuinely moral sentiment, only attribute that much more inner moral worth to their beneficence as they are refused all rewards of gratitude for it), but also because the love of mankind is here, as it were, stood upon its head, and the lack of love is even degraded to a license to hate one's lover.

(c) Malice, which is directly contrary to sympathy, is also
460   not foreign to human nature; when it goes as far as promot-

ing evil or wickedness itself, then as a special kind of malice it reveals a hatred of mankind, and appears in all its horrors. To feel one's well-being and even one's good conduct more strongly when another's misfortune or scandalous misstep sets off one's own condition in so much the brighter light is admittedly based on one of the natural laws of the imagination, namely, that of contrast. But to rejoice directly in the existence of such enormities as would destroy the general good of the world, and so to wish for such eventualities, bespeaks a secret hatred of mankind and is the direct opposite of loving one's neighbor, which is incumbent upon us as a duty. The arrogance of some people in uninterrupted prosperity and their self-conceit in their own good conduct (which, strictly speaking, is only their good luck in having so far evaded temptations to open vice), both of which the egotistical man credits to himself as merit, elicit this hostile satisfaction, which is directly opposed to our duty according to the principle of sympathy. This principle is shown in the maxim of the honest Chremes, as Terence has him say, "I am a man; everything which happens to mankind concerns me too." [9]

Of malice, the sweetest kind, which seems to have the greatest right—indeed, even obligation (as the desire for justice)—to aim at the harm of others without even looking to one's own advantage, is the desire for revenge.

Every deed which violates a man's rights deserves punishment, whereby the offense is avenged on the doer of the deed (and the wrong not merely redressed). Punishment, however, is not an act stemming from the private authority of the person wronged, but is an act of a court of justice distinct from him, which gives effect to the laws of a sovereign to whom all are subject. And when we regard men as being in a juridical situation (as is necessary in ethics), but only according to laws of reason (not civil laws), then no one has the authorization to inflict punishment and avenge a wrong suffered from men except him who is also the Supreme Moral Lawgiver. And this one alone (namely, God) can say, "Vengeance is mine; I

[9] [Terence, *The Self-Tormentor* I. 1. 25.]

will repay." [10] Thus it is a moral duty not only to refrain
from returning vengeful hatred for the hostility of others, but
even to refrain from summoning the Judge of the World to
vengeance. This is partly so because man is so saddled with
461   guilt of his own that he is much in need of pardon, but it is
especially so because no punishment, from whomever it might
be, may be inflicted in hate. Therefore, reconciliation (*placa-
bilitas*) is a duty of man, although it is not to be confused with
the weak toleration of wrongs (*ignava injuriarum patientia*)
which renounces stern (*rigorosa*) measures to forestall continued wrongs by others. For that would be to throw one's
rights at the feet of others and to violate man's duty to
himself.

Remark

All vices, which in themselves would make human nature hateful if they were taken (as qualified) in the sense
of principles, are, objectively regarded, inhuman, yet
human when they are subjectively considered, i.e., as experience acquaints us with our species. Although one
might in the impetuosity of abhorrence call some of them
devilish, just as their counterparts could be called angelic
virtues, nevertheless both concepts are only ideas of a
maximum, thought of as measures for comparing degrees
of morality, inasmuch as one assigns man his place in
either heaven or hell without making him an intermediate being occupying neither one nor the other. Whether
Haller may have hit it better with his "ambiguous hybrid
of angel and beast" [11] will be left undecided here. But
dichotomizing in a comparison of heterogeneous things
leads to no determinate concept at all, and the ordering
of beings according to distinguishing properties unknown
to us can do nothing to lead us to such a concept. The
first opposition (of angelic virtue and devilish vice) is exaggerated. The second, although men do, alas, fall into

[10] [Romans 12:19b.]

[11] [In his poem, *Über den Ursprung des Übels* ("Concerning the Origin
of Evil"), II, 107.]

bestial vices, no more warrants attributing to the species a predisposition to such vices than the deformation of some trees in a forest is a ground for making them a distinct kind of plant.

⚜ second section ⚜

CONCERNING THE MORAL DUTIES TO OTHER MEN ISSUING FROM THE RESPECT DUE THEM

§ 37

Moderation in claims generally, i.e., voluntary restriction of one's self-love in consideration of the self-love of others, is called modesty. The lack of this moderation (immodesty) regarding one's worthiness to be loved by others is egotism (*philautia*).[12] But immodesty in one's claims to be respected by others is self-conceit (*arrogantia*). The respect which I bear others or which another can claim from me (*observantia aliis praestanda* [13]) is the acknowledgment of the dignity (*dignitas*) of another man, i.e., a worth which has no price, no equivalent for which the object of valuation (*aestimii*) could be exchanged. Judging something to have no worth is contempt.

§ 38

Every man has a rightful claim of respect from his fellow men, and he is also bound to show respect to every other man in return.

Humanity itself is a dignity, for man can be used by no one (neither by others nor even by himself) merely as a means, but must always be used at the same time as an end. And precisely therein consists his dignity (personality), whereby he raises himself above all other beings in the world, which are not men and can, accordingly, be used—consequently, above

---

[12] ["Self-love" (*Selbstliebe*) as Kant uses the word does not have derogatory connotations. Compare § 27 and § 28 above, pp. 115 f. However, "egotism" (*Eigenliebe*) does.]

[13] ["Respect should be shown to others."]

all things. Even as he therefore cannot give himself away for a price (which would conflict with the duty of self-esteem), so can he likewise not act counter to the equally necessary self-esteem of others as men, i.e., he is bound to give practical acknowledgment to the dignity of humanity in every other man. Consequently, there rests upon him a duty regarding the respect which must necessarily be shown to every other man.

463

§ 39

To show contempt (*contemnere*) for others, i.e., to refuse them the respect which is owed man in general, is in all cases contrary to duty; they are, after all, men. To think but little (*despicatui habere*) of some people as compared to others is indeed sometimes unavoidable, but the external manifestation of such disregard is certainly an affront. Whatever is dangerous is no object of contempt, and therefore neither is the vicious. So if my superiority to the assaults of someone's vice justifies me in saying I contemn that person, it means only that no danger is involved, even though I might take no precautions against him, simply because he shows himself in his own depravity. Nevertheless, I cannot deny the vicious person all respect as a man; for though by his conduct he makes himself unworthy of it, it cannot be taken away from him, at least as far as his quality of being a man is concerned. So it is an outrage to inflict punishments that dishonor humanity itself (such as drawing and quartering, letting someone be torn to pieces by dogs, cutting off noses and ears). Such punishments are not only more grievous to one who loves honor (who claims the respect of others, as everyone must) than is the loss of life and possessions; they also make a spectator blush to belong to a race that can be treated in that way.

Remark

Hereupon is founded a duty to respect man even in the logical use of his reason: not to censure someone's errors under the name of absurdity, inept judgment, and the like, but rather to suppose that in such an inept judgment there must be something true, and to seek it out. In doing so, one should at the same time expose the deceptive semblance (the subjectivity of the grounds determining the judgment, which were held by mistake to be objective), and thus, while accounting for the possibility of error, preserve the mistaken individual's respect for his own understanding. For if a man uses such expressions to deny his opponent all understanding, how will he instruct the opponent that he has erred? Thus it is also with the reproach of vice, which must never burst out in complete contempt or deny the wrongdoer all moral worth, because on that hypothesis he could never be improved either—and this latter is incompatible with the idea of man, who as such (as a moral being) can never lose all predisposition to good.

464

§ 40

Respect for the law, which in its subjective aspect is referred to as moral feeling, is one and the same with the consciousness of one's duty. Therefore, showing respect for man insofar as he is a moral being (most highly esteeming his own duty) is also a duty which others have to him; and to be thus respected is a right to which he cannot renounce his claim. This claim is called love of honor, which manifests itself in outward behavior as respectability or decency (*honestas externa*). An offense against it is called scandal. To set an example of disrespect for decency, which might encourage imitations, is, to be sure, extremely contrary to duty. On the other hand, to take as a bad example what is merely contrary to common opinion (*paradoxon*), but otherwise good in itself, is foolish (since one holds what is not customary to be also not allowed). Such folly is pernicious and dangerous to virtue. For respect for others, which is owed them and which sets an example for men, cannot degenerate into a blind imitation (whereby custom, *mos,* is elevated to the dignity of a law), be-cause such a tyranny of popular manners would be contrary to the duty of man to himself.

§ 41

Omission of the bare duties of love is lack of virtue (*pecca-tum* [14]). But omission of the duty which proceeds from the re-spect due all men generally is a vice (*vitium*). For by neglect-ing the former, no man is wronged; but by omitting the latter, a man suffers injury with regard to his lawful claims. The former transgression is opposed to duty as its contrary (*contrarie oppositum virtutis*). But what not only is no moral ingredient but even cancels out the worth of what would otherwise benefit the subject is a vice.

Therefore, the duties to one's fellow man proceeding from the respect due him are expressed only negatively, i.e., this duty of virtue will be expressed only indirectly (by forbidding its opposite).

465

CONCERNING THE VICES VIOLATING THE DUTIES OF RESPECT FOR OTHER MEN

These vices are the following: (*a*) pride, (*b*) calumny, and (*c*) mockery.

A. PRIDE

§ 42

Pride [*Hochmut*] (*superbia* and, as this word expresses it, the inclination to swim always at the top) is a kind of ambi-tion (*ambitio*) according to which we demand that other men esteem themselves but little in comparison with us. Accord-ingly, pride is a vice which conflicts with the respect to which every man can make a lawful claim.

Pride is different from elevation of spirit (*animus elatus*), which, as a love of honor, is a concern to yield nothing of one's human dignity in comparison with other people (the

[14] ["Fault."]

latter is therefore usually joined with the adjective "noble");
for pride demands from others a respect which it denies them.
But elevation of spirit can itself become a fault and an offense
when it is simply a demand that other people occupy themselves with its importance.

Pride is, as it were, a solicitation of the ambitious person
for followers whom he believes himself entitled to treat con-
temptuously. That pride is unjust and is opposed to the respect owed mankind in general; that it is also folly, i.e., fri-
volity in the use of means for something which definitely has
no value as an end; yes, that it is even foolishness, i.e., an
offensive lack of understanding in using such means as must
produce in other people exactly the opposite of one's aim (for
the more a proud man tries to get the respect of others, the
more everyone refuses it to him)—all this is clear in itself. But
it might be less easily noticed that the proud man always, in   466
the depths of his soul, is mean. For he would not demand that
other people think little of themselves in comparison with
him did he not know that, were his luck to change, he would
not find it hard on his part to fawn upon others and give up
all claim to their respect.

B. Calumny

§ 43

Slander (*obtrectatio*), or calumny, by which I understand
not libel (*contumelia*), which is falsehood one is answerable
for to a court of law, but only the immediate inclination of
rumoring something prejudicial to the respect for others with
no particular purpose, is contrary to the respect owed humanity in general. For every given scandal weakens this respect
and makes it incredible; yet upon this respect depends the
impulse to what is morally good.

The intentional spreading (*propalatio*) of slurs upon the
repute of another, though it incurs no legal liability and the
slurs may even be true, so diminishes respect for humanity in
general that it casts the shadow of worthlessness upon our

species and makes misanthropy (unsociability) or contempt the prevailing way of thinking; or it dulls one's moral feeling through more frequent sight of such things, and thus inures one to them. It is therefore a moral duty that, instead of taking malicious pleasure in exposing the faults of others in order to assure oneself of being as good as, or at least not worse than, any other man, one should rather cast the veil of philanthropy over the faults of others, not merely by softening but also by silencing our judgments. Examples of respect shown to others may also incite in them an endeavor to deserve it. For this reason, a passion for spying on the morals of others (*allotrioepiscopia*) is plainly of itself an inquisitiveness offensive to the proper knowledge about mankind, and everyone may rightfully oppose it as a violation of the respect owed him.

467

C. MOCKERY

§ 44

Light-minded faultfinding and the propensity to expose other people to ridicule, or derision involved in making another person's faults the immediate object of one's amusement, is spite. It is entirely different from joking or making fun of apparent faults while in the intimacy of one's friends, for these are actually evidences of high spirit that sometimes overstep the rule of fashion (which is then not scoffing). But holding up to ridicule real faults or faults attributed as real with the intention of depriving a person of his deserved respect, and the propensity to do this, may be called bitter derision (*spiritus causticus*). It has something devilish in its enjoyment, and is therefore that much more a severe violation of the duty to respect other men.

To be distinguished from this is the jocular or even derisive retort (*retorsio jocosa*) to the insulting attacks of a contemptuous adversary, in which the jeerer (or, in general, a spiteful but impotent adversary) is in turn jeered down. This is a rightful defense of the respect one can demand from him.

But when the object is truly no joking matter but one in which reason necessarily takes a moral interest, then even though one's adversary may have been ever so derisive and may have given occasion for ever so much ridicule in return, it is more in keeping with the dignity of the object and with the respect due humanity to meet the attack either with no defense at all, or else with one conducted seriously and with dignity.

Remark

One will perceive that under the preceding title, virtues are not so much praised, as, rather, vices opposed to them are censured. But this is already implied by the concept of respect, which, as we are obligated to manifest it toward other men, is only a negative duty. I am not bound to venerate others (regarded merely as men), i.e., to show them positive reverence. The only respect which I am bound to by nature is that for the law generally (*reverere* 468 *legem*). And to obey this law with reference to other men, but not to venerate them generally (*reverentia adversus hominem*), nor to perform anything in the way of veneration toward them, is a universal and unconditional duty of man toward other men, which can be required of everyone as the respect originally owed to others (*observantia debita*).

The varieties of respect to be manifested toward other men according to the differences of their qualities or accidental circumstances, namely, of age, sex, birth, strength or weakness, or even of status and dignity (which depend in part upon arbitrary arrangements), cannot be set forth and classified in detail in *The Metaphysical Principles of Virtue*, since the concern here is only with the pure rational principles of respect.

◄® *second chapter* ®►

CONCERNING THE ETHICAL DUTIES OF MEN TO ONE ANOTHER WITH REGARD TO THEIR CONDITIONS

§ 45

In a system of pure ethics, these duties of virtue can indeed give no occasion for a separate chapter, for they do not contain principles obligating men to one another and thus cannot properly yield a part of *The Metaphysical Principles of Virtue.* They are only rules qualified according to the differences in the subjects to which the principle of virtue (which is formal) may be applied in cases issuing from experience (the material); and therefore they admit of no assuredly complete classification, as do no empirical divisions. Nevertheless, just as a "Transition from the Metaphysics of Nature to Physics," [15] having its own special rules, is required, so something similar is rightfully required of *The Metaphysics of Morals,* namely, applying pure principles of duty to cases of experience so as to schematize them, as it were, and to set them forth ready for morally-practical use. What conduct is proper toward men according to the moral purity or depravity of their conditions? What is proper in crude or in refined circumstances? What to the unlearned or to the learned? And if to the latter, then what is appropriate to them in the use of their knowledge as educated (polished) members of society or as specialists in their own fields (professional intellectuals)? And for the latter, again, what is fitting for those whose knowledge proceeds from technique or more from the spirit [*Geist*] and from taste? What conduct is suitable according to distinctions of status, age, sex, state of health, affluence or poverty, and so on? These considerations do not provide so many kinds of ethical obligation (for there is only one kind, namely,

15 [An unfinished work by Kant, part of the *Opus Postumum.*]

that of virtue in general), but only kinds of application (corollaries). They cannot, then, be set up as sections of ethics and as members of its systematic division (which must follow a priori from a concept of reason), but can only be appended to it. But even these applications belong to a complete presentation of the system.

◦ conclusion of the elements of ethics ◦
CONCERNING THE MOST INTIMATE UNION OF LOVE WITH RESPECT IN FRIENDSHIP

§ 46

Friendship (in its perfection) is the union of two persons through equal mutual love and respect. One easily sees that it is an ideal in which a morally good will unites both parties in sympathy and shared well-being. If it does not also cause life's entire happiness, the acceptance of this ideal in such mutual sentiment includes the worthiness to be happy, so that friendship among men is our duty. It is easy to see that although aiming at friendship, as a maximum of good sentiment toward one another, is no ordinary duty but rather an honorable one proposed by reason, yet perfect friendship is a mere idea (but still a practically necessary one), unattainable in every attempt to realize it.[16] For how is it possible to ascertain the equality of one of the requisite parts (e.g., mutual benevolence) of the very same duty as found in the one person's sentiments and in those of his neighbor? And even more, how can one discover the relation between the feeling for one duty and that for the other in the same person (e.g., the feeling of benevolence and that of respect)? And how can one discover whether, if the one person loves more ardently than the other, he does   470

16 [This sentence reads as follows in the first edition: "It is easy to see that friendship is a mere idea (but still a practically necessary one), unattainable, to be sure, in practice, but still to be striven for (as a maximum of good sentiment toward one another), and that friendship is no ordinary duty but an honorable one proposed by reason."]

not thereby lose something of the latter's respect, so that mutual love and esteem will be hard to bring into the subjectively symmetrical equilibrium which is, nevertheless, necessary for friendship? For love can be regarded as attracting and respect as repelling; and if the principle of the first bids an approach, that of the second demands that friends halt at a suitable distance from one another. This restriction of intimacy by the rule that even the best of friends should not become too familiar with one another contains a maxim which is valid not only for the superior in his relation to the inferior, but also vice versa. For the superior feels his pride injured before one realizes it and wants to see the respect of the inferior for him suspended for perhaps a moment, but not terminated; for once that respect is violated, it is irretrievably lost, even though its outward sign (ceremonial) is restored to its old ways.

Friendship thought of as attainable in its purity or completeness (between Orestes and Pylades, Theseus and Pirithoüs) is the hobbyhorse of the novelists. Against this, Aristotle says: My dear friends, there is no such thing as a friend! [17] The following remarks will call attention to the difficulties of such friendship.

Morally considered, it is certainly one's duty to point out a friend's faults to him, for this is to his best interests and thus is a duty of love. But the latter sees therein a lack of the respect which he expects; and he believes either that he has already fallen in the former's respect or, since he is watched by him and secretly criticized, that he is in constant danger of losing it. Or he even fancies that in being watched and supervised he has already been offended.

17 [Kant is probably referring to *Nicomachean Ethics* IX. 10 and 11, and *Eudemian Ethics* VII. 12, 1245b21, but his sentence is misleading. In fact, Aristotle, in discussing the mean in friendship, remarks that one who seems to have many friends is thought actually to have no real friend: having too many friends precludes the intimate sharing of true friendship.]

A friend in need—how much to be wished for (assuming that he is an active one, helpful at his own expense)! But it is also a great burden to feel oneself tied to the destiny of others and laden with alien responsibilities. Friendship, therefore, cannot be a bond aimed at mutual advantage, but must be purely moral; and the assistance which each may count on from the other in case of need must not be thought of as the end and determining ground of friendship (for thereby one person would partly lose the respect of the other), but only as the outward sign of their inner, heartfelt benevolence (without putting it to a test, which is always dangerous). Friendship is not based on advantage, for each friend is magnanimously concerned with sparing the other any burden, bearing any such burden entirely by himself, and, yes, even completely concealing it from the other; but each one, nevertheless, can always flatter himself with the idea that in case of need he could definitely count upon the other's help. But if one accepts a benefit from the other, then he can probably count on an equality in their love, but not in their respect; for he sees himself plainly as a step lower, inasmuch as he is obligated and yet not reciprocally able to obligate. Friendship, through the sweetness of the sensation arising from that mutual possession which approximates a fusion into one person, is at the same time something so tender (*teneritas amicitiae* [18]), that if it is left to rest upon feelings, and if this mutual communication and surrender are not underlaid with principles or with rules which prevent such mutual intimacy and limit such mutual love by demands of respect, then it is not for a moment secure against breaches. Such interruptions are usual among the uncultivated, although they never cause any termination of friendship (for common people fight with one another and yet they get on together [19]). Such people cannot part from one another, but likewise they cannot be at one, for the quarreling itself is necessary to them in order to taste the sweetness of

471

[18] ["Tenderness of friendship."]
[19] [*Denn Pöbel schlägt sich und Pöbel verträgt sich.*]

concord in reconciliation. But at all events the love in friendship cannot be emotion, because emotion is blind in its option
and evaporates in the sequel.

§ 47

Moral friendship (as distinguished from sensitive [*ästhetisch*] friendship) is the complete confidence of two persons in
the mutual openness of their private judgments and sensations, as far as such openness can subsist with mutual respect
for one another.

Man is a being intended for society (even though he is also
unsociable). In the cultivation of the social state he strongly
feels the need to open himself up to others (even without
thereby aiming at anything). But, on the other hand, he is also
constrained and admonished by his fear of the abuse which
others might make of this disclosure of his thoughts; and he
472   therefore sees himself compelled to lock up within himself a
good part of his judgments (particularly those concerning
other people). He might like to talk with someone about what
he thinks of the people with whom he associates, what he
thinks of the government, religion, and so on; but he must
not risk it because others, by cautiously holding back their
own judgment, might make use of his remarks to his own
detriment. He might also like to reveal to others his deficien-
cies and faults; but he must fear lest, if he presents himself
quite openheartedly, others conceal their shortcomings and
so make him lose their respect.

But if one finds a man of good disposition and understanding to whom he can open his heart with complete confidence,
without having to worry about such dangers, and moreover
with whom his opinions about things are in accord, then he
can give vent to his thoughts. Then he is not completely
alone with his thoughts, as if in prison, but enjoys a freedom
which he misses in the mass of men, among whom he must
keep himself to himself. Every man has his secrets and must
not blindly entrust himself to others, partly because of the

ignoble cast of most people's thinking, whereby they would use him to his disadvantage, and partly because many lack understanding in judging and in discriminating what bears repeating and what does not (indiscretion)—qualities that are seldom found together in one subject (*rara avis in terris, nigroque simillima cygno* [20]). The strictest friendship requires an understanding and trusted friend who considers himself bound not to share without express permission a secret entrusted to him with anyone else (though this other person be thought ever so reliable).

This (purely moral) friendship is no mere ideal, but (like the black swan) actually exists now and then in its perfection. On the other hand, that (pragmatic) friendship which burdens itself with the aims and purposes of other men (even though it does so from love) can have neither the purity nor the completeness requisite for an exactly determinant maxim; and so such friendship is but an ideal in wish. In its rational concept this ideal knows no bounds, but in experience it must necessarily always be very much restricted.

A friend of mankind in general (i.e., a friend of the entire race) is one who takes a sensitive [*ästhetisch*] interest (rejoicing) in the well-being of all men and will never disturb that well-being without inner regret. However, the expression "friend of mankind" has a somewhat stricter meaning than that of "philanthropist," which designates those who simply love mankind. For the former expression also contains the 473 representation of and the consideration for the equality of men, and hence the idea of one's being obligated to others at the same time as he obligates them through his beneficence— the idea of all men as brothers under one common father, who wants happiness for everyone. The relationship of a protector, as benefactor, to the person protected, and thus obligated to give thanks, is indeed a relationship of mutual love; but it is not one of friendship, because the respect owed by each to the other is not equal. The duty to be benevolent to men as their

[20] ["A rare bird on earth, very similar to a black swan." Juvenal, *Satires* II. 6. 165.]

friend (a necessary courtesy) and taking this duty to heart serve to guard against that pride which is wont to afflict those so fortunate as to possess the means of welldoing.

~✫ *supplement* ✫~
CONCERNING THE SOCIAL VIRTUES
(*virtutes homileticae*)

§ 48

It is one's duty both to himself and to others to use his moral perfections in social intercourse (*officium commercii, sociabilitas*) and not isolate himself (*separatistam agere*). To be sure, a person must make himself the immovable center of his principles; but nevertheless he must regard his sphere as part of an all-encompassing sphere of cosmopolitan sentiment, not so much in order to promote the good of the world as to cultivate the means that lead indirectly to it, namely, the agreeableness of society, sociability, mutual love and respect (affability and propriety, *humanitas aesthetica et decorum*). And so the Graces will accompany Virtue; it is even a duty to bring this about.

To be sure, these social graces are only externals or accessories (*parerga*), giving a comely virtuous appearance which deceives nobody, because everyone knows why he must assume it. They are small change indeed; but they do promote the moral feeling itself through the endeavor to bring appearance as near as possible to the truth, by the practice of accessibility, affability, courtesy, hospitality, mildness (in disagreeing without quarreling). All these, as mere modes of intercourse expressing obligations, at the same time obligate other people; and so they have an effect upon moral sentiment by making virtue something which is at least loved.

The question arises as to whether or not one is also permitted to associate with the wicked. One cannot avoid meeting them; to do otherwise one would have to leave the world. And even our judgment of them is not competent. But where

474

the vice is a scandal, i.e., a public display of contempt for a strict law of duty that, accordingly, carries infamy with it, one's existing association must be broken off or avoided as much as possible, even though the law of the land does not punish the offense. It must be broken off, since continued association with such a person deprives virtue of all honor, and puts it up for sale to anyone rich enough to corrupt a parasite with the pleasures of luxury.

II

THE METHODOLOGY OF ETHICS

THE DIDACTICS OF ETHICS

§ 49

The fact that virtue must be acquired (and is not innate) is contained already in the concept of virtue, and needs no appeal to anthropological information gleaned from experience. The moral capacity of man would not be virtue if it were not actualized by the strength of one's resolution in conflict with powerful opposing inclinations. Virtue is the product of pure practical reason insofar as the latter, in the consciousness of its superiority (through freedom), gains mastery over the inclinations.

That virtue can and must be taught follows from the fact that it is not innate; the philosophy of virtue [*Tugendlehre*] is thus a doctrine [*Doktrin*].[1] But because the power of exercising virtue's rules is not gained merely by instruction in how one should conduct himself to conform to the concept of virtue, the Stoics thought that virtue could not be taught by simple representations of duty or by exhortations, but that it must be cultivated and exercised by seeking to combat the internal foe within man (ascetically). For one cannot straightway do whatever he wills if he has not tried and exercised his powers beforehand. However, the determination to do what one wills must be embraced completely and all at once; other-

[1] [The word *Doktrin* is used here by Kant to denote a subject that is taught. *Lehre* also means "doctrine," and has usually been rendered thus in this translation; however, *Lehre* is roughly equivalent to "philosophy" and thus has a broader meaning than *Doktrin*. In § 49 and following, *Lehre* is rendered "philosophy" to distinguish it from *Doktrin*.]

wise that disposition (*animus*) which so capitulates to vice as to give it up gradually would be in itself impure and even vicious, and, consequently, could produce no virtue (since virtue is founded upon a single principle).

478

§ 50

Now, as for the method of this doctrine (and every scientific study must be methodical, else the treatment would be chaotic), it cannot be fragmentary but must be systematic, if the philosophy of virtue is to be represented as a science. The treatment can be either acroamatic, where all but the teacher are mere auditors, or erotematic, in which the teacher asks of his pupils what he wants to teach them.[2] This erotematic procedure in turn is either that of *dialogue,* in which the instructor seeks what he wants to teach in his pupils' reason, or that of *catechism,* which asks merely of the memory what is to be taught. For if anyone wants to ask something of another's reason, he can only do it through dialogue, i.e., teacher and student mutually questioning and answering one another. The teacher's questions direct his pupil's train of thought merely by developing the pupil's predisposition to grasp certain concepts through proposed cases (he is the midwife for his pupil's thoughts). The pupil, who thus becomes aware that he too is able to think, by his counterquestions (about obscurities or about his doubts that stand in the way of the propositions advanced) teaches his teacher how to question well; we learn by teaching (*docendo discimus*), as the saying goes. (For there is a demand made of logic—not yet sufficiently taken to heart—that it provide rules of inquiry appropriate to the aim of the inquirer, not always for determinant judgments only, but also for preparatory judgments (*judicia praevia*), by which a person is led to new thoughts. This is a subject which can indicate discoveries even to the mathematician and which is also often applied by him.)

2 [Kant derived these words from Greek: *akroamatisch* from the Greek *akroaomai,* "listen to," and *erotematisch* from *eromai,* "ask."]

§ 51

For the pupil who is still a novice, the first and most necessary doctrinal instrument of the philosophy of virtue is a moral catechism. This must precede the religious catechism, and cannot be expounded merely as an insertion interwoven with religious instruction, but must be separated as a selfsufficient whole; for the transition from the philosophy of virtue to religion can be made only through pure moral principles, since otherwise the avowals of religion would be impure. For that reason, even the greatest and most estimable theologians have hesitated to draw up and at the same time vouch for a catechism for statutory religious dogma, though one would think that the least he would be entitled to expect from the vast stores of their learning. 479

A moral catechism, on the other hand, as a fundamental doctrine [*Lehre*] of the duties of virtue, involves no such scruples or difficulty, because it can be developed (as far as its content is concerned) from common human reason and only needs to be adapted (formally) to the didactic rules of instruction. However, the formal principle of such instruction does not permit the use of the Socratic dialogue for this purpose because the student does not even know how he should put his questions; and so the teacher alone is the interrogator. But the answer which he methodically elicits from his pupil's reason must be drawn up and kept in definite terms that are not easily altered, so that it can be entrusted to the pupil's memory. In this way the catechistic method of teaching differs from the acroamatic method (where only the teacher speaks) and from the dialogistic (where both teacher and pupil question and answer one another).

§ 52

The experimental (technical) means for the cultivation of virtue is the good example of the teacher himself (his own conduct being exemplary) and the admonitory example of other people; for imitation is, for the still uncultivated man, the first determination of the will to accept maxims which he later makes for himself. Habituation is the establishment of a firm inclination by its more frequent gratification and without the use of any maxims; such habituation is a mechanism of sense rather than a principle of thought (whereby unlearning becomes subsequently more difficult than learning). But as for the power of an example (be it an example for good or bad) and what it offers for the propensity to imitate or be warned,[3] we must say that whatever others give us can be the foundation of no maxims of virtue. For these maxims consist just in the subjective autonomy of every man's practical reason; consequently the law, not the conduct of other men, must serve us as an incentive. The instructor therefore will not say to his bad pupil, "Take an example from that good (orderly, diligent) boy!" For that will only cause the pupil to hate the boy for putting himself in a prejudicial light. The good example (exemplary behavior) should not serve as a model but only as proof of the feasibility of what is in accordance with duty. Thus, it is not comparison with any other man (as he is) but with the idea of humanity (as he ought to be), and so with the law, which must supply the teacher with an infallible standard for education.

480

Remark

FRAGMENTS OF A MORAL CATECHISM

The teacher seeks in his pupil's reason what he wants to teach him; and if perhaps the student does not know

---

[3] "Instance" [*Beispiel*], a German word which one commonly uses for "example" [*Exempel*] as being equivalent to it, does not have the same meaning as "example." Taking an example and citing an instance in order to clarify an expression are completely different concepts. An example is a particular case of a practical rule insofar as this rule represents whether an action may be done or not. On the other hand, an instance is merely the particular (*concretum*) represented as contained according to concepts under the universal (*abstractum*), and is thus only a theoretical presentation of a concept.

the answer to the question, then (directing his student's reason) he suggests it to him.

1. Teacher: What is your greatest, yes, your whole desire in life?

Student: (remains silent).

Teacher: That everything should always go according to your wish and will.

2. What does one call such a condition?

Student: (remains silent).

Teacher: It is called happiness (constant well-being, a pleasant life, complete satisfaction with one's condition).

3. If you had all happiness (all that is possible in the world) in your possession, would you keep it all for yourself or share it with your fellow men?

Student: I would share it and make other people happy and contented also.

4. Teacher: That shows quite well that you have a good heart. But let us see if you have good understanding. Would you give the sluggard soft pillows to while away his life in sweet idleness? Or the drunkard wine and other 481 intoxicating spirits? Or the deceiver a charming appearance and captivating manners so as to dupe others? Or the violent person audacity and a hard fist so as to be able to overpower others? These are all so many means which each of these people wishes in order to be happy in his fashion.

Student: No, not that.

5. Teacher: So, you see, if you had all happiness at your disposal and the best will besides, you still would not, without reflection, bestow that happiness upon everyone who sought it, but would first inquire to what extent each person was worthy of happiness. But as for yourself, you would probably have no hesitation about first providing yourself with everything you reckon in your happiness?

Student: Yes.

Teacher: But does it not also occur to you to ask whether you yourself might be worthy of happiness?

Student: By all means.

Teacher: That something in you which strains after happiness is inclination. But that which restricts your inclination, on condition that you first be worthy of happiness, is your reason, and your being able by means of your reason to restrain and subdue your inclination is the freedom of your will.

6. The rule and direction for knowing how you go about sharing in happiness, without also becoming unworthy of it, lies entirely in your reason. This amounts to saying that you don't have to learn this rule of conduct by experience or from other people's instruction; your own reason teaches and even tells you what you have to do. For instance, if a situation presents itself in which you can get yourself or a friend a great advantage by an artfully thought out lie (and without hurting anybody else either), what does your reason say to that?

Student: I should not lie, though the advantage to me and my friend be as great as ever you please. Lying is mean and makes a man unworthy to be happy. Here is an unconditional constraint by a command (or prohibition) of reason, which I must obey. In the face of this, all my inclinations must be silent.

482   Teacher: What does one call this necessity, laid upon man directly by his reason, to act in accordance with its law?

Student: It is called duty.

Teacher: Accordingly, the observance of man's duty is the universal and sole condition of his worthiness to be happy; and these two are one and the same.

7. But if, besides, we are conscious of such a good and efficacious will, by which we think ourselves worthy (at least not unworthy) to be happy, can we make this the foundation of any secure hope of sharing in happiness?

Student: No, not upon that alone. For it is not always within our power to provide ourselves with it. Moreover, the course of nature does not adjust itself to our merit;

the fortunes of life (our welfare generally) depend upon circumstances which are far from being all within the power of man. Our happiness, therefore, remains always only a wish, which can never even become a hope unless some other power is added.

8. Teacher: Has reason its own grounds for assuming that there really is such a power that distributes happiness according to the merit and guilt of men, governs the whole of nature, and rules the world with supreme wisdom, i.e., for believing in God?

Student: Yes. For we see in those works of nature which we can judge of such extensive and profound wisdom that we cannot explain it to ourselves otherwise than as the inexpressibly great art of a Creator. From this Creator we also have cause to promise ourselves a no less wise regulation of the moral order, the supreme ornament of the world: a regulation, namely, that if we do not make ourselves unworthy of happiness by violating our duty, then we can hope to become partakers of it.

In this catechism, which ought to go through all the articles of virtue and vice, the greatest attention must be paid to the consideration that a command of duty is not founded upon the advantages or disadvantages of observing it, either for the man it ought to obligate or even for other people, but, rather, is founded quite purely upon moral principle. Any mention of advantages or disadvantages is only incidental, as a supplement that is dispensable in itself, but serves as a vehicle for the taste of those who are frail by nature. The ignominy of vice, not the 483 harmfulness of it (for the agent himself), must above all be strikingly represented. For if the dignity of virtue in action is not exalted above everything else, the very concept of duty disappears and dissolves into mere pragmatic prescriptions. Then the nobility of man in his own consciousness disappears, and he is for sale, to be bought at any price which tempting inclinations may offer him.

When these things have been wisely and accurately evolved from man's own reason according to the variety of the circumstances of age, sex, and rank which are encountered, then there is still something which must make the decision, which inwardly moves the soul and sets man in a position in which he cannot but regard himself with the greatest admiration for the original predisposition residing within him, the impression of which never fades away. When, at the conclusion of the student's instruction, his duties in their order are once more summarily enumerated (recapitulated) for him, when in each one of these duties he is made mindful of the fact that no evil, hardship, nor any of life's suffering, nor even threat of death—any or all of which might be inflicted upon him for remaining true to his duties—can rob him of his consciousness of being superior to such evils and being master of them, then the following question lies very close to him: What is that in you which may dare to do battle against all the forces of nature within you and round about you, and to conquer them when they come into conflict with your moral principles? When this question, whose solution completely transcends the power of speculative reason, but which nonetheless presents itself of its own accord, is taken to heart, then even the incomprehensibility of this self-knowledge must give the soul an exaltation which only animates it into more strongly holding its duty sacred the more it is assailed.

In this catechistic moral instruction it would be of the greatest advantage to moral education to present some casuistical questions with every analysis of a duty, and to let the assembled students test their understanding by having each one of them declare how he thinks the captious problem proposed to him might be solved. This is 484 so not only because such a procedure is a cultivation of the reason especially suited to the ability of a beginner (inasmuch as these questions, which concern what duty is, can be resolved far more easily than questions of speculation), and is, accordingly, the most appropriate kind of procedure for generally sharpening the understanding of the young; but this is especially so because it lies in the nature of man to love what he by his own work has brought to the condition of a science (whose outcome he now knows), and so the student by such exercises is drawn imperceptibly to serve the interest of morality.

But it is of the greatest importance in education not to intermix (amalgamate) the moral catechism with the religious catechism, still less to let it follow upon the latter, but always to bring the moral catechism to a state of the clearest insight and indeed with the greatest diligence and minuteness of detail. For otherwise nothing will come of religion later on but the hypocrisy of acknowledging one's duties from fear, and of feigning an interest in them which is not of the heart.

Second Section of the Methodology of Ethics

ETHICAL ASCETICS

§ 53

The rules for the exercise of virtue (*exercitiorum virtutis*) proceed from two frames of mind: a hardy spirit and a cheerful one (*animus strenuus et hilaris*), in obeying virtue's duties. For virtue not only has to combat obstacles whose overthrow requires the mustering of all one's forces, but also has to forgo many of the joys of life, whose loss can sometimes make the spirit gloomy and sullen. And what is done not with pleasure but as mere compulsory service has no inner worth for him who so responds to his duty. Such action is not loved; on the contrary, one thus involved avoids, as much as possible, occasions for practicing virtue.

The cultivation of virtue, i.e., moral ascetics, as far as the principle of the sturdy, spirited, and vigorous exercise of virtue is concerned, has the motto of the Stoics in view: Accustom yourself to bear the occasional misfortunes of life and to forbear its superfluous enjoyments (*assuesce incommodis et desuesce commoditatibus vitae*). This is a kind of dietetics for man, to keep him morally healthy. But health is only a negative kind of well-being; health itself cannot be felt. Something must be added which affords life agreeable enjoyment and is still simply moral. This something is the virtuous Epicurus' ideal of an ever joyful heart. For who should have more reason to be happy in spirit, even without finding it a duty to put himself in a cheerful state of mind and make it habitual, than he who is conscious of no intentional transgres-

485

sion and is secure against lapsing into it (*hic murus ahenëus esto,* etc. Horace [4])? Monkish ascetics, on the contrary, which from superstitious fear or hypocritical loathing of oneself goes to work with self-torture and mortification of the flesh, does not aim at virtue but at a fanatical purgation of sin by inflicting punishment upon oneself. Instead of morally repenting sins (i.e., with a view to improvement), such an ascetics wants to do penance for them through self-elected and self-inflicted punishment. But all of this is a contradiction, inasmuch as another person must always impose punishment. Moreover, such self-elected and self-inflicted punishment cannot engender the cheer that accompanies virtue and, even more, cannot take place without causing a secret hatred of virtue's commands. Ethical gymnastics consists only in such strife against the natural impulses as attains the magnitude of making us their master in circumstances threatening morality with danger; and so such gymnastics makes us hardy and cheerful in the consciousness of freedom regained. To repent of something (which is inevitable upon remembering former transgressions—and, what is more, it is a duty not to let this memory disappear) and to impose a penance upon oneself (e.g., fasting), not for dietetic but for pious reasons, are two very different moral precautions. The latter, which is joyless, gloomy, and sullen, makes virtue itself hateful and drives away its adherents. The discipline which man practices on himself can therefore become meritorious and exemplary only through the cheer which accompanies it.

4 ["Let this be our wall of bronze, to be conscious of no wrong, to pale under no transgression." Horace, *Epistles* I. 1. 60 ff.]

Conclusion

RELIGION AS A DOCTRINE OF DUTIES TO GOD LIES OUTSIDE THE LIMITS OF PURE MORAL PHILOSOPHY

Protagoras of Abdera began his book with the words, "Whether the gods are or are not, of this I know nothing to say." [5] The Athenians drove him off his land and out of the city for this, and his books were burned in the public assembly. (Quintilian, *Institutio Oratoria* III. 1.) [6] In this action, the judges of Athens certainly wronged him very much as men; but as government officials and judges they acted quite justly and consistently. For how could a man swear an oath unless it had been decreed publicly and legally on high authority (*de par le Sénat*) that there are gods? [7]

[5] *De diis, neque ut sint, neque ut non sint, habeo dicere.*

[6] [Natorp points out that the source is actually Cicero, *De Natura Deorum* I. 23. 63.]

[7] Of course later on a great and wise moral lawgiver completely forbade swearing as absurd and almost bordering on blasphemy. It is only in political matters that anyone still thinks this mechanical device, which is useful in the administration of public justice, is absolutely indispensable; and mitigating interpretations have been invented to evade the injunction against it. Although it would be absurd to swear in earnest that there is a God (because one must already have postulated the existence of God in order to be able to swear at all), the question still remains whether an oath may not be possible and valid, since one swears only upon the condition that there is a God (without making an issue of the thing, as Protagoras did). Indeed it may well be that all oaths taken sincerely and at the same time discreetly have been executed in no other sense. The fact that a person volunteers to swear simply that there is a

But granting this belief in God, and conceding the fact   487
that religion is an integral part of the general doctrine of
duties, there is now the question of determining the limits
of the science to which religion belongs. Must religion be considered a part of ethics (for there can be no question here of
the rights of men regarding one another), or must it be considered as lying completely outside the limits of a purely
philosophical ethics?

The formal aspect of all religion, expounded as the sum
total of all duties regarded as (*instar*) divine commands, belongs to philosophical ethics inasmuch as this aspect only expresses the relation of reason to the idea of God, which reason
makes for itself. A duty of religion is then not yet made into a
duty to (*erga*) God, taken as a being existing outside of our
idea, because we here abstract from such existence. That all
human duties should be conceived according to this formal
aspect (in which they are related to a divine will given a priori)
has only a subjectively logical basis. We cannot, of course,
make such obligation (moral necessitation) intuitable to ourselves without thinking of another being and his will (universally legislative reason is only this being's spokesman), namely,
God. But this duty regarding God (actually regarding the idea
we make of such a being) is a duty of man to himself, i.e., not
an objective one, as an obligation to render certain services to
another, but only subjective, for strengthening the moral incentive in our own legislative reason.

But as for the material aspect of religion, namely, the sum
total of duties to (*erga*) God, i.e., the worship to be rendered
him (*ad praestandum*), this aspect would contain particular
duties not proceeding from universally legislative reason alone,
and hence not knowable by us a priori but only empirically;

God seems, it is true, to be no dubious undertaking, be he a believer or
not. If there is a God (the deceiver will say), then I have hit it; if there is
no God, then nobody calls me to account and I bring myself into no
danger through such an oath. But is there then no danger involved, if
there is a God, in being caught in a deliberate lie planned to deceive even
Him?

and, accordingly, it could contain duties belonging as divine commands only to revealed religion. It could not, therefore, arbitrarily assume the existence of such a being or merely posit the idea of it for practical purposes, but would have to assert this existence as immediately or mediately given in experience. But such a religion, however it might be founded, would still constitute no part of pure philosophical ethics.

488 Religion, therefore, as a doctrine of duties to God, lies completely outside the limits of purely philosophical ethics; and this fact serves to justify the author of the present treatise in not having dragged religion in this sense into his ethics for the sake of completeness, even though that is customary.

To be sure, there can be a *Religion within the Limits of Reason Alone*.[8] But this is not derived from reason alone but is also based on truths of history and revelation, and contains only the agreement of pure practical reason with history and revelation (that they do not conflict with reason). Consequently, it is not pure religion but one applied to pre-existing history; and there is no place for such applied religion in ethics, insofar as ethics is pure practical philosophy.

CONCLUDING REMARK

All moral relations of rational beings containing a principle of the agreement of the will of one of them with the will of another can be reduced to love and respect; and, insofar as this principle is practical, the will's determining ground regarding love can be reduced to the other person's end, while the will's determining ground regarding respect can be reduced to the other person's right. If one of these beings (God) is such as to have nothing but rights and no duties regarding the other, and if, consequently, this other has only duties and no rights regarding the former, then the principle of the moral relation between them is transcendent. On the other hand, the moral relation of men

---

8 [*Religion innerhalb den Grenzen der bloßen Vernunft* first appeared in 1793. The second edition appeared in 1794.]

to men, whose wills mutually limit one another, has an immanent principle.

The divine purpose regarding the human race (the creation and guidance of man) cannot be conceived except as an end of love, i.e., God's aim is the happiness of mankind. But the principle of God's will regarding the respect (awe) owed him, i.e., the principle of divine right, which restricts the operations of divine love, can be none other than that of justice. One might say (in human terms) that God created rational beings as if it were from a need to have someone beside himself whom he could love, or by whom he could also be loved. But in the judgment of our own reason, the demand that divine justice (which is penal) makes upon us is not only just so great as, but even greater than this need of love (because the principle of such justice is restrictive). Reward (*praemium, remuneratio gratuita*) from the supreme being, however, cannot be derived at all from justice toward beings who have no rights and nothing but duties to him, but can be derived only from love and beneficence (*benignitas*). Still less can a claim for recompense (*merces*) be made of such a being; and a compensatory justice (*justitia brabeutica*) in the relation of God to man is a contradiction.

There is in the idea of the exercise of justice by a being who is superior to any injury that might be done to his ends something which cannot be reconciled with the relation of man to God; that something is the concept of a wrong which might be committed against the unlimited and inaccessible Ruler of the World. For there is here no question of juridical violations which men perpetrate against one another and upon which God, as penal judge, passes sentence; instead, the question here concerns the injury which is supposed to be done to God himself and to his right. The concept of such an injury is transcendent, i.e., it lies completely beyond any concept of penal justice for which we can supply an instance (as occurring among men), and it contains extravagant principles which cannot

489

at all be brought into accord with those principles we would use in cases within our experience and which are, consequently, for our practical reason entirely empty. The idea of a divine penal justice is here personified, but not as a particular judging being who exercises justice (for then contradictions with juridical principles would occur). Rather, justice is taken directly as substance (otherwise called eternal justice) which, like the fate (destiny) of the ancient philosophical poets, is even above Jupiter and pronounces what is right according to an iron, inflexible necessity that is for us inscrutable. Now for some instances of this justice.

(1) Punishment (according to Horace [9]) never lets the culprit, striding arrogantly before it, out of its sight, but ever hobbles after him until it catches him. (2) Blood innocently shed cries for revenge. (3) Crime cannot go unavenged; if punishment does not fall upon the culprit, then his posterity must pay for the crime. Or if punishment does not occur in his lifetime, then it must happen in a life after death,[10] and such a life after death is therefore explicitly assumed and gladly believed in so that the claim of eternal justice may be settled. (4) A right-thinking ruler once said that he did not want to let any bloodguilt come upon his country by pardoning a wicked murdering duelist for whom intercession was sought. (5) The price of sin must be paid, even should a completely guiltless

490

[9] [Horace, *Carmen Seculare* III. 2. 31 and 32.]

[10] The hypothesis of a future life may not even be mixed in here in order to represent the threatening punishment as complete in its fulfillment. For man, considered according to his morality, is not judged according to temporal conditions when he is judged as a supersensible object by a supersensible judge; the question is only about his existence. His earthly life, be it short, long, or even eternal, is only the existence of his earthly life as appearance; and the concept of justice needs no closer determination. For the belief in a future life does not, strictly speaking, come first in order that penal justice may be seen to have an effect upon that future life; but, conversely, the inference to a future life is drawn from the necessity for punishment.

man sacrifice himself in expiation (in which case surely the suffering he took upon himself could not properly be called punishment—for he himself has done no wrong). From this, one can see that this sentence is not attributed to any person administering justice (for such a sentence could not be pronounced without wronging other people), but rather that absolute justice, as a transcendent principle attributed to a supersensible subject, determines the right of this supersensible being to pass sentence. All of this, no doubt, is in keeping with the formal aspect of such a principle; but it conflicts with the material aspect of this principle, i.e., conflicts with the end, which is always the happiness of men. (6) In view of the eventual multitude of wrongdoers who let the register of their sins ever lengthen, it would seem that penal justice would not put the end of creation in the Creator's love (as one must think it is) but in the strict observance of the Creator's right (i.e., penal justice would make the right itself the end of creation, which is placed in the glory of God). But this, since justice is only the restrictive condition of God's goodness, seems to contradict the principles of practical 491 reason, according to which the creation of the world would have to have been foregone if it were to have yielded a product so contrary to the aim of the Creator (which can only have love as its ground).

One sees from this that in ethics, taken as the pure practical philosophy of internal legislation, only the moral relations of man to man are conceivable for us. But whatever passes for a relation between God and man completely transcends the bounds of ethics and is for us utterly inconceivable. And so, as was asserted above, ethics cannot extend itself beyond the limits of the duties of man to himself and to other men.

SUPPLEMENT

ON A SUPPOSED RIGHT TO LIE
BECAUSE OF PHILANTHROPIC CONCERNS[1]

In the periodical *France*[2] for 1797, Part VI, No. 1, page 123, in an article bearing the title "On Political Reactions"[3] by Benjamin Constant[4] there is contained on p. 123 the following passage:

"The moral principle stating that it is a duty to tell the truth would make any society impossible if that principle were taken singly and unconditionally. We have proof of this in the very direct consequences which a German philosopher has drawn from this principle. This philosopher goes as far as to assert that it would be a crime to tell a lie to a murderer who asked whether our friend who is being pursued by the murderer had taken refuge in our house."[5]

The French philosopher [Constant] on p. 124 [of the periodical *France*] refutes this [moral] principle in the following way:

"It is a duty to tell the truth. The concept of duty is inseparable from the concept of right. A duty is what in one man corresponds to the right of another. Where there are

1. [This essay appeared in September of 1799 in *Berlinische Blätter (Berlin Press)*, published by Biester. See H. J. Paton, "An Alleged Right to Lie" in *Kant-Studien* 45 (1953–54).]

2. [The periodical *Frankreich im Jahre 1797. Aus den Briefen deutscher Männer in Paris (France in the Year 1797. From Letters of German Men in Paris)*, published in Altona.]

3. [*Des réactions politiques* had appeared in May of 1796, and it was translated into German in this periodical *Frankreich*.]

4. [Henri Benjamin Constant de Rebecque (1767–1830), the renowned French statesman and writer.]

5. "J. D. Michaelis in Göttingen [Johann Daniel Michaelis (1717–91), professor of theology in the University of Göttingen] had propounded this unusual opinion even before Kant. But the author of this article [viz., Constant] has informed me that Kant is the philosopher referred to[6] in this passage."—K. F. Cramer. [Karl Friedrich Cramer (1752–1807), the editor of the periodical *Frankreich*, was formerly professor of Greek, oriental languages, and homiletics at Kiel until his dismissal in 1794 because of his open sympathy for the French Revolution, after which dismissal he became a book dealer in Paris.]

6. I hereby admit that this was actually said by me somewhere,[7] though I cannot now recollect the place.—I. Kant.

7. [Kant does say something similar in the "Casuistical Questions" appended to the article on "Lying" contained in the *Metaphysical Principles of the Doctrine of Virtue* (Part II of the *Metaphysics of Morals*). See the Royal Prussian Academy edition, Vol. VI, p. 431.]

no rights, there are no duties. To tell the truth is thus a duty, but is a duty only with regard to one who has a right to the truth. But no one has a right to a truth that harms others.''

The πρῶτον ψεῦδος⁸ here lies in the statement, ''To tell the truth is a duty, but is a duty only with regard to one who has a right to the truth.''

Firstly it must be noted that the expression ''to have a right to truth'' is mean- 426 ingless. One must say, rather, that man has a right to his own truthfulness (*veracitas*), i.e., to subjective truth in his own person. For to have objectively a right to truth would be the same as to say that it is a matter of one's will (as in cases of *mine* and *thine* generally) whether a given statement is to be true or false; this would produce an unusual logic.

Now, the first question is whether a man (in cases where he cannot avoid answering Yea or Nay) has the warrant (right) to be untruthful. The second question is whether he is not actually bound to be untruthful in a certain statement which he is unjustly compelled to make in order to prevent a threatening misdeed against himself or someone else.

Truthfulness in statements that cannot be avoided is the formal duty of man to everyone,⁹ however great the disadvantage that may arise therefrom for him or for any other. And even though by telling an untruth I do no wrong to him who unjustly compels me to make a statement, yet by this falsification, which as such can be called a lie (though not in a juridical sense), I do wrong to duty in general in a most essential point. That is, as far as in me lies I bring it about that statements (declarations) in general find no credence, and hence also that all rights based on contracts¹³ become void and lose their force, and this is a wrong done to mankind in general.

Hence a lie defined merely as an intentionally untruthful declaration to another man does not require the additional condition that it must do harm to another, as jurists require in their definition (*mendacium est falsiloquium in praeiudicium alterius*).¹⁴ For a lie always harms another; if not some other

8. [the first fallacy.]

9. I do not want to sharpen this principle to the point of saying ''Untruthfulness is a violation of one's duty to himself.'' For this principle belongs to ethics,¹⁰ but here the concern is with a duty of right [*Rechtspflicht*].¹¹ The *Doctrine of Virtue* [*Tugendlehre*] sees in this transgression only worthlessness, the reproach of which the liar draws upon himself.¹²

10. [As contained in the *Metaphysical Principles of the Doctrine of Virtue* [*Tugendlehre*], which is Part II of the *Metaphysics of Morals*.]

11. [Duties of right are treated in the *Metaphysical Principles of the Doctrine of Right* [*Rechtslehre*], which is Part I of the *Metaphysics of Morals*.]

12. [See the *Doctrine of Virtue*, Ak. VI, 429–31.]

13. [See the opus cited above in note 11, Ak. VI, 271–75.]

14. [a lie is a falsehood that harms another.]

human being, then it nevertheless does harm to humanity in general, inasmuch as it vitiates the very source of right [*Rechtsquelle*].

However, this well-intentioned lie can become punishable in accordance with civil law because of an accident (*casus*); and that which avoids liability to punishment only by accident can also be condemned as wrong even by external laws. For example,[15] if by telling a lie you have in fact hindered someone who was even now planning a murder, then you are legally responsible for all the consequences that might result therefrom. But if you have adhered strictly to the truth, then public justice cannot lay a hand on you, whatever the unforeseen consequence might be. It is indeed possible that after you have honestly answered Yes to the murderer's question as to whether the intended victim is in the house, the latter went out unobserved and thus eluded the murderer, so that the deed would not have come about. However, if you told a lie and said that the intended victim was not in the house, and he has actually (though unbeknownst to you) gone out, with the result that by so doing he has been met by the murderer and thus the deed has been perpetrated, then in this case you may be justly accused as having caused his death. For if you had told the truth as best you knew it, then the murderer might perhaps have been caught by neighbors who came running while he was searching the house for his intended victim, and thus the deed might have been prevented. Therefore, whoever tells a lie, regardless of how good his intentions may be, must answer for the consequences resulting therefrom even before a civil tribunal and must pay the penalty for them, regardless of how unforeseen those consequences may be. This is because truthfulness is a duty that must be regarded as the basis of all duties founded on contract, and the laws of such duties would be rendered uncertain and useless if even the slightest exception to them were admitted.

To be truthful (honest) in all declarations is, therefore, a sacred and unconditionally commanding law of reason that admits of no expediency whatsoever.

Monsieur Constant remarks thoughtfully and correctly with regard to the decrying of such principles that are so strict as to be alleged to lose themselves in impracticable ideas and that are therefore to be rejected. He says on page 123 [of the German translation of Constant's piece that appeared in the periodical *Frankreich*], "In every case where a principle that has been proved to be true appears to be inapplicable, the reason for this inapplicability lies in the fact that we do not know the middle principle that contains the means of its application." He adduces (p. 121) the doctrine of equality as being the first link of the social chain when he says (p. 122): "No man can be bound by any laws other than these to whose formation he has contributed. In a very limited society this principle can be applied directly and requires no middle principle in order to become a common principle. But in a very numerous society there must be added a new principle to the one that has been stated. The middle principle is this: individuals can contribute to the formation of laws either in their own person or through their representatives. Whoever wanted to apply the former principle to a numerous society without also using the middle principle would unfailingly bring

15. [This ensuing instance is similar to the one cited in note 7 above.]

about the destruction of such a society. But this circumstance, which would show only the ignorance or the incompetence of the legislator, would prove nothing against the principle.'' He concludes (p. 125) thus: ''A principle acknowledged as true must hence never be abandoned, however obviously there seems to be danger involved in it.'' (And yet the good man himself abandoned the unconditional principle of truthfulness on account of the danger which that principle posed for society, inasmuch as he could not find any middle principle that could serve to prevent this danger; and indeed there is no such principle to do the mediating here.)

If the names of the persons as they have here been introduced be retained, then the ''French philosopher'' confuses the action whereby someone does harm (*nocet*) to another by telling the truth when its avowal cannot be avoided with the action whereby someone does wrong to (*laedit*) another. It was merely an accident (*casus*) that the truth of the statement did harm [but not wrong] to the occupant of the house, but it was not a free act (in the juridical sense). For from a right to demand that another should lie for the sake of one's own advantage there would follow a claim that conflicts with all lawfulness. For every man has not only a right but even the strictest duty to be truthful in statements that are unavoidable, whether this truthfulness does harm [but not wrong] to himself or to others. Therefore he does not himself by this [truthfulness] actually harm [*nocet*] the one who suffers because of it; rather, this harm is caused by accident [*casus*]. For he is not at all free to choose in such a case, inasmuch as truthfulness (if he must speak [i.e., must answer Yea or Nay]) is an unconditional duty. The ''German philosopher'' will, therefore, not take as his principle the proposition (p. 124), ''To tell the truth is a duty, but is a duty only with regard to the man who has a right to the truth.'' He will not do so, first, because of the confused formulation of the proposition, inasmuch as truth is not a possession the right to which can be granted to one person but refused to another. But, secondly, he will not do so mainly because the duty of truthfulness (which is the only thing under consideration here) makes no distinction between persons to whom one has this duty and to whom one can be excused from this duty; it is, rather, an unconditional duty which holds in all circumstances.

Now, in order to go from a metaphysics of right (which abstracts from all empirical determinations) to a principle of politics (which applies these [metaphysical] concepts [of right] to instances provided by experience) and by means of this principle to gain the solution of a problem of politics in accordance with the universal principle of right, the philosopher will provide the following. First, he will present an axiom, i.e., an apodeictically certain proposition that arises directly from the definition of external right (the harmony of the freedom of each with the freedom of all others according to a universal law). [16] Second, he will provide a postulate of external public law (the will of all united according to the principle of equality without which no freedom would exist for any-

429

---

16. [See the opus cited in note 11, Ak. VI, 230–31.]

one). [17] Third, there is the problem of how to make arrangements so that in a society, however large, harmony can be maintained in accordance with principles of freedom and equality (namely, by means of a representative system). [18] And this will then be a principle of politics; and establishing and arranging such a political system will involve decrees that are drawn from experiential knowledge regarding men; and such decrees will have in view only the mechanism for the administration of justice and how such mechanism is to be suitably arranged. Right must never be adapted to politics; rather, politics must always be adapted to right.

The author says, "A principle acknowledged as true (I add, acknowledged as an a priori principle, and therefore apodeictic) must never be forsaken, however apparently danger is involved in it." But here one must understand the danger not as that of (accidentally) doing harm [*schaden*] but in general as the danger of doing wrong [*unrecht*]. [19] And such wrongdoing would occur if I made the duty of truthfulness, which is wholly unconditional and which constitutes the supreme juridical condition in assertions, into a conditional duty subordinate to other considerations. And although by telling a certain lie I in fact do not wrong anyone, I nevertheless violate the principle of right in regard to all unavoidably necessary statements generally (i.e., the principle of right is thereby wronged formally, though not materially). This is much worse than committing an injustice against some individual person, inasmuch as such a deed does not always presuppose that there is in the subject a principle for such an act.

430   The man who is asked whether or not he intends to speak truthfully in the statement that he is now to make and who does not receive the very question with indignation as regards the suspicion thereby expressed that he might be a liar, but who instead asks permission to think first about possible exceptions— that man is already a liar (*in potentia*). [20] This is because he shows that he does not acknowledge truthfulness as in itself a duty but reserves for himself exceptions from a rule which by its very nature does not admit of any exceptions, inasmuch as to admit of such would be self-contradictory.

All practical principles of right must contain rigorous truth; and the principles that are here called middle principles can contain only the closer determination of the application of these latter principles (according to rules of politics) to cases that happen to occur, but such middle principles can never contain exceptions to the aforementioned principles of right. This is because such exceptions would destroy the universality on account of which alone they bear the name of principles.

17. [See op. cit. in note 11, Ak. VI, 311.]

18. [See op. cit. in note 11, Ak. VI, 313–15.]

19. [See above at Ak. p. 428, where Kant distinguishes *nocet* from *laedit*.]

20. [in accordance with possibility.]

GERMAN-ENGLISH LIST OF TERMS

A

Achtung	respect
Affekt	emotion
Afterreden	calumny
Allgemeinheit	universality
Amphibolie	amphiboly
Anlage	predisposition
Anschauung	intuition
Anthropologie	anthropology
Antinomie	antinomy
Antrieb	impulse
Apathie	apathy
Asketik	ascetics
Ausführung	performance
Ausübung	exercise
Autokratie	autocracy
Autonomie	autonomy

B

Barmherzigkeit	soft-heartedness
Befolgung	obedience
Befugnis	authorization
Begehren	desire
Begehrungsver- mögen	faculty of desire
Begierde	appetite
Begriff	concept
Beispiel	instance
Belohnung	reward
Beobachtung	observance
Bescheidenheit	modesty
Bestimmungs- grund	determining ground
Bewegungs- grund	motive
Bewußtsein	consciousness

C

Charakter	character

D

Dankbarkeit	gratitude
Deduktion	deduction (justification)
Demut	humility
Didaktik	didactics

E

Ehrbarkeit	respectability
Ehrbegierde	ambition
Ehrliebe	love of honor
Eigendünkel	self-conceit
Einbildungs- kraft	imagination
Elementarlehre	doctrine of ele- ments
Empfänglich- keit	susceptibility
Empfindung	sensation
Endzweck	ultimate end
eng	strict
Erfahrung	experience
Erhabenheit	sublimity
Erkenntlichkeit	gratefulness
Erkenntnis	cognition, knowledge
Erlaubte, das	that which is allowed
Erscheinung	appearance
Ethik	ethics
Exempel	example
Exposition	exposition

F

Fähigkeit	ability
Falschheit	falsity
Fehler	fault
Fertigkeit	skill
Form	form

Formale, das	formal element	**I**	
Freiheit	freedom	Ideal	ideal
Freiheitsgesetz	law of freedom	Idee	idea
Freundschaft	friendship	Imperativ	imperative
Frohsinn	cheer	Inhalt	content
G		Interesse	interest
Gebot	command	**K**	
Gefräßigkeit	gluttony	Kargheit	miserliness
Gefühl	feeling	Kasuistik	casuistics
Gegenstand	object	kasuistische	casuistical
Geiz	avarice	Fragen	questions
Gelüsten	lustfulness	Katechismus	catechism
gerecht und	just and unjust	Kausalität	causality
ungerecht		Keuschheit	chastity
Gerechtigkeit	justice	Klugheit	prudence
Gerichtshof	court of justice	Kraft	power
Geschlechts-	sexual gratifi-	Kriecherei	servility
genuß	cation	Kultur	cultivation
Geschmack	taste	**L**	
Gesetz	law	Laster	vice
Gesetzgeber	legislator	Lauterkeit	purity
Gesetzgebung	legislation	Leben	life
Gesetzmäßig-	legality	Legalität	legality
keit		Leidenschaft	passion
Gesinnung	disposition	Liebe	love
Gesundheit	health	Logik	logic
Gewissen	conscience	Lüge	lying
Gewissenhaftig-	conscientious-	Lust und	pleasure and
keit	ness	Unlust	displeasure
Gewohnheit	habit	**M**	
Gleisnerei	hypocrisy	Materiale, das	material ele-
Glückseligkeit	happiness		ment
Glückseligkeits-	doctrine of	Materie	matter
lehre	happiness	Mathematik	mathematics
Gott	God	Maxime	maxim
Grad	degree	Mensch	man, human
Grundsatz	principle		being
Gymnastik	gymnastics	Menschenfeind	misanthrope
H		Menschen-	philanthropist
Handlung	action	freund	
Hang	propensity	Menschenhaß	misanthropy
Hochmut	pride		
Höflichkeit	politeness		

Menschenliebe	philanthropy	Regel	rule
Menschheit	humanity	Religion	religion
Metaphysik	metaphysics	Richter	judge
Methode	method		
Methodenlehre	methodology	**S**	
Mitfreude	rejoicing with	Sache	thing
Mitgefühl	compassion	Schadenfreude	malice
Mitleid	pity	Schuldigkeit	indebtedness
Mitleidenschaft	commiseration	Schwäche	weakness
Mittel	means	Seele	soul
Mittleres	mean	Selbst	self
Moralität	morality	Selbstbetäu-	self-stupefaction
N		bung	
		Selbstentlei-	suicide
Nächstenliebe	love of one's	bung	
	neighbor	Selbsterhaltung	self-preser-
Neid	envy		vation
Neigung	inclination	Selbster-	self-knowledge
Nötigung	necessitation	kenntnis	
Noumenon	noumenon	Selbstliebe	self-love
		Selbstmord	self-murder
P		Selbstschän-	self-abuse
Pedanterie	pedantry	dung	
Person	person	Selbstschätzung	self-esteem
Persönlichkeit	personality	Selbstsucht	selfishness
Pflicht	duty	Selbstzwang	self-constraint
Phänomenon	phenomenon	Sinn	sense
Philosoph	philosopher	Sinnlichkeit	sensibility
Philosophie	philosophy	Skandal	scandal
Physik	physics	Sollen, das	ought
Preis	price	Spielraum	latitude
Prinzip	principle	Spottsucht	derision
		Stolz	elevation of
R			spirit
Rachbegierde	desire for	Strafe	punishment
	revenge	Substanz	substance
Raum	space		
Realität	reality	**T**	
recht und	right and wrong	Tapferkeit	fortitude
unrecht		Tat	deed
Recht	right	teilnehmende	sympathetic
Rechtslehre	doctrine of	Empfindung	feeling
	right	Teilnehmung	sympathy
Rechtspflicht	juridical duty	Teleologie	teleology

Theorie	theory	Versoffenheit	drunkenness
Tierheit	animality	Versprechen	promise
Tod	death	Verstand	understanding
Trieb	drive	Vollkommen-	perfection
Triebfeder	incentive	heit	
Tugend	virtue	Vollständigkeit	completeness
Tugendlehre	doctrine of	Vorstellung	representation
	virtue		
Tugendpflicht	duty of virtue	**W**	
U		Wahl	a choice, option
		Wahrhaftigkeit	veracity
Übertretung	transgression	Weisheit	wisdom
Umgangstu-	social virtues	weit	broad
genden		Welt	world
Unkeuschheit	lewdness	Wert	worth, value
Unmäßigkeit	immoderation	Wesen	being
Unredlichkeit	insincerity	Widerstreit der	conflict of
Unterlassung	omission	Pflichten	duties
Untugend	lack of virtue	Wille	will
unzweckmäßig	unpurposive	Willkür	choice
Urheber	author	Wissenschaft	science
Ursache und	cause and effect	Wohlfahrt	welfare
Wirkung		Wohlgefallens,	complaisant
Urteil	judgment	Liebe des	love
Urteilskraft	faculty of judg-	Wohllust	lust
	ment	Wohltat	benefit
		Wohltätigkeit	beneficence
V		Wohltun	beneficence
Verachtung	contempt	Wohlwollen	benevolence
Verbindlichkeit	obligation	Wunsch	wish
Verbrechen	crime	Würde	dignity
Verdienst	merit	**Z**	
verdienstlich	meritorious		
Verhöhnung	mockery	Zeit	time
Verletzung	violation	Zufriedenheit	satisfaction
Vermögen	capacity, faculty	Zurechnung	imputation
Vernunft	reason	Zwang	constraint
Verpflichtung	obligation	Zweck	end
Verschuldung	offense	Zweckmäßig-	purposiveness,
Verschwendung	prodigality	keit	finality

INDEX

Ability (*Fähigkeit*), 9
Actions (*Handlungen*), free, 42 f., 115; in contrast to mere maxims, 47 f., 50-53, 109 f.; internal and external, 17-20; morally indifferent, 23
Allowed, that which is (*Erlaubte, das*), 22. Compare 21, 23
Ambition (*Ehrbegierde*), 81, 130
Amphiboly of the moral concepts of reflection (*Amphibolie der moralischen Reflexionsbegriffe*), 105-7
Animality (*Tierheit*), in man, 15, 44, 50, 59, 80, 85-90, 96 f., 109
Anthropology (*Anthropologie*), moral, xxxix, 16, 43, 65
Antinomy (*Antinomie*), regarding man's duties to himself, 78 f.
Apathy (*Apathie*), moral, 68
Appearance (*Erscheinung*), 92
Appetite (*Begierde*), 10; sensible, 67
Aristotle, 63, 94, 95n., 136
Ascetics (*Asketik*), ethical, 72 f., 154 f.
Author (*Urheber*), of an action, 23, 27; of the law, 27
Authorization (*Befugnis*), 22 f., 25, 28
Autonomy (*Autonomie*), of practical reason, xv f., xx-xxii, xxxiii f., xlvii f., lv, 41, 148
Avarice (*Geiz*), 63 f., 63n., 81, 93-96, 116 f.

Being (*Wesen*), human and not human, 73; subhuman and superhuman, 105

Beneficence (*Wohltätigkeit, Wohltun*), 52, 60 f., 112 f., 115-19, 122, 137, 139
Benefit (*Wohltat*), 118 f.
Benevolence (*Wohlwollen*), 52, 60 f., 88, 112-16, 135
Body and soul (*Körper und Seele*), 79 f.
Broad duties (*weite Pflichten*). See Duty
Brown, John, 5

Calumny (*Afterreden*), 131 f.
Capacity (*Vermögen*), 9, 11 f., 50
Casuistical questions (*kasuistische Fragen*), xl f., 84 f., 87 f., 89 f., 92 f., 96, 99 f., 118 f., 122 f.
Casuistics (*Kasuistik*), moral, 71, 73
Catechism (*Katechismus*), moral, 71, 147, 151-53; fragments of moral, 148-51
Cato, 89
Causality (*Kausalität*), 92; of the intelligible and sensible, 101n.
Cause and effect (*Ursache und Wirkung*), 85, 92
Chastity (*Keuschheit*), 86
Cheer (*Frohsinn*), 154 f.
Chesterfield, 89
Choice (*Willkür*), 11-13, 11n., 26 f., 48, 66, 110; form and matter of, 31, 37 f., 47
Choice, a (*Wahl*), 11n., 26 f.
Cochius, Leonhard, 41
Cognition (*Erkenntnis*), 9n.
Command (*Gebot*), 67, 103 f., 107, 109 f.
Commiseration (*Mitleidenschaft*), 121 f.

171